SCHOOL CHOICE AT THE CROSSROADS

School Choice at the Crossroads compiles exemplary, policy-relevant research on school choice options—voucher, private, charter, and traditional public schools—as they have been implemented across the nation. Renowned contributors highlight the latest rigorous research findings and implications on school vouchers, tuition tax credits, and charter schools in states and local areas at the forefront of school choice policy. Examining national and state-level perspectives, each chapter discusses the effects of choice and vouchers on student outcomes, the processes of choice, supportive conditions of school choice programs, comparative features of school choice, and future research. This timely volume addresses whether school choice works, under what conditions, and for whom—further informing educational research, policy, and practice.

Mark Berends is a Professor of Sociology and the Director of the Center for Research on Educational Opportunity at the University of Notre Dame, USA.

R. Joseph Waddington is Assistant Professor of Educational Policy Studies and Evaluation at the University of Kentucky, USA.

John Schoenig is the Senior Director of Teacher Formation and Educational Policy for the Alliance for Catholic Education (ACE) at the University of Notre Dame, USA.

SCHOOL CHOICE AT THE CROSSROADS

Research Perspectives

Edited by Mark Berends,
R. Joseph Waddington,
and John Schoenig

Routledge
Taylor & Francis Group

NEW YORK AND LONDON

First published 2019
by Routledge
711 Third Avenue, New York, NY 10017

and by Routledge
2 Park Square, Milton Park, Abingdon, Oxon, OX14 4RN

Routledge is an imprint of the Taylor & Francis Group, an informa business

© 2019 Taylor & Francis

The right of Mark Berends, R. Joseph Waddington, and John Schoenig to be identified as the authors of the editorial material, and of the authors for their individual chapters, has been asserted in accordance with sections 77 and 78 of the Copyright, Designs and Patents Act 1988.

Library of Congress Cataloging-in-Publication Data
A catalog record for this title has been requested

ISBN: 978-0-8153-8036-8 (hbk)
ISBN: 978-0-8153-8037-5 (pbk)
ISBN: 978-1-351-21331-8 (ebk)

Typeset in Bembo
by Deanta Global Publishing Services, Chennai, India

CONTENTS

PREFACE

School choice—in the form of vouchers, tuition tax credits, and charter schools—continues to expand. About one-quarter of the states in the U.S. have voucher programs and nearly 90 percent of the states have charter schools (including DC). In the foreseeable future, it is likely that these types of school choice programs will continue to expand as freedom and choice are an important aspect of our culture and as we continue to address the challenges of an educated citizenry.

This edited volume brings together the nation's leading experts on school choice to inform educators, educational leaders, policymakers, researchers, and the general public to provide the latest rigorous research findings and implications on school vouchers, tuition tax credits, and charter schools. After a brief introduction that highlights what the chapters cover, we move into "where we are" describing what the current state of research is on vouchers, tuition tax credit programs, and charter schools. The volume then addresses what we know about the social context of school choice. Researchers have moved on beyond making simple comparisons of traditional public schools to voucher or charter schools. Although researchers have been able to employ a range of rigorous methods to assess the impact of vouchers and charter schools, there is the increasing importance of understanding the social context and the mechanisms that may explain the conditions under which school choice is effective or not.

The chapters assembled here are written by some of the nation's empirical thought leaders on school choice, including emerging scholars and those who have examined school choice throughout their careers. The authors presented preliminary versions of the chapters at a national invitational conference hosted by the Institute of Educational Initiatives and the Center for Research on Educational Opportunity (CREO) at the University of Notre Dame.

The aim of the conference was to inform educators, policymakers, and research-ers by convening leading researchers to address not only whether vouchers and charter schools "work," but also the conditions under which choice is effective and whether school choice addresses educational inequalities between different racial/ethnic and socioeconomic groups. Each chapter is published in the name of the author(s) and the views expressed do not necessarily reflect those of the University of Notre Dame, the Institute of Educational Initiatives, CREO, partnering institutions, or sponsoring agencies.

We gratefully acknowledge Fr. Tim Scully who encouraged this conference to take place at Notre Dame and all of the work of Natalie Mayerhofer and Kathleen Kennedy in handling the planning and logistics of the conference. We are grateful for their attention to detail, good humor, and sense of calm. Thanks, too, to Matthew Rice, who helped bring together important details for the book. We are also grateful to Heather Jarrow and Rebecca Collazo of Routledge for their encouragement, patience, and professionalism in bringing this volume together. Finally, we thank the benefactors to Notre Dame, the Institute for Educational Initiatives, and CREO who have made possible our continued research on school choice policy.

SECTION I
Introduction and Overview

1

INTRODUCTION

School Choice at the Crossroads

*Mark Berends, R. Joseph Waddington, and
John Schoenig*

Education is at a crossroads. So too is school choice. In December 2015, President Barrack Obama signed the *Every Student Succeeds Act* (ESSA), which reauthorized the 50-year-old *Elementary and Secondary Education Act* (ESEA) and aims to increase educational opportunities among all students. After signing the bill, which focuses on public schools, President Obama said, "We reaffirm that fundamentally American ideal—that every child, regardless of race, income, background, the ZIP code where they live, deserves the chance to make their lives what they will."

With ESSA, testing and accountability remain, but the authority to implement the new law falls on states—a significant change from the federal oversight of *No Child Left Behind Act* of 2001. Because ESSA is established, researchers and policymakers can examine how states vary in its implementation. We can continue to monitor how well certain groups of students are doing and whether achievement gaps are closing. And as the new administration in Washington builds its school choice platform, we can also study the effects of choice on America's children and families.

At the time of their election in 2016, President Donald Trump and Vice President Mike Pence were strong proponents of school choice. Their nomination and subsequent confirmation of U.S. Secretary of Education Betsy DeVos reflected this administrative priority. Ms. DeVos is a champion of charter schools and voucher programs (publicly funded scholarships that allow parents to send their children to any school—public or private, religious or nonreligious). When she stated her goals for school choice in an interview in *Philanthropy Magazine*, she sounded much like President Obama: "That all parents, regardless of their zip code, have had the opportunity to choose the best educational setting for their children. And that all students have had the best opportunity to fulfill their God-given potential."

Ms. DeVos's influence has resulted in a significant expansion of charter schools—in particular in her home state of Michigan, where over 70 percent of charter schools are run by for-profit Educational Management Organizations (EMOs). Interestingly, despite pronounced criticism of Michigan charter schools generally—especially the Detroit area charter sector—a Center for Research on Education Outcomes (CREDO) (2013) study found charter school attendance was positively associated with reading and mathematics gains across the state and in Detroit. Nationally, the picture is more varied: Some charter schools have had strong, positive effects on student achievement, some have had negative effects, and some have had no effect. The effects vary across all student subgroups—by race/ethnicity, socioeconomic status, and students with special learning needs. On balance, however, charter schools tend to have a small positive effect in mathematics (Berends, 2015; Betts & Tang, chapter 5). The next wave of research calls for studies of the conditions under which charters are effective or not.

Under the leadership of DeVos and the new administration, voucher programs may also continue to expand for many more American families. To date, such programs have been limited to low or modest income families. The administration believes that education dollars should go directly to every American family: "The money will follow the student," the president has said. "That means the student will be able to attend the public, private, charter, or magnet school of their choice—and each state will develop its own system that works best for them." In other words, the implementation of these initiatives would see federal, state, and local funding combined so that families—regardless of income—receive the average per-public expenditure (about $12,000–$13,000) to choose where to send their children to school.

No doubt states like Indiana, Ohio, Florida, and Louisiana, which have significantly increased choice options in recent years, are eager to see federal support for choice enacted. Others fear that voucher expansion will wreak havoc on the public school system leading to increased privatization of America's schools (Ravitch, 2010, 2013).

And so it is that we stand at a crossroads. With unprecedented stated ideological support at the federal level, a growing portfolio of state-funded charter and voucher programs, and a growing push for change in K–12 education, the conversation regarding the expansion of publicly funded educational choice is only likely to amplify in the years ahead. As a result, we are confronted with a host of questions, perhaps most notably: Will expanding school choice policies work? For whom? Under what conditions?

This edited volume will inform the answers to these questions by compiling exemplary, policy-relevant research on school choice options—voucher, private, charter, and traditional public schools—as they have been implemented across the nation. In addition, we will highlight research in states and local areas, like Indiana, which educational leaders have said is at the forefront of school choice policy (DeVos, 2017). Now home to the nation's largest voucher program in terms of participation, Indiana has also nearly doubled its number of charter schools in the last five years. As such, the state provides a strong test case for transferring local policies to the nation as a whole.

The introduction and chapters are based on papers presented at a major national invitational conference hosted by the Institute of Educational Initiatives and the Center for Research on Educational Opportunity (CREO) at the University of Notre Dame. With national and state-level experts, the chapters will examine areas such as the effect of choice and vouchers on student outcomes, the processes of choice, supportive conditions of school choice programs, comparative features of school choice, and future research. The goal of these chapters is to address whether school choice works, for whom, and under what conditions—thus further informing educational research, policy, and practice.

The volume begins with chapters addressing the current state of research on school voucher programs that provide government funding to families so that they can send their child to a private school, offsetting the cost of tuition either fully or partially. Some of the chapters in this section also address some of the variations of school vouchers, including tax credit programs and educational savings accounts. The section provides a history of voucher and tax credit programs, the supply side of private schools in voucher programs, and a review about voucher effects on student achievement. The next major section includes several chapters about charter schools, including what we know about the effects on student outcomes, educational innovation, processes related to charter school organizations and policy implementation, and variation in effects of charter schools on student outcomes. In the final sections, national experts address the challenges of understanding the context of school choice, focusing on a variety of future research challenges, such as what outcomes to focus on, the policies and practices that make choice schools successful, the importance of addressing equity and access within the politics of school choice, and broadening our perspective of choice based on what we know from other countries. Together, the authors provide important perspectives of what we know about major school choice initiatives and where we need to go in future research and policymaking.

Voucher and Tax Credit Programs

To begin, John Witte examines educational vouchers and tax credit scholarship programs since they came into existence in the early 1990s and tracks their progress over time. Although there are a number of ways to support private school families with public monies, Witte's chapter addresses two programs that provide publicly funded vouchers or "scholarships" to students to attend private schools: (1) direct voucher programs that provide government money to families to attend private schools; and (2) more complex organizational tax credit programs, allowing individuals and corporations to receive tax credits for donations to organizations that then award "scholarships" to students to attend public or private schools.

Witte offers several overall conclusions concerning vouchers. First, although there exist 23 active voucher programs, they occur in only 12 states and the District of Columbia. This could be interpreted as a quite modest expansion since the first program in Milwaukee in 1990. Clearly, the 168,532 students enrolled in these programs nationwide is minuscule compared to the approximately 55 million public school students (0.3 percent). A second conclusion is that voucher programs come in many varieties—e.g., the four statewide programs and the largest form of voucher to aid students with some form of disability (12 of the 23 programs).

Tax credit programs are in some ways similar to voucher programs. First, there seems to be some momentum building for these programs in that 11 of 21 programs have been enacted since 2011. Second, they also come in many varieties. Finally, vouchers and tax credits both are the creatures of Republican-led legislatures and were created almost exclusively by Republican governors. Although this is clear, the chapter also describes the political constraints that ironically may lead to some Republicans opposing these forms of education choice and some Democrats supporting them.

In Chapter 3, Megan Austin expands the scope of research on the supply side of school voucher programs by identifying a new type of cost to schools that participate: organizational and social costs associated with admitting, enrolling, and educating a new population of students while continuing to support already enrolled students. She finds that schools generally maintained generous admissions policies but received more transfer applications, increasing the administrative work of gathering prior school records, evaluating students' academic performance, making a placement decision, and orienting students to the school's expectations. Schools used the admissions process to begin integrating new students prior to enrollment. In most schools, comments and reactions from already enrolled students and their parents, teachers, and other members of the community had the potential to disrupt schools' strong sense of community. Principals devoted sizeable amounts of time to respond to comments and communicate the value of voucher program participation for all students and the broader community.

Patrick Wolf and Anna Egalite provide an important review in Chapter 4 of what we know about the effects of private school choice on student achievement. They point out that parental school choice has existed in the U.S., by law, for over a century. Traditionally, school choice involved families moving to a neighborhood with good public schools or self-financing private schooling, both of which tend to be difficult for low-income families to manage. Contemporary education policies allow parents in many areas to choose from among public schools and often also private schools using a voucher or tax-credit scholarships. The newest form of school choice is Education Savings Accounts (ESAs), which make a portion of the funds that a state spends on children in public schools available to their parents in spending accounts that they can use to customize their children's education. Opponents claim that expanding private school choice yields no educational benefits to participants. Wolf and Egalite's review of the empirical research on private school choice finds evidence that private school choice tends to deliver modest positive achievement benefits to participating students, but the effects are somewhat inconsistent. The results of experimental studies tend to be somewhat more positive than the results from quasi-experimental evaluations.

Charter Schools

To begin the section on charter schools, it is helpful to have an overview of where we stand on student achievement outcomes after a quarter of a century of charter school reform. In Chapter 5, Julian Betts and Emily Tang provide that overview with their ongoing meta-analysis of high-quality charter school studies. Their meta-analysis includes the research on charter schools and student achievement, with a focus on lottery-based studies and rigorous value-added studies. On average, for the limited set of charter schools, locations, and years that have been studied to date, charter schools are producing higher achievement gains in math relative to traditional public schools in elementary and middle but not high schools. For reading achievement, charter schools are, on average, producing higher gains in middle schools but not in elementary or high schools. For both math and reading, middle school studies tend to produce the highest effect sizes of all of the grade groupings. The literature shows a large variation in estimated charter school effects across locations, and some studies also show large variations within a given city or state. Betts and Tang also examine some of the factors related to these differences and provide a link to the more detailed analyses.

School choice advocates argue that providing schools with greater autonomy should result in more innovative practices. Because much of the current research has not thoroughly examined this issue, Mark Berends, Roberto V. Peñaloza, Marisa Cannata, and Ellen B. Goldring ask in Chapter 6 if charter schools are more innovative than traditional public schools? With data from teachers and principals, the authors compare a variety of innovative organizational and instructional practices between charter and traditional public schools. Their findings reveal some innovative practices differ across school types, but further research is needed to understand how innovative practices cohere into a system of instruction and whether innovative instructional designs are related to student outcomes, such as academic achievement gains. With the exploratory findings from their research, the authors hope to set the stage for future research to examine how innovation indicators moderate and mediate charter school effects on student achievement.

In Chapter 7, Madeline Mavrogordato takes a deeper dive into innovation among teachers in two charter schools. Although arguments for charter schools emphasize the freedom and autonomy that charter schools have to be innovative, Mavrogordato's data reveal that how autonomy translates to teachers can vary across settings and the way schools are organized. Charter schools are given considerable autonomy from the bureaucracy that school choice proponents argue has plagued traditional public schools for many years. In theory, this autonomy should spur positive educational innovation that would otherwise be stifled.

Using qualitative data from interviews with 33 teachers across two case study charter schools, Mavrogordato explores the extent to which the claims about charter schools' autonomy and innovation are reflected in the work teachers do. She finds that school leaders play an important role in shaping the extent to which the autonomy charter schools possess filters down to teachers. Moreover, teachers sometimes purposefully enact innovative practices as a result of autonomy, but at other times these practices are a result of having to improvise in an effort to overcome a challenge or compensating for resources that are lacking.

Claire Smrekar and Madeline Mavrogordato in Chapter 8 examine the policy context of charter school *adoption* and *implementation* in Indianapolis—the only city in the U.S. with independent mayoral authorizing authority. Their study identifies specific *implications* of this hybrid of mayoral control, including expanded civic capacity and innovation diffusion across Indianapolis area public school systems. This qualitative chapter utilizes over 30 in-depth interviews conducted with key stakeholders. Legislative, state, and school district documents and reports were analyzed for descriptive evidence of expanded civic capacity, school innovation, and charter/non-charter school competitive pressures. The case of Indianapolis reframes the mayoral role in education reform and expands the institutional framework for charter school authorizing.

In Chapter 9, Mark Berends and Joseph Waddington examine the effects of different school types—unique in school effects research—on student outcomes. Although researchers have examined school effects for decades, they have rarely been able to examine the variability of effects of different school types with longitudinal student achievement records. With such data for students in grades 3–8 in the Indianapolis urban area, Berends and Waddington examine how the effects of different school types—charter, magnet, Catholic, other private, and traditional public—on student achievement growth and engagement (absences and suspensions). They focus particularly on charter schools to see if the impact on student outcomes varies by charter school authorizer (Mayor's Office or not) or by a student's race/ethnicity or socioeconomic status. They find that students who switch from public to charter schools in Indianapolis experience achievement gains from baseline in math and English/language arts of nearly 0.2 standard deviations by their third year enrolled in a charter. This contrasts with students switching from public to magnet or private schools, who experience an average loss from baseline of nearly the same amount in mathematics. However, students in charters are nearly 16 percentage points more likely to be suspended than their public school peers. The positive achievement and negative suspension impacts are strongest for students attending Mayor's Office-authorized charters, Black students, and students receiving free or reduced-price lunches. The chapter ends with a discussion of the findings in the context of recent studies and describes the authors' plans for future research that will continue to examine the variability within these school types over time by collecting additional school measures that may help to explain the findings.

Understanding the Context of School Choice

This final section begins with Collin Hitt, Patrick Wolf, and Michael McShane presenting in Chapter 10 their findings from the most thorough meta-analysis yet conducted on the effect that school choice has on educational attainment. It also considers the vital question of how attainment effects correlate with achievement effects. One would presume that the programs that produced the largest achievement impacts would produce the largest attainment impacts too. The authors find otherwise. They use an expansive definition of school choice, including private school voucher programs, charter schools, early college high schools, magnet schools, vocational schools, and other forms of public school choice. In total, they include studies of more than 20 programs, which provide 39 unique estimates of the impact that school choice programs have had on both achievement and attainment. They find that while the achievement impacts of school choice programs are inconsistent, perhaps on balance weakly positive, the impacts on attainment are consistently positive. This pattern implies that some programs have produced clearer attainment impacts than achievement impacts. Altogether the authors find that achievement impacts are weak predictors of attainment impacts. If test score gains are neither a necessary nor a sufficient condition for producing long-term gains in crucial student outcomes, then current approaches to accountability for school choice programs are questionable at best. The authors' findings suggest that focusing on test score gains may lead regulators to favor schools whose benefits could easily fade over time and punish schools that are producing long-lasting gains for their students.

An original hope for charter schools was that they would serve as an educational laboratory, and that promising educational approaches could be identified from the most successful charter schools. Research has found great variation in the effects of charter schools on student achievement. In Chapter 11, Philip Gleason reviews the research literature on what policies and practices are used by the most successful charter schools. Key findings include strong evidence of factors associated with positive charter school impacts including long school days or years, comprehensive behavioral policies with rewards and sanctions, and a mission that prioritizes boosting student achievement. More limited evidence suggests that successful charter schools give teachers frequent feedback and coaching, encourage and facilitate the use of student data to help teachers improve their practices, and provide high dosage tutoring to students. Other charter school characteristics, policies, and practices have been found to be uncorrelated with their impacts, including the school's age, CMO affiliation, funding, average class size, teacher qualifications, and efforts to encourage parent involvement. The chapter concludes with a discussion of possible next steps for research to learn more about what makes charter schools successful.

In Chapter 12, Janelle Scott, Elizabeth DeBray, Christopher Lubienski, Johanna Hanley, Elise Castillo, and Samantha Hedges focus on the politics of research on school choice, emphasizing the need to pay attention to equity and access. Incentivist educational policies advance from the logic that public school systems cannot improve because they are not structured to be externally accountable, and that actors within the system are not positioned in ways that would allow them to sense and respond to competition. A key aspect of charter schools' theory of action is that increased freedom will produce not only greater academic outcomes, but also redress inequality. The role of charter schools in redressing or widening equity has advocates and detractors, many of whom are active in funding incentivist reforms (reforms that aim to provide incentives to individuals and institutions to be more effective) and producing or promoting evidence to policymakers on their promise or pitfalls. This chapter presents evidence from research in Los Angeles Unified School District (LAUSD) to investigate the multiple forms of evidence intermediary organizations (IOs) are producing and promoting, and how political contexts might inform policymakers' and IOs' use of it. Charter schools have proliferated in LAUSD, as in other urban school districts, making LAUSD an important case to examine how evidence on charter school equity operates in local contexts, and how national and state-level politics inform evidence use.

In the final chapter, Helen Ladd takes a broader perspective when discussing school choice, focusing on variation in policy contexts. The combination of self-governing schools and expanded parental choice of schools poses great challenges for education policymakers who are primarily responsible for furthering the public and shared interests in education. Ladd points out the private and public benefits of schools and the public interest in providing *all* children the opportunity to flourish. To illustrate the challenges of protecting the public interest within the tension emerging from self-governance and the expansion of school choice, she focuses on the growth of charter schools in Durham, North Carolina and then discusses the implications for other initiatives in the U.S. to address this tension through the development of compacts among different school sectors within a district to work together toward common ends. Although more research is necessary on whether compacts among sectors resolve the tension between self-governing schools and parental choice, their existence brings to the forefront the conflicts between public and private interests and the need for system-wide accountability policies to address these conflicts.

As school choice continues to expand in the form of vouchers, tuition tax credits, and charter schools, the experts assembled in this volume raise many important findings and challenges for policymakers, educators, and researchers to consider. Although we know a great deal about the impact of voucher programs and charter schools since they were established nearly three decades ago, the authors point the way toward additional work that can further our understanding about the conditions under which school choice is effective and ineffective. Our hope is that readers will learn from the authors of the chapters that follow and also engage in the work yet to be done.

References

Berends, M. (2015). Sociology and school choice: What we know after two decades of charter schools. *Annual Review of Sociology*, 41(15), 159–80.

CREDO. (2013). National Charter School Study. Sanford, CA: CREDO.

Devos, B. (2017). Keynote Address Opening Doors, Opening Windows. Indianapolis, IN: American Federation for Children National Policy Summit.

Ravitch, D. (2010). Choice: The story of an idea. *The death and life of the great American school system: How testing and choice are undermining education.* New York: Basic Books.

Ravitch, D. (2013). *Reign of error: The hoax of the privatization movement and the danger to America's public schools.* New York: Alfred Knopf.

SECTION II
Where We Are

2

EDUCATIONAL VOUCHERS AND TAX CREDIT SCHOLARSHIP PROGRAMS IN THE UNITED STATES

1990–2017

John F. Witte

This chapter addresses the two major state programs that provide public funds to send students to private schools in the United States. These programs do not account for the totality of educational choice, which has become a prominent feature of K–12 education in America. The chapter does not analyze public charter schools, open enrollment, schools for alternative public education (including virtual education), post-secondary options, or magnet schools. I will briefly discuss some of those programmatic options in section II below.

Private school choice challenges longstanding traditions in American education. In the modern era of education in America, dating to the mid-nineteenth century, the vast majority of students attended public schools, organized and run by local school districts. Originally these districts were often one-room schools. They were consolidated in the twentieth century, but compared to other countries, the approximately 14,000 U.S. school districts is a very large number.

Private schools always existed, initially for the elite. Beginning at the end of the nineteenth century private schools expanded quickly because Catholics created schools following a major meeting of Catholic bishops in 1883. Their objection was the control of public schools by Protestants and the use of the Protestant St. James Bible as a primary classroom text. Private school enrollment leveled at about 12 percent with about 90 percent of those students attending religiously affiliated schools for most of the twentieth century (Witte, 2000).

Prior to the late 1980s public school students were assigned a public school based on their residential area or by a magistrate overseeing an integration order. Families in public schools had few choices—their children were assigned a school.

Enter school choice. Minnesota and Wisconsin were path-breaking school choice states. Minnesota led as early as 1967 with the nation's first tuition tax credit program. That was followed beginning in the 1980s by alternative schools for at-risk students, private school provision for post-secondary options, and in 1992, with the first public charter schools. Wisconsin followed quickly with post-secondary options and charter schools, but most importantly enacted the first private-school low-income voucher program in Milwaukee, which began in 1990. Florida was the first state to follow in the 1990s with a statewide failing schools voucher program (later deemed unconstitutional relative to the Florida constitution), and the first corporate tax credit scholarship program. In addition, a number of states, now almost all, passed legislation creating charter schools, and open enrollment that allowed public school students to enroll in districts other than their residential district.

The two choice programs that involve the most students are those within the public-school sector: open enrollment and charter schools. In 2016–17 open enrollment was available in 46 states, of which 42 allowed inter-district transfers. Of these, mandatory programs existed in 28 states (Wixom, 2017). Although national statistics are not available, in many states open enrollment probably accounts for more student choice than any other program. Also, in the 2016–17 school year, charter schools in 35 states served three million students or approximately six percent of all public K–12 students (David et al., 2017, p. 2). As described below these programs involve many more students than the major private-school choice programs. The reason is undoubtedly that open enrollment and charters allow choices only within the public school sector and thus garner more broad-based political support.

This chapter focuses exclusively on private-school choice. There are a number of ways to support private school families using public monies. I focus on the two programs that provide publicly funded vouchers or "scholarships" to students to attend private schools. These are: (1) direct voucher programs that provide government money to families to attend private schools, and (2) more complex organizational tax credit programs. The latter allow individuals and corporations to receive tax credits for donations to organizations that then award "scholarships" to students to attend public or private schools. The organizational tax credit programs differ from the original individual tax credit program enacted in 1967 in Minnesota, and now existing in many states. The individual tax credit programs allow parents to get a credit or deduction on their state taxes for tuition or expenses they incur for their own children.

The chapter is divided into three further sections. The next section describes the growth and forms of voucher and organizational tax credit programs from 1990 to 2017. I will also analyze the political environment in which these programs were enacted and expanded. That political environment will be Republican, but I will also discuss the exceptions—the rare Democratic governors and legislatures supporting choice. Finally, I will focus on the states with the largest impacts in 2017 to understand why these state programs affect many more students than others. A subsequent section analyzes the legal and political constraints on the expansion of private-school choice. Legal issues involve the lingering "Blaine Amendments" in almost all states, and their importance relative to the federal constitutional situation defined in *Zelman v. Simmons-Harris* (2002). Discussion of political constraints is set within the overwhelming Republican support for voucher programs but also acknowledges the tensions that exist in both parties on educational choice. The final section appraises the political and policy impact of private-school choice initiatives and it offers some speculative comments on the future and importance of educational choice.

Vouchers and Tax Credits for Organizational Scholarship Programs

Vouchers

The idea of educational vouchers dates to a seminal paper by Milton Friedman in 1955, widely distributed as a chapter in his book *Capitalism and Freedom* in 1962. Friedman argued for a full universal system in which all families would be given a set amount of money in terms of a "voucher" to purchase education for their children at any school in the market—public or private. Schools would be free to enroll whom they decide; utilize whatever curricula and pedagogical approaches they wish; and of course, be religiously affiliated or not (Friedman, 1962).

The voucher programs that emerged three decades after Friedman's seminal idea did not come close to his universal formula. They were, and remain, far from the revolutionary change Friedman advocated. The first, in Milwaukee, WI, as originally conceived, was: limited to low-income families (175 percent of the poverty line or less) residing in Milwaukee who had been in public schools the prior year or not enrolled in school; capped at 1,500 students; and limited to secular private schools (Witte, 2000). Most of these restrictions on voucher programs in Wisconsin have been removed through incremental changes in the Milwaukee program. Additional programs in Wisconsin include a longstanding program for Racine, and recently statewide and special needs programs (see Table 2.1). The restriction to secular schools was lifted in 1996 along with a major increase in the student enrollment cap. That led to a lawsuit based on both a Wisconsin Blaine Amendment and a First Amendment argument. The Wisconsin Supreme Court ruled in favor of the program changes in a 4–3 decision, following a highly contested Supreme Court race in which the pro-choice justice was aided by election practices that were also challenged in court. In 2012, the family income limit was raised to 300 percent of the poverty line and the eligible residential area was expanded to Milwaukee County.

A second low-income voucher program began in 1995 in Cleveland, OH. It had a more modest voucher but became the U.S. Supreme Court test case in the famous *Zelman v. Simmons-Harris* (2002) decision, which upheld the constitutionality of vouchers. Subsequent to the Cleveland program, Ohio has passed four other voucher programs of various types, with the largest being a statewide program enacted in 2005 (Table 2.1).

TABLE 2.1 Educational Voucher Programs in the United States

State	Program	Year Enacted	Students 2016–17	Funds 2016–17	Lower House When Enacted	Upper House When Enacted	Governor When Enacted
Arkansas	Succeed Scholarship Program for Student with Disabilities	2015	62	$500,000	Rep.	Rep.	Rep.
Florida	John McKay Students with Disabilities	1999	31,550	$357,000,000	Rep.	Rep.	Rep.
Georgia	Special Needs Scholarship Program	2007	4,154	$23,495,631	Rep.	Rep.	Rep.
Indiana	Choice Scholarship Program	2011	34,299	$146,051,106	Rep.	Rep.	Rep.
Louisiana	Students Scholarships for Excellence	2008	6,695	$39,000,000	Dem.	Dem.	Rep.
Louisiana	School Choice Pilot Program for Students with Exceptionalities	2010	339	$1,000,000	Dem.	Dem.	Rep.
Maryland	Broadening Options Program	2016	2,405	$4,500,000	Rep.	Rep.	Rep.
Mississippi	Dyslexia Therapy Scholarship	2012	164	$816,720	Rep.	Rep.	Rep.
Mississippi	Speech-Language Therapy Scholarship	2013	0	$0	Rep.	Rep.	Rep.
N. Carolina	Opportunity Scholarship Program	2013	5,515	$24,840,000	Rep.	Rep.	Rep.
N. Carolina	Children with Disabilities Scholarships	2013	1,083	$10,028,166	Rep.	Rep.	Rep.
Ohio	Cleveland Scholarship Program	1995	8,003	$33,444,695	Rep.	Rep.	Rep.
Ohio	Autism Scholarship Program	2003	3,477	$60,629,336	Rep.	Rep.	Rep.
Ohio	Educational Choice Scholarship Program	2005	21,815	$86,543,018	Rep.	Rep.	Rep.
Ohio	John Peterson Special Needs Scholarship Program	2011	4,930	$35,415,773	Rep.	Rep.	Rep.
Ohio	Income-Based Scholarship Program (Expansion of Ed Choice Program)	2013	7,574	$17,712,565	Rep.	Rep.	Rep.
Oklahoma	Lindsey Nicole Henry Scholarships for Students with Disabilities	2010	553	$4,248,000	Rep.	Rep.	Dem.

(continued)

TABLE 2.1 Continued

State	Program	Year Enacted	Students 2016–17	Funds 2016–17	Lower House When Enacted	Upper House When Enacted	Governor When Enacted
Utah	Carson Smith Special Needs Scholarship Program	2005	985	$5,042,836	Rep.	Rep.	Rep.
Washington D. C.	D.C. Opportunity Scholarship Program	2004	1,154	$11,143,483	Rep.	Rep.	President
Wisconsin	Milwaukee Parental Choice Program	1990	27,982	$201,900,000	Dem.	Dem.	Rep.
Wisconsin	Racine Parental Choice Program	2011	2,531	$18,000,000	Rep.	Rep.	Rep.
Wisconsin	Wisconsin Parental Choice Program	2013	3,057	$22,300,000	Rep.	Rep.	Rep.
Wisconsin	Special Needs Scholarship Program	2015	205	$2,578,800	Rep.	Rep.	Rep.
TOTAL			**168,532**	**$1,106,129**	**19R;3D**	**19R;3D**	**21R;1D**

A third program, started by Governor Jeb Bush in Florida, was of a different design. The Florida Opportunity Scholarship Program, which began in 2000, allowed students who were attending failing schools under the Florida school report card system, to obtain vouchers to attend other schools, either public or private.[1] It, however, suffered a different fate in the courts in that the Florida Supreme Court ruled it violated the "uniform education" provision of the Florida constitution. A subsequent Florida voucher program was the first in the country to target students with disabilities, but it was never challenged in court. That program has grown to be larger in size than the Milwaukee Parental Choice Program in terms of both students and funding.

Of recent interest, primarily for its meteoric rise in the number of students using vouchers and the funds contributed by the state, is the Indiana Choice Scholarship Program enacted in 2011. It is already the largest program in the country in terms of students served (see Table 2.1 and Austin, Chapter 3). Of the four largest voucher programs (Florida Disability Scholars, Milwaukee, and Ohio being the others), all but Indiana have grown over a number of years, following a number of incremental changes to the initial legislation. Indiana has achieved a large scale in just six years, and thus for strong voucher proponents, may serve as model legislation in the future.

The Indiana program is statewide, with a number of eligibility categories (Indiana Department of Education, 2018). For regular students (not in one of the categories below), eligibility is limited to students from families with incomes below 150 percent of reduced-free lunch eligibility ($68,265 for a family of four in 2016–17). However, the program also grants eligibility to: siblings of scholarship recipients; students with an Individual Education Plan (disability) and a family income of 200 percent or less of reduced-free lunch; those transferring from the corporate tax credit program (Table 2.2); and those in a school that received an F rating on the state report card in the prior year if family income meets the 150 percent rule.

The scholarship amount is set each year by the state and awards are based on family income with students with family incomes of 100 percent of the reduced-free lunch level ($45,510 for a family of four) receiving 90 percent of the state scholarship level. Those between 100 percent and 150 percent receive only 50 percent of the scholarship level.

Schools in the Indiana voucher program also have to meet a number of standards. They must be: accredited; administer state tests; not discriminate on enrollment; submit several annual financial reports; do criminal background checks on all employees; and provide the state full access to schools including classroom observations, and review of all curricula and instructional materials.

Although the program was capped at 7,500 the first year and 15,000 in year two, beginning in 2013–14, enrollment was unlimited. It has been estimated that 60 percent of Indiana public school students were eligible for vouchers in 2013 (Alliance for School Choice, 2014, p. 67). Although the many rules and

TABLE 2.2 Scholarship Tax Credit Programs in the United States

State	Program	Year Enacted	Students 2016–17	Funds 2016–17	Lower House When Enacted	Upper House When Enacted	Governor When Enacted
Alabama	Tax Credits for Contributions to Scholarship Granting Organizations	2013	3,955	13,822,620	Rep.	Rep.	Rep.
Arizona	Individual School Tuition Organization Tax Credit	1997	52,554	$100,959,059	Rep.	Rep.	Rep.
Arizona	Corporate School Tuition Organization Tax Credit	2006	20,076	$54,597,804	Rep.	Rep.	Dem.
Arizona	Lexie's Law	2009	936	$5,000,000	Rep.	Rep.	Rep.
Florida	Florida Tax Credit Scholarship	2001	98,889	$559,082,031	Rep.	Rep.	Rep.
Georgia	Georgia Scholarship Tax Credit Program	2008	13,600	$58,000,000	Rep.	Rep.	Rep.
Illinois	Invest in Kids Program	2017	NA	NA	Dem.	Dem	Rep.
Indiana	Corporate and Individual Scholarship Tax Credit Program	2009	9,424	$17,563,037	Dem.	Rep.	Rep.
Iowa	Individual and Corporate School Tuition Organization Tax Credits	2006	10,771	$16,200,000	Dem.	Dem.	Dem.
Kansas	Tax Credit for Low-income Students	2014	188	$790,000	Rep.	Rep.	Rep.
Louisiana	Tuition Donation Rebate Program	2012	1,706	$7,005,905	Rep.	Rep.	Rep.
Montana	Tax Credits to Student Scholarship Organizations	2015	25	NA	Rep.	Rep.	Dem.
Nevada	Educational Choice Scholarship Program	2015	1,061	$5,500,000	Rep.	Rep.	Rep.
New Hampshire	Education Tax Credit Program	2012	178	$347,096	Rep.	Rep.	Dem.
Oklahoma	Equal Opportunity Education Scholarship	2011	1,645	$2,747,473	Rep.	Rep.	Rep.
Pennsylvania	Educational Improvement Tax Credit	2001	30,469	$62,100,000	Rep.	Rep.	Rep.
Pennsylvania	Educational Opportunity Scholarship Tax Credit	2012	11,417	$44,213,700	Rep.	Rep.	Rep.
Rhode Island	Rhode Island Corporate Scholarship Tax Credit	2006	415	$1,588,537	Dem.	Dem.	Rep.
South Carolina	Educational Credit for Exceptional Needs Children	2013	1,958	$10,000,000	Rep.	Rep.	Rep.
South Dakota	Partners in Education Tax Credit	2016	280	$325,000	Rep.	Rep.	Rep.
Virginia	Educational Improvement Scholarships Tax Credits	2012	2,419	$10,183,623	Rep.	Split (20–20)	Rep.
TOTAL			**261,966**	**$973,025,885**	**17R; 4D**	**17R; 3D**	**18R; 3D**

regulations in this program are a far cry from that envisioned by Milton Friedman almost 70 years ago, it does represent design compromises that allow many to access the program while also establishing a robust set of accountability measures.

There are several overall conclusions that emerge from Table 2.1. First, although there exist 23 active voucher programs, they occur in only 12 states and the District of Columbia. This could be interpreted as a quite modest expansion since the first program in Milwaukee in 1990. Clearly, the 168,532 students enrolled in these programs nationwide is minuscule compared to the approximately 55 million public school students (0.3 percent).[2] However, many states may have awaited the U.S. Supreme Court decision in 2002, and 12 programs have been enacted since 2011, with one eliminated in a school district in Colorado because of a change in school board membership (see Section III). I return to the issue of voucher expansion in discussing political and legal constraints in the next section and conclusion.

A second conclusion from Table 2.1 is that voucher programs come in many varieties. To date, only four are statewide programs and none approach in any way the wide-open voucher system proposed by Milton Friedman. If anything, the largest single category (12 programs of 23) are vouchers to aid students with some form of disability. These programs are obviously politically popular in that they affect very vulnerable populations. A more cynical interpretation might be that public school districts are willing, even eager, to have the state and private schools bear the burden of educating their most expensive students.

Finally, the last three columns in Table 2.1 reveal a consistent, overtime association between enacting voucher legislation and control of state government by Republicans. Of the 23 programs, when enacted, only three lower and upper houses were controlled by Democrats, and only one program was enacted when a Democrat was governor. Oklahoma Governor Brad Henry, a moderate Democrat, had 10 years' prior experience in the state Senate. The program he signed into law was a very modest disability voucher program that after seven years only served 553 students statewide. Thus, as I noted more than a decade ago (Witte, 2000), education voucher programs remain Republican programs in almost all states.

Tax Credits for Organizational Scholarships

Educational tax credit programs vary considerably in their provisions. In this chapter, I am limiting the discussion to tax credit programs that allow individuals or corporations to make tax free contributions to organizations, which in turn provide "scholarships" to students to attend schools using donated funds. I am not discussing individual tax credit programs because organizational tax credits closely approximate voucher programs described above in that they end with specific students getting vouchers (always called "scholarships" not vouchers) to attend either public, but mostly private schools.[3]

Having said that, one aspect of organizational tax credit programs (hereafter "tax credit programs") is that they vary enormously in their provisions.

An excellent resource on these programs is a very detailed state-by-state analysis of these tax credit programs written by the Foundation for Opportunity in Education. It describes the variance across states in 24 major provisions and five additional miscellaneous parameters on which these programs differ (Foundation for Opportunity in Education, 2013). These include the types of organizations allowed, eligibility of students, the amount of donations that are tax free, caps on the amount that can be given and the overall expenditures, the purposes of the scholarships, and many other factors.

There are several differences in these programs, which are depicted in Table 2.2, from straightforward voucher programs. First, they are more recent, with the first program being enacted in Arizona in 1997, with two others following in Florida and Pennsylvania in 2001. These three programs are by far the largest, accounting for 57 percent of the students receiving scholarships in the country. All have relatively wide eligibility and have been expanded and have grown in popularity over time. Another difference is that only two of the 16 programs specifically target students with special needs—Lexie's Law in Arizona (2009) and the South Carolina Exceptional Needs program (2013).

There are also some factors that are similar to voucher programs. First, there seems to be some momentum building for these programs in that 11 of 21 programs have been enacted since 2011. In addition, as with voucher programs there has been consistent incremental expansion of programs. One study found that of the seven programs begun before 2010, six have been considerably expanded. These include the three largest programs (Arizona, Florida, and Pennsylvania), which explains their size relative to the rest of the programs (Bednick, 2013).

Second, as with vouchers, most programs have been enacted under Republican regimes. Fifteen of 21 were passed with Republicans controlling the lower house, senate, and governorship. There is one unique exception, however. The Iowa Scholarship Tax Credit Program, which applies to both individuals and corporations, was enacted in 2006 when Democrats were in control of both houses of the legislature, and Democrat Tom Vilsack was governor. Vilsack was a former mayor, and state senator, and was elected in 1998 as the first Democratic governor in 30 years. He was re-elected in 2002. The bill was passed with very wide margins of 75 to 19 in the House and 49 to one in the Senate. In addition, the program has a relatively generous eligibility provision, applying to families with incomes of 300 percent of the poverty line ($70,650 for a family of four in 2013) or less. The program had a budget cap of $8.75 million when first enacted but that cap was lifted by unanimous votes of both legislative houses in 2013.

Summary

There has been enormous attention in the educational literature and media given to vouchers and their close cousin organizational tax credit programs. However, in scope they account for far less educational choice than other programs that operate within the public sector, especially open enrollment and charter schools. Together both types of voucher programs enrolled only 430,498 students of the 55 million students in public schools (0.78 percent). However, more states seem to be enacting programs in recent years, and existing programs have expanded incrementally over time.[4] This does not, however, mitigate the fact that after a quarter century, these programs remain few, small, and in the case of vouchers, often targeted on special needs students. What this suggests is that there may be considerable constraints on educational vouchers. I next explore two forms of constraints: legal and political.

Legal and Political Constraints on Education Voucher Programs

Legal Constraints

The potential legal constraints on vouchers come from both the U.S. and state constitutions. Ironically, the latter may be more important. The major obstacle in the U.S. Constitution is the First Amendment. That challenge was settled in the 2002 *Zelman v. Simmons-Harris* decision based on the Cleveland voucher program. At issue was whether vouchers that provided public monies to send students to private schools violated the "establishment" clause of the First Amendment.[5] In the main majority opinion of the 5–4 decision, Chief Justice Rehnquist emphasized that payments that provided needed benefits went directly to the parents and that individual choices between various types of schools made the program one of parental choice and neutral with respect to religion. He wrote:

> [The] Ohio program is entirely neutral with respect to religion. It provides benefits directly to a wide spectrum of individuals, defined only by financial need and residence in a particular school district. It permits such individuals to exercise genuine choice among options public and private, secular and religious. The program is therefore a program of true private choice.

Thus, the Supreme Court ruled the Ohio program did not violate the establishment clause of the First Amendment and was therefore constitutional. It would appear that tax credits for organizational scholarships also would fit within the *Zelman* ruling.

It was thought that following *Zelman* there would be a flood of new voucher programs. As indicated in Tables 2.1 and 2.2, there has been some acceleration in the creation of these programs, but hardly a flood. The reason lies in both constraints provided by state constitutions, and the general politics of private school choice.

State legal constraints to vouchers come in two possible forms. First, all state constitutions have provisions specifying that the state has a duty to provide some degree of public education. However, nearly all the states go further and specify that that provision must be free, equal, and uniform. It is the equal and uniform clauses that provide the potential problems for vouchers in that opponents can argue that support of private schools creates an unequal and non-uniform option for those attending private schools with publicly funded vouchers.

An important example of this constraint was the State of Florida Supreme Court decision to rule the Florida Opportunity Scholarship Program in violation of the uniform education provision of the Florida constitution. The court ruled that the Opportunity Scholarship Program violated article IX, section 1(a) of the Florida Constitution: "Adequate provision shall be made by law for a uniform, efficient, safe, secure, and high quality system of free public schools."[6] Students were allowed to continue to use the program to attend public schools if their school failed. State precedents do not carry the weight of U.S. Supreme Court rulings, but the Florida case was a rather straightforward application and it struck down a major program in a very large state. Florida did not try to resurrect that program in a modified form but rather instituted organizational tax credit programs and the first voucher program for students with disabilities. Of interest politically is that the latter program has never been challenged in court even though on the surface it would appear to fail the same constitutional provisions as the broader school voucher program.

The 2013 North Carolina state voucher program was also challenged under state constitutional standards and an injunction initially prevented it from enrolling students. However, the North Carolina challenge was unsuccessful. In July 2015, the North Carolina Supreme Court upheld their voucher program 4–3, declaring "using tax dollars for education was a public purpose." As in almost all court rulings on vouchers, the vote followed precise party lines with the four supporting judges being Republicans (Blythe & Hui, 2015).

The second state-level legal constraint on voucher and scholarship tax credit programs comes from the famous *Blaine Amendments* that were added to many state constitutions in the latter years of the nineteenth and early years of the twentieth century. These amendments were named after Massachusetts Congressman James G. Blaine who became very concerned about the effects on public education of the large influx of European Catholics beginning in the latter half of the nineteenth century. Some historians have claimed that Blaine was trying to protect the rights of Catholics and particularly the emerging Catholic schools following the American Bishops 1983 decree that all Catholic parishes had to create Catholic schools, and that Catholic families had a duty to send their children to these schools. Most, however, adhere to the more straightforward scenario that Blaine wanted to protect the Protestant approach to public education that included the Protestant St. James Bible as a primary text.[7]

Regardless of the motivation, James Blaine first attempted in 1875 to insert a clear amendment in the U.S. Constitution that would have prevented any public money from being provided in support of religious public schools. Failing that amendment, he turned to states in a concerted campaign. He was ultimately highly successful in that currently all but 11 states have some form of Blaine amendment in their constitutions.[8]

One of the first Blaine amendment cases, and the first Blaine amendment loss for voucher programs, was in state court in Arizona. A unique aspect of the Arizona case was the rare occasion that a program targeted for students with disabilities was the subject of the lawsuit. In 2006 Arizona passed two targeted voucher programs. The Arizona Scholarships for Students with Disabilities Program was modeled after Florida's McKay Scholarship Program. The Displaced Pupils Choice Grant Program provided students in foster care with vouchers to attend either public schools or qualified private schools of their choice. The two program were consolidated in one lawsuit, *Caine vs. Horne*.[9] It challenged their constitutionality based on Arizona's Blaine amendment that reads: "Section 10. No tax shall be laid or appropriation of public money made in aid of any church, or private or sectarian school, or any public service corporation." A March 2009 unanimous decision sided with the plaintiffs and ruled both programs unconstitutional. The opinion, written by Judge Michael D. Ryan, contained the key passage: "These programs transfer state funds directly from the state treasury to private schools. That the checks or warrants first pass through the hands of parents is immaterial."

However, when the voucher opponents tried to have the program eliminated on establishment clause grounds, citing *Zelman*, the U.S. Supreme Court upheld the programs by a 5–4 vote in April 2011. The court ruled there was no violation of the establishment clause. Interestingly, no other cases against targeted voucher programs for students with disabilities have been brought in other states.

Another Blaine amendment case that had dragged on for years in the courts was recently decided politically. Douglas County, a wealthy district in Colorado, passed a voucher program in 2011 through its school board. Judge Michael Martinez issued a permanent injunction stopping the Douglas County voucher program because it violates the state constitutional provision of funds for schools "controlled by any church or sectarian denomination" (Carroll, 2011). The case was appealed to the U.S. Supreme Court which ruled in July 2017 that the state court should reconsider. However, after voucher opponents were elected to the Douglas County School Board in November 2017, the board voted in December 2017 to rescind the program.

An important challenge to a tax credit program was overturned on a technicality by the New Hampshire Supreme Court in 2014. The New Hampshire Education Tax Credit Program was enacted in 2012. It was immediately challenged in court in part due to the state Blaine amendment. The New Hampshire's Blaine amendment reads: "[No] money raised by taxation shall ever be granted or applied for the use of schools or institutions of any religious sect or denomination" (New Hampshire Constitution, Part II, article 83). One of the important issues in this case was if there was actually government money involved, in that, as the defendants argued, the money used "never falls into the tax collector's hands" because it is a credit, and thus is never paid in taxes. If the plaintiffs had succeeded in New Hampshire, given that only two of the 17 states with scholarship tax credit programs do not have Blaine Amendments (Louisiana and Rhode Island), nearly all tax credit scholarship programs could be in jeopardy. However, the New Hampshire Supreme Court sidestepped the central issue by ruling that the plaintiffs did not have standing in that they suffered no direct injury (*Duncan v. State of New Hampshire*, 2014). There has not been a subsequent legal effort to overturn the program.

These cases collectively indicate that one aspect of the politics of school vouchers is whether legal challenges are raised. But there are also other more overt political challenges to voucher-type programs.

Political Constraints

A number of years ago I tried to capture the essence of the politics surrounding school choice with the phrase "choice theatre" (Witte, 2000). Some 18 years later much represented by that image is still at work. The issue crystallizes opposing forces on several dimensions. There is the clash between a regulated/bureaucratic and a market approach to the provision of a good that is both individual and collective. Those clashes line up with both the left–right and the partisan Democratic–Republican dimensions. Choice supporters also portray their plight as a small cadre of revolutionaries struggling against the colossus of the education establishment with both organizations for management (administrators and school boards) linking arms with their employees and their powerful teachers' unions.[10] And all of this continues to attract media attention, which is increasingly split on the issue. On one side they highlight failing and struggling minority families and students seeking redress from a non-caring education establishment, while on the other choice is portrayed as an effort to destroy public education as we have known it for hundreds of years. The end result is very good theater.

But unlike some theatrical productions, in this case there is much truth in the countervailing images. Although the pro-choice forces are very persistent and well organized, the array of opposition groups and organizations is overwhelming. An organization called Public Schools First (2014) lists 38 organizations that overtly oppose vouchers, with short statements of opposition from most of them. They not only include the major teachers' unions, both of which also state they support charter schools, but also the Elementary Principals Association and the Secondary Principals Association. However, peak "management organizations," also are strongly opposed, including the American Association of School Administrators and the National School Boards Associations. In addition, the Parent Teacher Association of America is strongly opposed. To wrap up the inclusiveness of the opposition, the NAACP and several other Black education associations are listed as well as Jewish and even Hindu organizations. On many of their individual websites, the organizations provide local memberships with "talking points" against vouchers to be used in local debates.

This group conflict extends to the partisan nature of support for and against choice. With only the exception of an Iowa tax credit scholarship program, enactment of these programs has repeatedly proven to be one-sided: Republicans champion vouchers and Democrats oppose. And the recent increase in program enactment may have been spurred by recent increases in Republican control of state legislatures and governorships.

With increasing Republican control, the question arises as to why there have not been more programs enacted? There are at least four possible answers. First, there simply may not have been enough time to form coalitions to overcome the unified opposition of powerful education groups. In that scenario there may well be more legislation coming. Second, the opposition is simply too strong and is able to mobilize, or perceive to mobilize, public school supporters from parents to former public school students. Third, and tied to the second, the legal issues loom large and the prospects of lawsuits may deter even the most diehard choice supporters.

However, the fourth reason for the paucity of voucher initiatives may be deeper and more important for the future. Although when enacted the partisan divide on vouchers is apparent, that may be deceptive—the positions within each party may not be as clear when legislation is being considered. Thus some Republicans may be wary of extended and extreme private-school choice options. The wariness derives from several forces. First, there may simply be moderates in their ranks that at a minimum do not see choice as an important agenda item, or even worse as a danger to them if they come from a split district. Second, although Republicans in the main favor markets and do not embrace teacher unions, they also are likely to be fiscal conservatives who view providing public monies to all private schools as a potential budget buster. Third, most Republican districts are in the suburbs or small to medium-sized cities where constituents are likely to be much more positive about the performance of their public schools. These Republicans may be able to put the brakes on choice initiatives even when their party has political control.

The same wariness, in the reverse, may creep into some Democrats. Some moderate Democrats may view vouchers as a reform worth trying or at least listening to the debate. This could be reinforced if their constituents come from the inner cities where they are well aware of the education problems and constituent dissatisfaction with those schools. The effects of these defectors from the mainstream Democratic view opposing choice may prevent wholesale dismantling of choice programs when Democrats come to power, and they may also induce compromises with the wary Republicans to block the more extreme choice initiatives from reaching a political decision.

The combined effects of all these forces: strong and hostile interest group opposition but facing well-organized and determined supporters and non-unified legislative parties may create a form of gridlock that prevents anything but incremental changes, while allowing those programs affecting students with disabilities to advance because few have the nerve to oppose efforts to help those students. This constellation of factors fits well into an environment of legal uncertainty created by the possible constitutional barriers outlined above. [11]

Wither Educational Choice

The combined history of legislation and the analysis of the legal and political barriers, suggests that private school choice is likely to grow at a relatively slow pace, with most of the growth coming through expansion of new and existing choice programs. Most programs begin very modestly, some stay that way and others expand quite dramatically. The one exception and possible model for statewide voucher advocates is the recently enacted program in Indiana that began statewide with a very large eligibility pool of students and impressive growth in students using vouchers. However, the strength of the Republican majorities and the presence of the Milton Friedman Foundation in Indianapolis may prove to be unique factors that limit replication of these results in other states. The forces above and the longer-term slow growth in voucher-type programs suggest that Indiana may be the exception rather than the rule for the future.

The looming question, as I write this chapter in February 2018, is what may happen at the national level with the combined Republican control of Congress and the presidency of Donald Trump. As of this writing, the most obvious actions have been the appointment of choice supporter Betsy DeVos as secretary of education and promises by the administration to fund school choice at the national level, including vouchers. However, nothing has been done and it appears little will be done before the mid-term, 2018 elections.[12] If Republicans retain control of Congress, constraints on the politics of school choice, described above, may be tested for the first time at the national level.

Finally, I titled this section as "wither educational choice," not "wither private-school choice," because I did not want this essay to leave the impression that the school choice movement as a whole has failed. Some 30 years ago there effectively was no individual choice in American education apart from families moving their residence or enrolling their children in private schools and paying tuition. Over those 30 years, as noted in the introduction to this chapter, numerous venues for choice have been enacted. In some districts, for example, over half the schools are charter schools that offer a wide range of choices by location and pedagogy. For example, in the fall of 2018, all schools in New Orleans will be charter schools. Open enrollment continues to grow and post-secondary options are wildly popular with families. A recent effort to add further regulations to the first post-secondary options program in Minnesota engendered immediate protests from parents, students, and secondary education providers (Nathan, 2014).

In closing, I argue that choice has forever changed the culture and environment of American education. Families, politicians, and those in education realize that the era of dominance by school administrators and officials is over. Once the choice genie was out of the bottle, it was impossible to put it back in. The only legislative repeal of a voucher program was a short-term hiatus for the D.C. Scholarship Program.[13] Although cases are pending in the courts, they have only ultimately repealed the first Florida voucher program in 2006. And that program was superseded by alternative forms of voucher programs. Once options are created, especially in situations where students are failing, families will insist they remain and even expand. And school districts and state agencies are adapting to and accommodating those demands. Given the dimensions and longevity of the public school structure in America that is not a trivial reform.

Notes

1 At the time Florida was grading schools on an A to F scale. Failing schools were defined as schools receiving a grade of F in the prior year or having three consecutive years of D grades.
2 This is, however, an expansion from 115,582 voucher students reported in this chapter for the 2013–14 school year.
3 It could be argued, as defendants in a New Hampshire court case are doing, that public monies are not actually being used in these programs. The assumption they are making is that because the funding comes from tax credits it is never actually in public tax collector hands. For my purposes, even if a court accepts such an argument, these tax credits are classic tax expenditures and thus directly deprive the government of taxes to the benefit of those receiving the credit. Thus in outcome they directly parallel voucher programs that use general purpose public funds.
4 These programs are perfectly designed for incremental expansion because each contains numerous policy "levers" that can be addressed by advocates at different times. For example, geographic limits can be attacked using the argument, why just Milwaukee or Cleveland?—certainly there are poor students in other cities. Caps on the number of students can be viewed as arbitrary, especially in the face of waiting lists. Eligibility categories can be added and income limits raised.
5 The First Amendment to the U.S. Constitution reads in part: "Congress shall make no law respecting an establishment of religion, or prohibiting the free exercise thereof …".
6 Florida Supreme Court Official Opinion: SC04-2323-John Ellis "Jeb" Bush, ET AL *v.* Ruth D. Holmes, ET AL.
7 See Green, 2010 for a detailed discussion of the Blaine movement.
8 The eleven states without Blaine amendments are Arkansas, Connecticut, Louisiana, Massachusetts, Maryland, New Jersey, North Carolina, Rhode Island, Tennessee, Vermont, and West Virginia.
9 *Caine vs. Horne,* CV-08-0189-PR.
10 Two images from prior works capture this asymmetric struggle. Many years ago Paul Peterson suggested that the choice movement was reminiscent of Jedi warriors of Star Wars fame. Some 10 years later I included in a book on the Milwaukee voucher program a 1996 presidential cartoon created by a Colorado cartoonist that portrayed President Clinton as Goliath supported by the massive armies of the school establishment, and opponent and choice supporter Senator Robert Dole as David, slingshot and all. See Peterson, 1990, p. 73; Witte, 2000, p. 176.
11 Given this conclusion, it nevertheless remains that future state elections will still be critical. If Republicans significantly increase their control at the state level, we

can anticipate more voucher legislation. What is less clear is what Democrats will do if they gain control in states with voucher programs. The only repeal of a major program of which I am familiar is that of the Washington D.C. voucher program, which followed an all-out blitz by major establishment groups and abandonment of the program by President Obama. And that program was later restored. In Wisconsin there were two years of unified Democratic control of the legislature and the governor (2008–10), yet there were no major setbacks for the voucher program.

12 After spending 30 minutes on the U.S. Department of Education website, I was not able to find a single promotional reference to voucher or private school choice. Searches for "educational choice" led to repeated references to links to "public school choice," usually directing parents on how to choose a public school. A search on "vouchers" only came up with an explanation of what they were and a listing of programs by state.

13 With the Democrats in control in 2009, the five-year reauthorization of the Washington D.C. Scholarship Program was defeated, but allowed to continue for the students already enrolled. That was changed, and the whole program was reauthorized for five years as part of the *Omnibus Reconciliation Act* of 2011. Reputedly Speaker Boehner (R-OH) and President Obama agreed on this reauthorization as a final piece of that *Omnibus Act*.

References

Alliance for School Choice. *Yearbook: 2016–17*. Washington D.C.

Bednick, J. (2013). *Scholarship tax credit programs*. Cato Institute.

Blythe, A. & Hui, T. K. (2015). North Carolina Supreme Court upholds school voucher program. Retrieved from ably@newsobserver.com and khui@newsobserver.com.

Carroll, V. (2011). *The Denver Post* (online), August 20.

David, R., Melsa, K., & Pendergrass, S. (2017). *A growing movement*. National Alliance for Public Charter Schools.

Friedman, M. (1962). *Capitalism and freedom*. Chicago: University of Chicago Press.

Foundation for Opportunity in Education. (2013). Education credit programs: An analysis of provisions.

Green, S. (2010). *The second disestablishment: Church and state in the 19th century*. Oxford University Press.

Indiana Department of Education. (2018). *Choice scholarship program annual report: Participation and payment data*. Indianapolis, IN: Author (Office of School Finance).

Nathan, J. Internet Blog. 18 May, 2014.

Peterson, P. (1990). Monopoly and competition in American education. In *Choice and control in American education, volume 1*, edited by W. S. Clune & J. F. Witte. New York: Falmer Press.

Public Schools First, Inc. (2014). Retrieved from www.publicschoolsfirstin.org/wp-content.

Witte, J. F. (2000). *The market approach to education: An analysis of America's first voucher program*. Princeton, N.J. Princeton University Press.

Wixom, M. A. (2017). *50-state comparison: Open enrollment policies*. Denver Co. Education Commission of the States.

Zelman v. Simmons Harris. 2002. *536 U.S. 639* (2002).

3

ORGANIZATIONAL AND SOCIAL COSTS OF SCHOOLS' PARTICIPATION IN A VOUCHER PROGRAM

Megan Austin

The effectiveness of school voucher programs is a major concern for policymakers, practitioners, and researchers. This focus on effectiveness, most often measured by how well students in voucher schools perform on achievement tests compared with their public school counterparts, has resulted in the proliferation of research studies focused on the demand side of school choice—the students and parents (Cowen et al., 2013; Greene et al., 1999; Howell et al., 2002; Lareau & Goyette, 2014; Rouse, 1998; Witte et al., 2014; Wolf et al., 2013; Waddington & Berends, 2017; Shakeel et al., 2016; Zimmer & Bettinger, 2015). Although important for understanding whether voucher programs achieve their aims, these studies say very little about how or why programs produce the results they do. To answer those questions, more research is needed that focuses on the supply side of voucher programs (Abdulkadiroglu et al., 2015; Austin, 2015; McShane, 2015; Sude et al., 2017). Vouchers by themselves do not change student outcomes. The vouchers are a mechanism to facilitate access to a set of schools that are theorized to better educate students (Austin & Berends, in press; Berends, 2015; Sude et al., 2017).

Some recent work has focused on how the supply of voucher schools available to students is determined, examining either the factors that influence school participation in a voucher program or the characteristics of schools that participate (Austin, 2015; Howell & Peterson, 2006; Sude et al., 2017). However, this work generally does not extend to the experiences of private schools once they begin participating in a voucher program. For voucher programs to be effective, the schools that enroll voucher students must be able to function effectively. At the school organizational level, schools that struggle to meet program requirements or adapt to the regulatory and non-regulatory demands associated with participating in a voucher program are more likely to be distracted from the business of providing an effective education to their students. Although much more research is needed on the supply side of school choice, some extant research has begun to build our understanding of how schools respond to the financial and regulatory costs of participating in a voucher program.

This chapter expands the scope of that research to a new type of cost: organizational and social costs associated with admitting, enrolling, and educating a new population of students while continuing to support already-enrolled students. I draw on interviews with the principals of 10 Catholic schools that chose to participate in the Indiana Choice Scholarship Program (ICSP) beginning in its first year to identify the major social costs schools face and examine how schools deploy their organizational resources to address these costs. In Indiana, Catholic schools participated at a near-universal rate and accounted for about 70 percent of all participating schools in 2011–12 (Austin, 2015). The diverse sample of Catholic schools in this study, therefore, allows a nuanced look at a subset of schools that vary widely along potentially important dimensions such as financial stability, student body demographics, and academic standards. At the same time, these schools are similar with regard to potential confounding factors like religiosity, which could affect schools' early implementation experiences.

Burdens of School Voucher Participation

A handful of studies show that schools are sensitive to the burdens of voucher program administration (e.g., Egalite, 2015; Stuit & Doan, 2013; Sude et al., 2017). This literature has identified two major types of costs associated with participating in voucher programs: financial and regulatory (Sude et al., 2017). Financial costs include the costs associated with meeting program requirements—the staff time required to manage paperwork, for example—and costs associated with additional student enrollment, such as purchasing additional desks, textbooks, and other supplies or hiring additional teachers. Egalite (2015) finds that schools consider financial costs to be a major factor in their decision to participate or not in a voucher program.

Regulatory costs are those associated with meeting the requirements of a voucher program. When schools choose to participate in a voucher program, they become subject to increased oversight and accountability from the state. Participation requires schools to comply with requirements such as participating in state standardized testing and publicly reporting test results, meeting curricular or licensure standards, and reporting on program administration (Stuit & Doan, 2013; Sude et al., 2017). A 2013 analysis identified Indiana's voucher program as the second most heavily regulated program in the country (Stuit & Doan, 2013). Some studies have found that regulations can be a deterrent to schools considering participating in voucher programs (Egalite, 2015; Stuit & Doan, 2013); other work suggests that programs' specific regulations are less of a barrier than some schools' general desire to retain autonomy and avoid state oversight (Austin, 2015; Kisida et al., 2015).

To the financial and regulatory costs to schools of participating in a voucher program this chapter adds school organizational and social costs involved in accepting and supporting voucher recipients. These costs include administrative work to adapt to the academic, social, and behavioral needs of voucher recipients while maintaining academic standards, school identity, and responsiveness to students and families already attending the school (Austin, 2014).

Most voucher programs have income eligibility requirements that limit participation to students from low-income families; in Indiana, modest-income families are also eligible.[1] In many locations, including Indiana, voucher recipients are disproportionately African American, Latino, and multi-racial (Austin, 2014; Figlio, 2009; Morgan, 2001; Waddington & Berends, 2017). In Indiana, program regulations in the ICSP's first two years required students to have previously attended a public school (see Austin, 2015 for details). Due to these two sets of requirements, participating schools often experienced an influx of new students from demographic backgrounds that differed from the schools' existing demographic composition and who often had experienced a very different set of academic and behavioral expectations in their previous schools than those they encountered in their schools of choice.

Austin (2015) finds that the majority of Indiana private schools that chose to participate in the ICSP were most concerned with factors related to the organizational and social costs of participating. These organizational and social concerns are even more pronounced for Catholic schools than for other private schools, and they dwarf participating schools' concerns over any of the ICSP's regulatory requirements other than the program's admissions criteria, which is closely tied to the social impacts of accepting voucher students.

As Figure 3.1 illustrates, participating Catholic schools were most concerned about the potential costs of participating in the voucher program that were not related to program regulations (those in the non-regulatory category). They were least concerned about the program regulations that carry the highest regulatory burden compared to other voucher programs nationwide (those in the high burden category; Stuit and Doan, 2013). In part, this may be because many of Indiana's Catholic schools already participated in state testing and complied with other state accreditation requirements to be eligible to participate in athletic programs. This prior familiarity and experience with state regulations likely eased schools' concerns about the regulatory costs involved in becoming a voucher school. However, these schools still may experience some regulatory burden. For example, Austin (2015) found that the increased reporting requirements were a source of frustration for some schools.

Financial regulations, which carry less burden in Indiana than in other voucher programs, fell between the two in terms of schools' level of concern. The ICSP allows private schools to charge tuition over and above the amount of a voucher (about $4,500 at the elementary school level in 2011), so schools that charge higher tuition rates do not have the financial disincentive

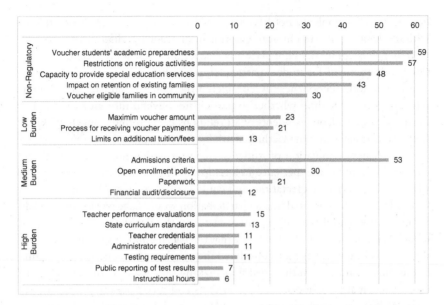

FIGURE 3.1 Percentage of Catholic schools participating in the Indiana Choice Scholarship Program that said each non-regulatory potential impact or regulation was "very important" or "extremely important" when weighing the decision to participate. Regulations are classified as low, medium, or high burden based on Stuit and Doan's (2013) measure of regulatory burden.

to participate that schools in other locations do (Stuit & Doan, 2013; Sude et al., 2017). In Indiana, as a result, the most prevalent tuition-related cost is that of voucher funds left on the table. Many voucher schools, especially Catholic schools, have a funding model that sets tuition rates below the cost to educate students. Because the maximum voucher amount for a school is calculated based on the school's tuition rate, many schools receive less than the maximum amount because they have set their tuition rates artificially low.

Compared to financial and regulatory costs, organizational and social costs were of much greater concern to participating Catholic schools. The social costs of participation include those associated with enrolling a new population of students who are not accustomed to the academic, social, behavioral, and religious norms of the Catholic schools. When weighing their participation decisions, 59 percent of participating schools stated that voucher students' academic preparedness was "very important" or "extremely important." Schools were similarly concerned about whether the program would allow them to uphold their admissions criteria—53 percent of respondents said admissions regulations were very or extremely important. Forty-eight percent of respondents said their capacity to provide special education services weighed heavily in their decision to participate. As will be discussed further in the results section, most Catholic schools do not have the capacity to meet the needs of students with moderate to severe physical, emotional, or academic disabilities.

Indiana's program does not place any restrictions on schools' religious activities or requirements for student participation in religious activities, but 57 percent of Catholic schools heavily considered the potential impact on religious activities when deciding whether to participate. Several interviewees emphasized that they welcome students of all religious backgrounds, but they expect students to respect that the Catholic faith is a core characteristic of their school identity. A new population of students, many of whom may not be Catholic and do not have prior experience in a religious school, may take more time to adapt to the religious expectations and could disrupt the school culture.

In addition, the potential impact participation would have on families already attending the school was an important factor in the decisions of 43 percent of schools, and 30 percent of schools felt that the social context surrounding their schools was important as they considered the number of voucher-eligible families in the community in their decision-making processes. As this chapter will show, participating schools faced social costs and made organizational investments to help new students adjust to academic, social, behavioral, and religious norms of the Catholic schools and address challenges to the school community that came with participation.

Literature Review

Admissions and Enrollment

Some opponents of school choice argue that schools of choice cream-skim the highest performers from public schools, thus reducing the social cost of accepting students who are lower-performing academically or behaviorally (Lacireno-Paquet et al., 2002; Stewart & Wolf, 2014; Zimmer et al., 2011). The ICSP admissions regulations require schools to follow the same admissions process for all students. However, even the same admissions process may produce different outcomes for different populations of students. Some studies have found evidence that schools use admissions requirements to screen for better-prepared students and make decisions about who to admit that are "focused on maintaining an advantageous market position" and therefore exclude or limit access for the highest-need populations (Jennings, 2010; Lubienski et al., 2009). Schools may create barriers to entry through enactment of admissions standards, behind-the-scenes exclusionary practices (Jennings, 2010), or activities that appear neutral but impose a burden on certain types of families, such as requiring attendance at an evening open house when transportation options are limited and low-income parents are working extra hours (Jennings et al., 2016; Pattillo et al., 2014; Sattin-Bajaj, 2011).

Other critics of voucher programs suggest that private schools control access by expelling students who do not meet the school's academic or behavioral standards, although some research suggests that this is not the case (Howell & Peterson, 2006; Peterson, 2009). Exclusionary admissions or disciplinary practices may be intentional, to minimize the organizational and social challenges that can occur when admitting a new population of students accustomed to different academic and behavioral norms. Other practices, such as offering informational materials only in English, may be unintentional as schools minimize the burden of a new program by simply maintaining their usual processes. In still other cases, schools may seek out opportunities to attract and enroll new types of students. This may be especially true of Catholic schools, the majority of which were motivated to participate in the ICSP due to the program's alignment with their mission to serve all students (Austin, 2014, 2015).

School Community

Serving a more diverse population of students may challenge Catholic schools' communities, which tend to be characterized by high levels of social closure (Carbonaro, 1998; Coleman & Hoffer, 1987; Morgan & Sørensen, 1999). Coleman and Hoffer's (1987) study on public and private high schools first suggested that Catholic schools are embedded in a unique type of community, in which both social norms and sanctions are embedded into the social structure of the community, helping to "both reinforce and perpetuate that structure" (p. 7). Bryk and colleagues expanded on this early research, finding that Catholic schools are distinctive in their emphasis on "building and nurturing a school community" (Bryk et al., 1993). They defined Catholic schools' communal organization as having three critical components: "(1) a set of shared values among members of the school community (administrators, teachers, students, and parents); (2) a set of shared activities, both academic and non-academic in nature; and (3) a distinctive set of social relations among school members" fostered by an "ethic of caring" (1993, p. 277). This strong school community is an end in itself; it also helps foster a climate of academic success (Bryk et al., 1993; Eide et al., 2004; Sikkink, 2012). Maintaining the school's community while integrating a new population of students into the school is a new challenge for many voucher schools (Morgan, 2001). Catholic schools' concern over how participation may affect their religious identity reflects this challenge, as religious identity plays a major role in the focus on shared values and activities that contribute to maintaining a strong community.

Similarly, the data presented above show that Catholic schools heavily weighed both the existing school community and the community of potential voucher students surrounding the school in their decisions to participate. As will be shown in the results, schools in our sample often focused their recruiting efforts on messaging through existing ties to individual families or their broader religious communities. Still, even schools that enroll students with some prior connection to the school community may face a backlash from parents of already enrolled students. In studies of how parents choose schools for their children, parents overwhelmingly express a preference for rigorous academics (Altenhofen et al., 2016; Billingham & Hunt, 2016; Denice & Gross, 2016; Harris & Larsen 2015). Parents are often less explicit about the role of racial preference in their school choices, but multiple studies have found that White parents, in particular, use a school's racial and socioeconomic composition as a proxy for school quality (Goyette, 2008; Goyette et al. 2012; Holme, 2002). Existing parents who are concerned about how voucher students may influence a school's academic rigor, or who consider students' race or socioeconomic status an indicator of their academic or behavioral capacity, may not welcome the new students. Existing parents whose socioeconomic status is similar to that of voucher students may feel resentful that they do not qualify for the same financial aid because they already committed to a Catholic education for their children. Both threaten the cohesiveness of a school's community.

To date, little research has examined how schools accepting voucher students approach these challenges (Austin, 2014). In this chapter, I contribute to this new research focus by highlighting the non-regulatory organizational and social costs of voucher program participation, which in Indiana's heavily regulated voucher program are of greater concern to Catholic schools than are most regulations. I identify two major areas of school administration that are influenced by these costs—admissions and enrollment policies and practices, and parent engagement—and analyze how school principals accept and mitigate the costs in these areas that come with accepting voucher recipients.

Methods

To examine schools-level responses to organizational and social costs of voucher program participation, I draw on in-person, semi-structured interviews with principals at 10 Catholic schools in Indianapolis and northern Indiana that participate in the ICSP. Indiana's Catholic schools participate in the ICSP at a near-universal rate, which suggests that Catholic schools' participation is not conditioned on school organizational characteristics apart from their religious orientation. The schools vary widely along potentially important dimensions such as financial stability, student body demographics, and academic standards.

Schools selected for qualitative interviews were purposively sampled to reflect the population of participating schools in terms of school size, relative financial stability, and population served prior to voucher participation. Schools were also chosen to maximize variability in terms of the number and proportion of voucher students enrolled at each school. The sample includes eight elementary and two secondary schools. All 10 schools are located in urban areas. School sizes range from less than 100 students to over 1,000 students. Schools' student bodies were composed of between three percent and 32 percent voucher students in 2011–12; all of the schools increased their voucher student enrollment in 2012–13.

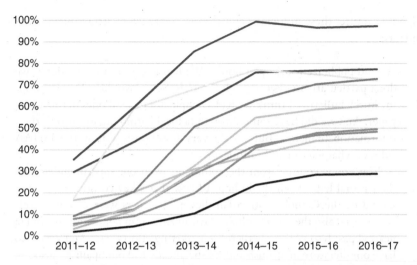

FIGURE 3.2   Voucher Student Enrollment as a Percentage of Total Student Enrollment by School Year for all Interview Schools.

Figure 3.2 shows voucher enrollment at each of the case study schools as a percentage of total enrollment. Schools are not labeled or linked to enrollment numbers to protect their anonymity.

All interviews were coded in Atlas.ti using a two-stage coding process. First, open coding was used to identify major ideas, themes, and issues (Emerson et al., 2011), and a set of codes then was developed from the first stage and applied to the data using a top-down coding framework.

Results

Voucher Student Recruitment and Admissions

Interviewed schools reported that it was uncommon for them to reject students, whether they were voucher recipients or traditional applicants. Similarly, schools did not change their admissions practices—under Indiana's voucher law, schools could keep their existing admissions policies but were required to apply them equally to voucher students as well as non-voucher students. Many schools focused their efforts to attract new students to their immediate religious communities, but this often meant reaching out to a more demographically and socioeconomically diverse set of families.

Most of the Catholic schools interviewed mentioned focusing initial recruiting efforts within their religious community. At the high school level, this approach is influenced by the Indiana High School Athletic Association (ISHAA) rules against recruiting, but it is also influenced by Catholic schools' emphasis on community and mission, a major driver of Catholic school participation in the voucher program (Austin, 2015). One high school principal's response captures these influences and schools' approach to attracting voucher students:

> We did publicize [our] open house. We had to be careful. We don't, we don't particularly market to public schools. So we would publicize things in church bulletins. I think we had a couple just general ones in the newspaper. And we did have some through [a local Latino organization], their information branches. But we do very fastidiously follow the ISHAA rules of what we can and cannot do.
>
> You know, coming from the comments from our superintendent and the pastoral letter from the bishop, I knew that a key constituency for us should be the Catholic Latino families. […] Others were certainly welcome—and also there is a Catholic African American population around [a nearby] parish so you know there's a marketing effort there. And we try to have our literature in Spanish and we specifically had our Spanish-speaking employees or our students with us when we spoke in certain areas of town.
>
> *(School 10)*

The above school reached out to several diverse communities. Other schools focused efforts on informing a large pool of eligible families within their own communities, through word of mouth or via communications directly to parishioners. Latinos are growing rapidly as a proportion of the U.S. Catholic population (Matovina, 2012; Pew Research Center, 2015), and several school communities reflected this demographic shift. A principal of a school with a sizeable existing Latino population reported that they were marketing to a similar population in the broader parish:

> with having such a huge population in our Sunday religious education [classes], we have over 1,000 students in our Sunday religious ed, and 75 percent of them are Latino. So that's who we market to, and we're not really—although we did […] put it on the marquee [sign in front of the school] out there.
>
> *(School 3)*

An elementary school principal of a school that had not previously enrolled many Latino students focused on parish outreach and word of mouth through current students, but made changes to marketing materials:

> We've mostly done our marketing just to the parish. Other than that, we sent [five postcards] home with our current students and said, 'Give this to five of your friends, and tell them about [our school].' All of our enrollment, everything now is in English and in Spanish, which again is a learning curve because we tend to get that form and [send it out the

following day]. Now, it has to go to somebody and be translated. We'll get better at that.

(School 3)

While the above school increased its racial/ethnic diversity, other schools reached out to a more socioeconomically diverse set of families within their communities than they already were serving. Of voucher-eligible families who enrolled, one principal said, "I think the majority of them already knew of the school. I think their issue was financially, can we make this work" (School 6). Another principal reported marketing to families who attended the parish but could not previously afford to attend the school:

We've done a lot in the past two years with the parish, with our priest, who's very actively involved with getting recruitment for the school. Prior to vouchers, nobody thought they could afford it. It was just a pipe dream. [Families thought,] "My kind of family doesn't go to a private school," and so educating from the pulpit has been really helpful as well.

(School 8)

By focusing recruiting efforts on families attending the school's parish or other nearby parishes and relying on word of mouth advertising, schools increased the likelihood that incoming students would be familiar with the schools' social and religious norms. At the same time, the families targeted by these efforts were often more demographically and socioeconomically diverse than currently enrolled families, and came from schools with different academic, cultural, and behavioral expectations. Schools relied on their admissions practices to address some of these challenges—though most often through screening-in practices, rather than screening-out applicants.

The admissions processes schools described invariably applied to both voucher recipients and traditional applicants—per Indiana law, schools could not have different admissions standards for voucher and non-voucher recipients. Several principals emphasized that they have rejected both non-choice students and choice students (School 10). One principal stated, "that was kind of a key question for many of the private schools and Catholic schools—can we still say no to a student that might not be a good mix for our student population?" But, at least during the admissions process, very few students were dismissed as "not a good mix." Instead, principals at both the elementary and high school levels typically described generous admissions policies that focused not on screening out students whose academic or disciplinary records showed cause for concern but rather on communicating expectations and identifying the student's needs.

Most schools described a simple application form that could often be completed online. Schools would then request academic, behavioral, and attendance records from any schools that applicants had previously attended, if an applicant was seeking to transfer rather than to start in the school's lowest grade. By its nature, the process was generally more involved for students transferring into the school than for students entering at the school's lowest grade level, as transfer students had prior school records and were more diverse in their prior school experiences. In the years under study here, when most voucher recipients were required to have attended a public school prior to receiving a voucher, the ICSP did create a higher volume of transfer students to shepherd through the admissions, orientation, and placement process.

Several principals described student interviews as part of the process for all applicants; others requested an interview only in cases where prior records showed cause for concern. For example, one elementary school principal described their interview policy as follows:

> If the documentation does show some red flags, we'll pull the family in for an interview with the student and just ask them, "Why do you want in eighth grade to come to [our] school?" It typically happens with the older grade levels.
>
> *(School 3)*

The most common "red flags"—a term used by several principals—mentioned were prior disciplinary problems, very low prior academic performance, and moderate to severe special needs. Of these, however, principals treated only special needs that could not be met as a reason not to admit a student. Principals treated most prior academic and disciplinary problems as reasons to have a conversation with an applicant, but not—in the vast majority of cases—to deny admission. One elementary school principal's response typifies the approach taken at the majority of sampled schools:

> We look at their grades. Grades are not that big of a deal, though. We've accepted kids who had very low grades because when they got here they turned it around. It's a different environment. But I think the main thing is behavior. But that's it. We really don't have anything that weeds kids out [...] We make sure we can accommodate their needs and support them academically. Behaviorally, we see if we can support them. We look at their discipline records. We're just not into taking everyone's problems. We do look at that. That's not to say that a student who had a discipline issue at another school doesn't come here and do very well. But basically that's it. We don't discriminate academics. [...] Pretty much we open the doors to whoever wants to come and be a part of it. Really, the only reason why a family would be denied is if we felt like we couldn't meet their needs.
>
> *(School 3)*

Another elementary school principal echoed the challenge of students transferring in at older grades, especially students with extremely low prior academic performance:

> It's going to be more difficult as you're older, because we have pre-algebra in seventh, algebra in eighth and you're going to get thrown in to the middle of that. If you're unprepared, then you're really going to have difficulty so … you look at it and you make a determination if the student can be brought up to speed in time, in a reasonable time.
>
> *(School 6)*

However, the school's decision for these students was not whether to admit them or not, but whether to place them: "And then if you do not think that they can [be brought up to speed], that they would benefit from another year of preparation or retention, then you offer to bring them in if they're willing to repeat the grade" (School 6).

Similarly, even students with more extreme disciplinary or academic challenges were usually admitted, often following an interview that gave principals a chance to discuss school expectations. One principal, at a school that had not rejected any students, responded:

> If a family comes in and says, "My student's been expelled from such and such school," that, obviously, is going to send up flags and it has to be an investigation of what happened and why and some background information. You have to get that from the previous schools, and just find out what's going on before there's going to be any kind of acceptance into the school. That would be the big thing.
>
> *(School 8)*

Even if Catholic schools do not use the admissions process to screen out voucher recipients, simply having an admissions process may serve as a barrier to some applicants (Jennings, 2010). One of the principals interviewed indicated that the school uses its admissions processes as a mechanism to encourage the least motivated students to self-select out of the applicant pool. After years of open enrollment (including several years prior to the ICSP), this high school began requiring students complete both a brief formal application online and an in-person interview. The principal explained the motivation as follows:

> What we believe is, we used to say we had the hotel method of admissions. Checked in and checked out. You just kind of signed in, paid your bill, and came in. And with that, I think, comes a level of, pardon my expression, but riff-raff. And they just check in, and two months later after they've wreaked havoc with your building for a

couple weeks, they're checking out and going to a different school. With this process, those people, they just don't go through the process. They're not going to go online. They're not going to fill out an application. They're not going to write essays. They're not going to come in for an interview. They're just not going to do all that. They'll say, "You know what, honey? Let's just go to School X and be done." So we've done, I don't know, 400 or 500 interviews. We've probably only denied five or six kids in five or six years. Less than one kid a year. I think as we – as I've looked back on a couple of them, academics in terms of just woeful academic skill set with no real sense that it is of a concern to them. That's probably the driving force on most of them. In the interview, the one that probably screams the loudest is the kid doesn't have any desire to do this. He doesn't want to be here, wants to be in his local public school where he's grown up. And you can just see it's destined for failure from the get-go.

(School 4)

Viewing the admissions process as a means to screen out unmotivated students was not the norm among interviewed schools. However, several schools identified students who do not "have any desire" to be in a Catholic school as more likely to struggle than those with prior academic or behavioral challenges who were open to moving to the Catholic school.

Voucher Student Departures

In the ICSP's first two years, seven to nine percent of voucher recipients exited their private voucher school mid-year, to return to a public school or enroll in a different voucher school (Indiana Department of Education, 2016); overall, about 20 percent of voucher recipients exit their voucher school either during or between school years (Austin et al., 2018; Waddington & Berends, 2017). In our interviews, principals identified 35 specific cases in which voucher recipients left their Catholic school in one of the first two years of the voucher program—approximately 5 percent of all voucher recipients who enrolled in the 10 interviewed schools. Interviewers collected information on the total number of students, voucher recipients, and voucher recipients who did not remain in their school, as well as the reasons students left, whether because they were asked or chose to do. Table 3.1 provides a summary of these responses. We do not have complete information on the number of non-voucher recipients who left each school to compare the rates of attrition for voucher and non-voucher recipients. However, four principals reported losing similar or somewhat higher percentages of non-voucher recipients than voucher recipients.

Overall, the most common type of exit was students who were asked to leave because of behavioral problems. This group comprised approximately

TABLE 3.1 Reasons Voucher Recipients Left Interview Schools in Year 1 or Year 2 of the ICSP

Reason Left	Asked by School or Chose to Leave	Number of Students	Number of Schools
Behavior	Asked	10	4
Family situation	Chose	5	2
Not meeting behavioral/academic expectations	Asked	3	1
Residential move	Chose	3	1
Academics	Chose	3	1
Academics	Asked	2	1
Couldn't meet special needs	Asked	2	1
Homeschool	Chose	2	1
Not a good fit	Chose	1	1
Incarcerated	N/A	1	1
Unspecified	Chose	3	1

Note: Table shows primary reason for departure for all 35 individual voucher recipients identified by principals as having left one of the 10 Catholic schools interviewed. In each interview, principals were asked whether any voucher students had left the school and if so, why they left.

one-third of all leaving voucher students. Although the type and severity of behavior problems varied, one principal's response illustrates that typically students were asked to leave due to ongoing problems, rather than single incidents:

> And that's what ended up happening specifically to the one student we asked not to come back last year. You know? I'm meeting with you every day, and every day, we're going over the same thing. You can't take things out of peoples' lockers. You can't tell your teacher you turned in this [assignment when you didn't], and we're just having those every single day, every single day. And it was like we exhausted everything we know, and we sometimes were dealing with certain behaviors we're just not equipped to deal with.
>
> *(School 3)*

Another 23 percent left because of changes in their family situation (e.g., foster care, parental divorce) or residential location made travel to the school difficult. About 17 percent were asked to leave due to academic challenges and another 9 percent chose to leave due to academic challenges. One elementary school principal who had three students choose to leave over the program's first two years identified the reasons as follows:

> [it was] because of academics. I think the parents were disappointed in the grades which the children were getting and I'm not sure how well some of them might have felt like they fit into the classroom. There was one little girl that seemed to have a very strong personality and there were two other students in her class that also had strong personalities so

> I'm not sure if there was just a little contention upon who got their way
> but I think it was primarily academics.
>
> *(School 7)*

A high school student's choice to leave his school was due to more general dissatisfaction: "It just wasn't a good fit for him. And I will say this. The older sibling is here and has been successful. The younger sibling just didn't like it. I understand that" (School 4).

Of the students who left in this sample, 17 were asked to leave, 17 chose to leave, and one was incarcerated. Although this sample is not representative of the full set of voucher schools or student departures, it provides some initial insight into reasons for voucher student exit from voucher schools.

Impact on the Community

Despite real challenges that accompanied the arrival of many voucher students, schools' leadership tended to embrace the program and worked to frame a potentially disruptive decision as in alignment with their emphasis on community and their shared values. Of parents' and teachers' responses to comments that voucher recipients were bringing down their school's academic and behavioral standards, one principal said:

> The [school leadership] had conversations about this. What do you think?
> Do you think this is the best thing for our schools? Because we knew
> that once we opened the door to kids who came in on the Choice program that they were going to be behind. They were going to be behind
> socially, emotionally, [...] academically. And that meant we were going
> to have to step up our game even more. I mean we could've sat back and
> said, "No, we don't want this because our kids are okay where they are."
> But that's not our mission. Our mission is to serve as many kids as we can.
>
> *(School 5)*

Although leadership focused on the big-picture school mission tended to embrace this view, factors at the program, parent, and student level all presented challenges to Catholic schools' strong community orientation. One principal sums this up in the following:

> I think there's still that sporadic, "Why are we doing this? [Are we] going
> to get too entangled with the government? Is the climate of the school
> changing?" We have a strong, I would say, community based, almost
> family based school. People appreciate that climate. They appreciate the
> safety. They appreciate the nurturing climate that exists here. Some people, I think, have a sense that that might be impacted. I don't think it has.
>
> *(School 4)*

At the program level, the ICSP's eligibility regulations created a backlash among families already enrolled at the school who met the financial criteria for a voucher but were ineligible because they already attended the Catholic school. One principal said:

> I think there's a lotta hurt feelings, honestly, because our families who have been here can't afford tuition. They are also on food stamps and received TANF and government assistance, but because they were here, that disqualifies them automatically. And some parents are very mad that they still have to pay tuition every month when according to financial income, [they] should be able to get a voucher.
>
> *(School 8)*

This frustration fostered divisiveness at several schools. Another principal described parents of non-voucher students as having "a little bit of us-versus-them mentality. There's that animosity because they still have to pay and they don't" (School 6).

School leadership felt this frustration as well; when asked what, if anything, about the ICSP they would change, many principals' first response was expanding the program to financially eligible children already attending a private school.[2] Schools took practical steps to ease this frustration for families, as one elementary school principal details:

> We just tried to dig deeper or when they get behind on the tuition they're already turning in what can I do to write it off, or help them through it, or find a donor who can cover it for them—because they do struggle but they made the choice without having that voucher in hand. I feel very guilty for them; empathetic that they are struggling and there's somebody right next to them who doesn't have that struggle because they chose to enroll at a different time.
>
> *(School 1)*

Another type of backlash to schools' decision to enroll voucher recipients was that of parents whose objections to schools' participation in the ICSP were based in prejudiced or racist stereotypes of voucher students. All 10 principals interviewed reported receiving at least some negative or derogatory comments from parents about "voucher kids" and their perceived impact on school academics or culture. Principals reported spending a good deal of time responding to the objections of already-enrolled parents to potential or perceived problems with enrolling voucher students in the school. One principal described objections to the idea of voucher student enrollment:

> I think one of the challenges that I face is that I could lose some of my families who have been here because they just don't get it – that everybody has a right

to this kind of education, not just the people who pay a little money, that we're not going to change because we accept the Choice scholarships. We're still going to expect a certain level of academic standards, behavioral standards. We're still going to expect that. I have heard comments from parents who have been here before that said that they did not like the idea that kids were coming in and changing the school culture. I have heard that they felt like some of the kids who came in were going to change the academic standards. So yeah there is that feeling that they're going to change our school and make our school different. We've worked very hard at trying to dispel that.

(School 5)

These conversations took place on "back channels," with parents talking to one another but not directly to the principal (School 6). Another principal reported similar conversations with parents who were quick to assume new students who cause trouble are voucher students, especially if they are students of color:

It seems to me that the children are doing fine. We do have here and there the kind of, I would say, kind of vulgar, by adults, [comments about] "voucher kids" and ironically, they base their decision on whether that's a voucher kid frequently on race and I know of specific examples where their assumption that a kid who maybe, you know, is a bit of trouble-maker something was a voucher kid, they were 100% wrong. That was not a voucher student that they were talking about. And they do that, "voucher kid, voucher kid" thing rather than [referring to them as] a student who's just receiving a choice scholarship, and they make that distinction as if there's something wrong with that. However, [the parents commenting are] receiving the parish subsidy; you know, they don't seem to see that that's an equivalent kind of aid that they're receiving.

(School 9)

The principal points out that parents often treat voucher recipients differently than recipients of other forms of financial aid, in part because of the association between financial eligibility for a voucher and students' race. In response, many principals addressed the discord created by both the decision to participate in the voucher program and the arrival of voucher students by working to remind teachers and families of the school mission and shared values that define their community. Principals made explicit efforts to rebut negative assumptions about voucher students, by speaking out on an ad hoc basis in response to parent complaints or, in some cases, by preparing formal remarks or presentations. The principal of School 9 continues her comments from above:

But that's, I think, it's educating. It's educating people, it's having people I think really walk our faith and, it's kind of, when it comes right into your life instead of being able to talk about 'Oh, I'm going to send my dollars there,' [now it's] 'oh I'm actually going to live with people that are struggling?' I think it's a wonderful challenge for us to be able to live our faith more fully.

Principals also directed this messaging toward students and teachers in the schools. Some new students—both voucher and non-voucher recipients—did bring academic or behavioral challenges to the classroom that affected both already-attending students and teachers, and both groups also occasionally expressed frustration, though to a lesser extent and more often in response to real behaviors than in the case of parents. One principal reported investing in a new disciplinary approach in response to more numerous and serious behavioral challenges than in the past and recounted a conversation with a teacher who was frustrated by the change:

> And one of my teachers said this to me, and I'm like, "You're right," [he said,] "We're spending so much energy on about eight percent of our fifth through eighth grade population right now where 92 percent are doing exactly what they should be. Why are we spending all this time on that? Why have them here?" Which I won't necessarily agree with that, but I see his point on why are we having to revamp and redo and come up with a new idea for eight percent of the kids.
>
> *(School 3)*

Although students and teachers had a better sense of who was and was not receiving a voucher than did parents, official information on voucher receipt was not shared with teachers. As a result, students and teachers also made assumptions about voucher recipients' identities, which principals worked to counter:

> There were some comments from some of the students, some of the adults in the building, [about] the "voucher kids" and I very specifically started the year, "we don't call them voucher kids. They're students. Didn't matter where they're coming from, and you don't know who they are. And you're making assumptions if you think students in the lower level classes or the students of color are all voucher kids because that's not the case." So I think ... yeah, just assumptions were made and we did our best to sort of [counter], we don't talk like that because that's an unfair label to put on children. It doesn't matter who's paying the bill, whether it's the state or the parents. We're still going to give them the best services we can.
>
> *(School 10)*

Conclusion

Participating schools did face organizational and social costs of participating in the ICSP. Because the ICSP required most students to have attended a public school for at least one year, participating schools experienced increased numbers of transfer student applications. Although schools generally maintained generous admissions policies, the increase in transfer applications required more administrative work to gather prior school records, evaluate students' academic performance and make a placement decision, and orient students to the school's expectations. Schools used the admissions process to begin integrating new students prior to their enrollment. This approach potentially reduced the disruptive influence of the arrival of a new population of students, even as schools welcomed students whose prior academic and behavioral records posed major challenges for administrators and teachers.

In most schools, comments and reactions from already-enrolled students and their parents, teachers, and other members of the community also had the potential to disrupt schools' strong sense of community. Principals devoted sizeable amounts of time to respond to such comments and communicate to the school community the value of voucher program participation for all students and the broader community. Schools' strong sense of mission motivated the extra efforts to foster both new student integration and acceptance from existing families. This clear vision was an important support as schools addressed significant organizational and social challenges. Schools should be prepared to experience and address these challenges when choosing to participate in a voucher program.

Notes

1 Students whose family income is up to 100 percent of the income limit for free and reduced-price lunch (FRPL) program eligibility are eligible for a voucher that covers 90 percent of tuition and fees; students whose family income is up to 200 percent of the FRPL eligibility cutoff are eligible for a voucher that covers 50 percent of tuition and fees.
2 In 2013, the Indiana voucher law was amended to open up several pathways to eligibility for students already attending private schools. However, these opportunities were not available in the program's first years, covered by this study.

References

Abdulkadiroglu, A., Pathak, P. A., & Walters, C. R. (2015). *School vouchers and student achievement: Evidence from the Louisiana Scholarship Program* (NBER Working Paper No. 21839). Cambridge, MA: National Bureau of Economic Research.

Altenhofen, S., Berends, M., & White, T. G. (2016). School choice decision making among suburban, high-income parents. *AERA Open, 2*(1), 1–14.

Austin, M. J. (2014). Sector effects following changes in student composition: The case of school vouchers. Paper presented at the Midwest Sociology of Education Conference, Notre Dame, IN.

Austin, M. J. (2015). Schools' responses to voucher policy: Participation decisions and early implementation experiences in the Indiana Choice Scholarship Program. *Journal of School Choice, 9*(3), 354–79.

Austin, M. J. & Berends, M. (In Press). School choice and learning opportunities. In *Handbook of the sociology of education in the 21st century*, edited by Barbara Schneider. New York: Springer.

Austin, M. J., Waddington, R. J., & Berends, M. (2018). Voucher pathways and student achievement in Indiana's Choice Scholarship Program. Paper presented at the Russell Sage Foundation Using Administrative Data for Science and Policy Conference, New York, NY.

Berends, M. (2015). Sociology and school choice: What we know after two decades of charter schools. *Annual Review of Sociology, 41*, 159–80.

Billingham, C. M. & Hunt, M. O. (2016). School racial composition and parental choice: New evidence on the preferences of white parents in the United States. *Sociology of Education, 89*(2), 99–117.

Bryk, A. S., Lee, V. E., & Holland, P. B. (1993). *Catholic schools and the common good*. Cambridge, MA: Harvard University Press.

Carbonaro, W. (1998). A little help from my friends' parents: Intergenerational closure and educational outcomes. *Sociology of Education, 71*(4), 295–313.

Coleman, J. C. & Hoffer, T. (1987). *Public and private high schools: The impact of communities*. New York: Basic Books.

Cowen, J. M., Fleming, D. J., Witte, J. F., Wolf, P. J., & Kisida, B. (2013). School vouchers and student attainment: Evidence from a state-mandated study of Milwaukee's Parental Choice Program. *Policy Studies Journal, 41*(1), 147–67.

Denice, P. & Gross, B. (2016). Choice, preferences, and constraints: Evidence from public school applications in Denver. *Sociology of Education, 89*(4), 300–20.

Egalite, A. J. (2015). Choice program design and school supply. In *New and better schools: The supply side of school choice* edited by M. Q. McShane (pp. 163–84). Lanham, MD: Rowman & Littlefield Publishers.

Eide, E. R., Goldhaber, D. D., & Showalter, M. H. (2004). Does Catholic high school attendance lead to attendance at a more selective college? *Social Science Quarterly, 85*, 1335–52.

Figlio, D. N. (2009). Voucher outcomes. In *Handbook of research on school choice* edited by M. Berends, M. G. Springer, D. Ballou, & H. J. Walberg (pp. 321–38). New York, NY: Routledge.

Goyette, K. A. (2008). Race, social background, and school choice options. *Equity and Excellence in Education, 41*(1), 114–29.

Goyette, K. A., Farrie, D., & Freely, J. (2012). This school's gone downhill: Racial change and perceived school quality among whites. *Social Problems, 59*(2), 155–76.

Green, J. P., Peterson, P. E., & Du, J. (1999). Effectiveness of school choice: The Milwaukee voucher experiment. *Education and Urban Society, 31*(2), 190–213.

Harris, D. N. & Larsen, M. F. (2015). *What schools do families want (and why)? School demand and information before and after the New Orleans post-Katrina school reforms*. New Orleans, LA: Education Research Alliance for New Orleans.

Holme, J. J. (2002). Buying homes, buying schools: School choice and the social construction of school quality. *Harvard Educational Review, 72*(2), 177–205.

Howell, W. G. & Peterson, P. E. (2006). *The education gap: Vouchers and urban schools*. Washington, DC: Brookings Institution Press.

Howell, W., Wolf, P. J., Campbell, D., & Peterson, P. E. (2002). School vouchers and academic performance: Results from three randomized field trials. *Journal of Policy Analysis and Management, 21*(2), 191–217.

Indiana Department of Education. (2016). *Choice scholarship program annual report: Participation and payment data.* Indianapolis, IN: Indiana Department of Education Office of School Finance, July. Retrieved from https://www.doe.in.gov/sites/default/files/choice/2015-2016-choice-scholarship-program-report-final-july-update.pdf.

Jennings, J. L. (2010). School choice or schools' choice? Managing in an era of accountability. *Sociology of Education, 83*(3), 227–47.

Jennings, J. L., Corcoran, S. P., Dinger, S., Sattin-Bajaj, C., Cohodes, S., & Baker-Smith, C. (2016). Administrative complexity as a barrier to school choice: Evidence from New York City. Paper presented at the annual meeting of the Sociology of Education Association, Asilomar, CA.

Kisida, B., Wolf, P. J., & Rhinesmith, E. (2015). *Views from private schools: Attitudes about school choice programs in three states.* Washington, DC: American Enterprise Institute.

Lacireno-Paquet, N., Holyoke, T. T., Moser, M., & Henig, J. R. (2002). Creaming versus cropping: Charter school enrollment practices in response to market incentives. *Educational Evaluation and Policy Analysis, 24*(2), 145–58.

Lareau, A. & Goyette, K. (2014). *Choosing homes, choosing schools.* New York: Russell Sage Foundation.

McShane, M. Q. (2015). *New and better schools: The supply side of school choice.* Lanham, MD: Rowman & Littlefield Publishers.

Matovina T. (2012). *Latino Catholicism: Transformation in America's largest church.* Princeton, NJ: Princeton University Press.

Morgan, S. (2001). Counterfactuals, causal effect heterogeneity, and the Catholic school effect on learning. *Sociology of Education, 74*(4), 341–74.

Morgan, S. & Sørensen, A. (1999). Parental networks, social closure, and mathematics learning: A test of Coleman's social capital explanation of school effects. *American Sociological Review, 64*(5), 661–81.

Pattillo, M., Delale-O'Connor, L., & Butts, F. (2014). High-stakes choosing. In *Choosing homes, choosing schools* edited by A. Lareau & K. Goyette (pp. 237–67). New York: Russell Sage Foundation.

Peterson, P. (2009). Voucher impacts: Differences between public and private schools. In *Handbook of research on school choice,* edited by M. Berends, M. G. Springer, D. Ballou, & H. J. Walberg. New York, NY: Routledge.

Pew Research Center. (2015). *America's changing religious landscape.* Washington, DC: Pew Charitable Trusts.

Rouse, C. E. (1998). Private school vouchers and student achievement: An evaluation of the Milwaukee Parental Choice Program. *Quarterly Journal of Economics, 113*(2), 553–602.

Sattin-Bajaj, C. (2011). Communication breakdown: Informing immigrant families about high school choice in New York City. In *School choice and school improvement,* edited by M. Berends, M. Cannata, & E. B. Goldring (pp. 147–73). Cambridge, MA: Harvard Education Press.

Shakeel, M. D., Anderson, K. P., & Wolf, P. J. (2016). *The participant effects of private school vouchers across the globe: A meta-analytic and systematic review.* Fayetteville, AR: University of Arkansas, Department of Education Reform (Working Paper 2016–07).

Sikkink, D. (2012). Religious school differences in school climate and academic mission: A descriptive overview of school organization and student outcomes. *Journal of School Choice, 6*(1), 20–39.

Stewart, T. & Wolf, P. J. (2014). *The school choice journey: School vouchers and the empowerment of urban families.* New York, NY: Palgrave Macmillan.

Stuit, D. & Doan, S. (2013). *School choice regulations: Red tape or red herring?* Washington, DC: The Thomas B. Fordham Institute.

Sude, Y., DeAngelis, C. A., & Wolf, P. J. (2017). Supplying choice: An analysis of school participation decisions in voucher programs in Washington, DC. *Journal of School Choice, 12*(1), 8–33.

Waddington, R. J. & Berends, M. (2017). Early impacts of the Indiana Choice Scholarship Program: Achievement effects for students in upper elementary and middle school. Paper presented at the annual meeting of the Society for Research on Educational Effectiveness, Washington, DC.

Witte, J. F., Wolf, P. J., Cowen, J. M., Carlson, D. E., & Fleming, D. J. (2014). High-stakes choice: Achievement and accountability in the nation's oldest urban voucher program. *Educational Evaluation and Policy Analysis, 36*(4), 437–56.

Wolf, P. J., Kisida, B., Guttmann, B., Puma, M., Eissa, N., & Rizzo, L. (2013). School vouchers and student outcomes: Experimental evidence from Washington, DC *Journal of Policy Analysis and Management, 32*(2), 246–270.

Zimmer, R. W. & Bettinger, E. P. (2015). Beyond the rhetoric: Surveying the evidence on vouchers and tax credits. In *Handbook of research in education finance and policy*, H. F. Ladd & M. E. Goertz (pp. 447–66). New York: Routledge.

Zimmer, R., Gill, B., Booker, K., Lavertu, Stephanie, & Witte, J. F. (2011). Charter schools: Do they cream skim, increasing student segregation? In *School choice and school improvement*, edited by M. Berends, M. Cannata, & E. B. Goldring (pp. 215–32). Cambridge, MA: Harvard Education Press.

4

DOES PRIVATE SCHOOL CHOICE IMPROVE STUDENT ACHIEVEMENT?

A Review of the Evidence

Patrick J. Wolf and Anna J. Egalite

The U.S. has had over a century of experience with school choice in one form or another. Because the public school's system of residential school assignment links housing choices to school choices, the most common mode of school choice throughout the twentieth century was a family's selection of a neighborhood in which to live (Tiebout, 1956). As any real estate agent can attest, school quality is reflected in housing and rental prices. Estimates suggest that families are willing to pay 2.5 percent more (or $6,688 in 2017 dollars) for a house zoned to a school whose test scores are 5 percent higher than average (Black, 1999). This public school quality premium is almost identical to the average tuition charge of $6,890 at Catholic schools in the U.S. (CAPE, 2018). Thus, public-school-choice-by-mortgage is almost an exact substitute, at least in terms of price, for the most common form of private schooling in the nation.

This situation creates access barriers for families unable to afford houses in areas with effective schools, as prices for even low-quality housing can be substantially inflated because of proximity to a desirable school. Approximately 27 percent of public school parents reported moving to their current neighborhood so their child could attend the zoned public school for that community (Grady & Bielick, 2010). This figure is highest among whites (29 percent) and Asians (36 percent), the non-poor (30 percent), and those living in suburban communities (33 percent). Nearly 11 percent of the K–12 student population self-finances private schooling, with low-income students under-represented among this distinctive population (Synder & Dillow, 2015).

For families restricted by their economic circumstances, more formalized government-funded school choice systems have developed. The most controversial modern school choice programs expand student options to private schools. Although fewer than half a million US students participate in private school choice, the number of students and programs have experienced remarkable growth in the past decade, a cause for alarm among school choice opponents and celebration among supporters. This chapter reviews the empirical evaluations of the achievement effects of private school choice programs in the U.S., including voucher programs and tax credit scholarship programs.

Overview of Private School Choice Programs

We define a private school choice program as any government initiative that provides a substantial amount of up-front financial assistance for parents to enroll a child in a private school. Private school choice programs come in four types. The first programs were established in Maine and Vermont in the latter half of the nineteenth century and continue to operate today (Maddaus & Mirochnik, 1992; McClaughry, 1987). Students living in towns in these two states that lack public schools serving their grade-level receive public funding to attend a private, non-religious school instead.[1] These "Town Tuitioning" programs are sometimes excluded from counts of private school choice programs, because they were not established explicitly to provide private schooling options for students and they exclude religious schools from participation. We include them here as the original private school choice programs because they have the practical effect of expanding parental school choice and later private school choice programs enacted for Milwaukee and Montana also were limited to secular private schools.[2] In 2016–17, the Maine Town Tuitioning program enrolled 5,727 students and the Vermont program served 3,350 (EdChoice, 2017).

The second type of private school choice is school vouchers. Vouchers provide government funds for students to attend state-approved private schools willing to participate in the program. Participating students must meet eligibility guidelines, which vary but generally require students to be low-income, have a disability, or be enrolled in a public school that has been rated in need of improvement. The first school voucher program was launched in Milwaukee in 1990 and the most recent one in Maryland in 2016. The Indiana Choice Scholarship Program is the largest voucher program in the U.S., enrolling 34,299 students in 2016–17 (Schultz et al., 2017).

The third type of private school choice initiatives are tax credit scholarship programs. These systems provide state tax credits to donors to nonprofit organizations that provide private school tuition scholarships to students. Most programs provide less than a dollar-for-dollar credit to donors but some do return all of the contributor's donation up to a statutory maximum. The fact that the funds supporting tax credit scholarships never actually enter government coffers makes such programs more likely to withstand legal challenges in the 38 U.S. states with so-called "Blaine Amendments" that restrict government funding of religious organizations. The Florida Tax Credit Scholarship Program was the first such program, established in 2001. It also is the largest of all the private school choice programs, serving 98,889 students in 2016–17 (Schultz et al., 2017). The newest tax credit scholarship program—the Invest In Kids Scholarship Tax Credit Program—was enacted in Illinois in 2017.

Education Savings Accounts (ESAs) are the fourth and most recently developed form of private school choice. An ESA is an expenditure account, established by the government, funded by a portion of the amount that the government would have spent on a student had they instead attended a public school. Parents can spend the funds on state-approved educational expenses such as private school tuition, tutoring, educational therapy, textbooks, and online instruction (Butcher & Burke, 2016). The first ESA program—the Empowerment Scholarship Accounts program—was established in Arizona in 2011. The most recent ESA program— the North Carolina Personal Education Savings Account Program—was enacted in 2017. Florida's Gardiner Scholarship Program is the largest ESA initiative in the U.S., serving 8,047 students with special needs in 2016–17 (Schultz et al., 2017).

Some states provide personal tax credits and deductions to families for private school expenses. Families also now can use tax-advantaged 529 savings plans to pay for private school tuition so long as the language in their state's laws regarding such accounts aligns with federal law. We do not count personal tax credits and deductions as private school choice programs because they involve government pay-backs and their assistance is too modest, typically amounting to less than $1,000 per child annually. Low-income families are unlikely to benefit from them.

How common is private school choice in the U.S.? The American Federation for Children's *School Choice Yearbook* (Schultz et al., 2017) includes the count of private school choice programs that most closely matches our definition. We subtract from their list personal tax credit programs in Alabama and South Carolina but add to it the Town Tuitioning programs in Maine and Vermont. These adjustments leave us with a count of 52 private school choice programs in 28 states plus the District of Columbia serving slightly more than 450,000 students or 0.7 percent of the total K–12 student population in 2016–17. For simplicity, throughout this chapter we will refer to them, collectively, as "choice programs."

Generally, the 52 choice programs can be distinguished along five key dimensions:

- *Jurisdiction*: Is eligibility limited to a single district, city, county, or an entire state?
- *Student Eligibility*: Is the program universal or is eligibility targeted to particular types of students such as the poor, students with disabilities, or military families?
- *Private School Regulation*: Do participating private schools have to be accredited? If so, by whom? Which assessments must they administer? Are they required to share test score results? If so, with whom—just parents, just the state, or the public? Are there accountability sanctions associated with student performance on specific assessments? Must they submit financial

audits? Can they administer admissions tests to screen out certain students based on academic ability or otherwise discriminate in admissions?

- *Value*: What is the maximum value of the voucher or scholarship? Does it vary by grade level? Can it cover education expenses beyond tuition?
- *Program Cap*: Is there a limit to the total number of participating students in a given year? If so, is this cap a hard limit or does it move from year to year? In cases in which the cap is reached, must states or schools employ a lottery to determine which students can participate?

The most recently established private school choice programs differ from earlier programs along three dimensions: (a) They are more likely to feature universal student eligibility; (b) they are more likely to apply statewide; and (c) they are more likely to involve ESAs. In the next section, we discuss these three developments in greater detail.

Recent Private School Choice Programs

Early choice programs, such as the Cleveland Scholarship and Tutoring Program, which began in 1996, restricted participation to low-income students. This legacy is apparent in the characteristics of well-established programs still operating today. Of the 52 choice programs in the U.S., nearly half (n=24) means-test applicants to determine program eligibility or service priority (Schultz et al., 2017). An additional 19 programs, including over 12 percent of all private school choice enrollees in 2014–15, are available only to students with disabilities. As school choice has become more commonplace in the United States, program eligibility has expanded to incorporate a broader swath of students. The newest choice programs—the Indiana Choice Scholarship Program and the Wisconsin Parental Choice Program, for example—have more inclusive income eligibility requirements than earlier programs did, and broader geographical reach, extending across an entire state instead of a single city.

The ESA model, with its ability to customize a child's education, is emerging as a popular type of private school choice. At the start of 2015, ESA programs existed only in Arizona and Florida. Since that time, four of the 11 newly enacted private school choice programs have been ESAs, in Mississippi, Nevada, North Carolina, and Tennessee.

Concerns about Private School Choice Programs and Achievement

As the expansion of choice programs continues, critics have claimed that support for school choice runs counter to the evidence regarding its effectiveness (Ravitch, 2011). Private school choice programs might fail to improve student test scores for any of four reasons. First, scholars have demonstrated that student academic achievement depends in large part on student background factors such as family income and parental incarceration (Egalite, 2016). Some school choice skeptics use this reasoning to argue that changing the school without changing the student will have little positive effect on student achievement (Condliffe et al., 2015). Other critics worry that parents will choose poorly when selecting a school for their child (Lauder & Hughes, 1999; Smith & Meier, 1995). A third claim is that traditional public schools actually are better than private schools at boosting student achievement (Lubienski & Lubienski, 2013). Finally, critics claim that private schools may be effective at teaching advantaged students but are ineffective at serving the kinds of disadvantaged students who participate in school choice programs (Fuhrer, 2013). If private school choice programs targeted at disadvantaged students tend to improve student test scores, doubt would be cast upon all four of these claims against school choice. In the next section, we seek to shed light upon these disputes by reviewing the empirical research on the effects of private school choice programs on the test scores of participating students.

Research Evidence on Vouchers

As of the date that this chapter went to press, researchers had conducted 23 empirical analyses of the reading achievement effects of private school choice programs in the US (Table 4.1a) and 23 assessments of the math achievement effects of such programs (Table 4.1b). The first study of school choice achievement effects focused on the Milwaukee Parental Choice Program. Witte (1998) reported no statistically significant achievement effects of the program in reading or math after four years. The most recent study, by Waddington and Berends (2018) of the Indiana Choice Scholarship Program, similarly found no significant achievement effects in reading but negative effects in math. In the intervening 19 years, however, the achievement effects reported from private school choice studies followed interesting patterns that defy easy characterization (Abdulkadiroglu et al., 2018; Anderson & Wolf, 2017; Barnard et al., 2003; Bettinger & Slonim, 2006; Bitler et al., 2014; Cowen, 2008; Dynarski et al., 2017; Figlio, 2011; Figlio & Karbownik, 2016; Greene, 2001; Greene et al., 1998; Jin et al., 2010; Krueger & Zhu, 2004; Metcalf et al., 2003; Mills & Wolf, 2017; Peterson et al., 1998; Peterson et al., 2003; Rouse, 1998; Waddington & Berends, 2018; Witte, 1998; Witte et al., 2012; Wolf et al., 2013).

In reading, 10 studies have reported positive effects, 11 have found no statistically significant differences between the choice students and control or comparison groups, and two have reported negative achievement effects. In math, eight studies have reported positive effects, 11 have found no differences, and four have reported negative achievement effects. Using standard vote-counting methods in summarizing results, with a positive result counting +1, a null result 0, and a negative result −1, private school choice programs score +8 in improving reading achievement and +4 in boosting math achievement. That pattern is not the whole story.

TABLE 4.1A Participant Achievement Effects of Private School Choice Programs in the United States on Reading Test Scores

Study	Study Type	Location	Study Year	Outcome Year	Overall Findings
Waddington & Berends	QED	Indiana	2018	4	-.14 standard deviations
Abdulkadiroglu et al.	Experimental	Louisiana	2018	1	-0.08 standard deviations
Dynarski et al.	Experimental	D.C. IV	2017	1	Null
Anderson & Wolf	Experimental	D.C. III	2017	4	+9 points
Mills & Wolf	Experimental	Louisiana	2017	3	Null
Figlio & Karbownik	QED	Ohio	2016	3	-0.31 standard deviations
Bitler et al.	Experimental	New York	2014	3	Null
Wolf et al.	Experimental	D.C. II	2013	4	+5 points
Witte et al.	QED	Milwaukee	2012	4	+0.15 standard deviations
Figlio	QED	Florida	2011	1	+4 points
Jin et al.	Experimental	New York	2010	1	Null
Cowen	Experimental	Charlotte	2008	1	+8 points
Krueger & Zhu	Experimental	New York	2004	3	Null
Barnard et al.	Experimental	New York	2003	1	Null
Peterson et al.	Experimental	New York	2002	3	+7 percentiles, subgroups
Peterson et al.	Experimental	D.C. I	2002	3	Null
Peterson et al.	Experimental	Dayton, OH	2002	2	+8 percentiles, subgroups
Metcalf et al.	QED	Cleveland	2003	5	Null
Greene	Experimental	Charlotte	2001	1	+6 percentiles, combined
Greene et al.	Experimental	Milwaukee	1999	4	+6 percentiles
Peterson et al.	QED	Cleveland	1998	1	+5 percentiles
Rouse	Experimental	Milwaukee	1998	4	Null
Witte	QED	Milwaukee	1998	4	Null

Notes: "Study Year" refers to year of publication; QED stands for quasi-experimental design. A "null" finding is one that was not statistically significant at p < .05. Overall findings taken from the authors' preferred statistical model. Findings that are positive and statistically significant appear with no shading while those that are null appear with light shading and those that are negative and statistically significant appear with dark shading.

TABLE 4.1B Participant Achievement Effects of Private School Choice Programs in the United States on Math Test Scores

Study	Study Type	Location	Study Year	Outcome Year	Overall Findings
Waddington & Berends	QED	Indiana	2018	4	Null
Abdulkadiroglu et al.	Experimental	Louisiana	2018	1	−0.41 standard deviations
Dynarski et al.	Experimental	D.C. IV	2017	1	−7 points
Anderson & Wolf	Experimental	D.C. III	2017	4	Null
Mills & Wolf	Experimental	Louisiana	2017	3	Null
Figlio & Karbownik	QED	Ohio	2016	3	−0.54 standard deviations
Bettinger & Slonim	Experimental	Ohio	2006	1	Null
Bitler et al.	Experimental	New York	2014	3	Null
Wolf et al.	Experimental	D.C. II	2013	4	Null
Witte et al.	QED	Milwaukee	1998	4	Null
Figlio	QED	Florida	2011	1	+4 points
Jin et al.	Experimental	New York	2010	1	+4 points, subgroups
Cowen	Experimental	Charlotte	2008	1	+7 points
Krueger & Zhu	Experimental	New York	2004	3	Null
Barnard et al.	Experimental	New York	2003	1	+5 points, subgroups
Peterson et al.	Experimental	New York	2002	3	+12 percentiles, subgroups
Peterson et al.	Experimental	D.C. I	2002	3	Null
Peterson et al.	Experimental	Dayton, OH	2002	2	Null
Metcalf et al.	QED	Cleveland	2003	5	Null
Greene et al.	Experimental	Milwaukee	1999	4	+11 percentiles
Peterson et al.	QED	Cleveland	1998	1	+9 percentiles, subgroups
Rouse	Experimental	Milwaukee	1998	4	+8 points
Witte	QED	Milwaukee	2000	4	Null

Notes: "Study Year" refers to year of publication; QED stands for quasi-experimental design. A "null" finding is one that was not statistically significant at p < .05. Overall findings taken from the authors' preferred statistical model. Findings that are positive and statistically significant appear with no shading while those that are null appear with light shading and those that are negative and statistically significant appear with dark shading.

From 1995 through 2011, the achievement effects of voucher and voucher-type programs were consistently in the range of null (no statistically significant difference) to positive. In reading, seven studies reported achievement gains either overall or for policy-relevant subgroups of students while the other seven found only null effects, for a vote-count score of +7. In math, the record was slightly more encouraging, with five studies observing null effects but eight reports concluding that private school choice had a positive effect on student math scores, a net of +8. That pattern changed starting in 2012. Since then, the reading effects of choice programs have been decidedly mixed, reported to be positive in three studies, null in four, and negative in two, for a net score of only +1. The voucher record on math achievement shifted even more dramatically, from tilting positive prior to 2012 to tilting negative since then. No recent private school choice study has reported positive math effects, six have observed null effects, and four have reported negative effects, for a net score of −4. The negative math impacts reported for the Ohio EdChoice Program (Figlio & Karbownik, 2016) and at least initially for the Louisiana Scholarship Program (Abdulkadiroglu et al., 2018; Mills & Wolf, 2017) have been disturbingly large.

Does the pattern of results vary by the rigor of the research design? Some reviews of the private school choice achievement effects have focused exclusively on those from experimental evaluations (Shakeel et al., 2017; Forster, 2016). Experimental evaluations randomly assign students to receive or not receive a private school voucher. Experiments are viewed by many social scientists as the "gold standard" for evaluation because they give us great confidence that any differences between the experimental "treatment" and "control" groups are actually caused by the program and not some other factor (Mosteller & Boruch, 2002). Quasi-experimental evaluations use various techniques to try to approximate the conditions of experiments. If those techniques work in the context of the evaluation, quasi-experiments can produce causal results similar to those of true experiments (Cook et al., 2008; Bifulco, 2012). We do not pass judgment on whether the specific quasi-experiments in our set satisfy the conditions for causal claims or not. We merely separate them out from the experiments to assess if research design matters much in determining if private school choice programs benefit students in terms of achievement.

Research design does appear to matter somewhat when interpreting the results from school choice achievement studies (Tables 4.2a and 4.2b). The 16 experimental evaluations of the reading effects of choice programs (six studies conducted after 2012 and 10 studies conducted prior to 2012) produce a vote-counting net score of +6 (i.e., +1 when evaluating those studies conducted after 2012 and +5 when evaluating those studies conducted prior to 2012), while the seven quasi-experimental studies (three studies conducted after 2012 and four studies conducted prior to 2012) only produce a net score of +2 (i.e., 0 when evaluating those studied conducted after 2012 and +2 when evaluating those studied conducted prior to 2012). Similarly, the math findings from experimental school

TABLE 4.2A Vote-counting Analysis of Scores from Various Subgroups of Studies on the Participant Achievement Effects of Private School Choice Programs in the United States, Post-2012

Group	Positive	Null	Negative	Net Score
Experimental Reading	2	3	1	+1
Quasi-Experimental Reading	1	1	1	0
Experimental Math	0	2	2	-2
Quasi-Experimental Math	0	0	2	-1
Totals	3	7	5	-2

Notes: Positive findings are statistically significant at $p < .05$ and count +1. Null findings are not statistically significant and count 0. Negative findings are statistically significant at $p < .05$ and count -1.

TABLE 4.2B Vote-counting Analysis of Scores from Various Subgroups of Studies on the Participant Achievement Effects of Private School Choice Programs in the United States, Pre-2012

Group	Positive	Null	Negative	Net Score
Experimental Reading	5	5	0	+5
Quasi-Experimental Reading	2	2	0	+2
Experimental Math	6	6	0	+6
Quasi-Experimental Math	2	3	0	+2
Totals	15	16	0	+15

Notes: Positive findings are statistically significant at $p < .05$ and count +1. Null findings are not statistically significant and count 0. Negative findings are statistically significant at $p < .05$ and count -1.

choice evaluations generate a net score of +4 while the quasi-experimental findings score 0. The private school choice achievement results are somewhat more positive if drawn from experimental than quasi-experimental studies.

Discussion and Conclusions

Over the past decade, support for school choice policies has evolved. Prominent supporters and public intellectuals, including Terry Moe, no longer refer to school choice broadly as a "panacea" (Chubb & Moe, 1990), but instead write about the importance of focusing on choice program design. At the extreme, several prominent education commentators have gone so far as to declare private school choice to be dead or, at best, a "failed experiment" (Anrig, 2008; Ravitch, 2011; Stern, 2008). School choice, however, is not dead. Fifty-two programs operate in 28 states plus the District of Columbia, providing access to private schools for over 450,000 students. The new programs enacted in recent state legislative sessions have tended to be statewide as opposed to urban, open to more than just low-income students, and take the form of Education Savings Accounts that permit families great latitude in customizing their child's education.

Evaluations of school voucher programs have generated important findings regarding the effects of vouchers on participating students. Overall, they indicate that the effect of school choice programs on student test scores largely tends to be null or positive, with important exceptions. The achievement results from voucher studies were more positive prior to 2012. The results since 2012 have been decidedly mixed regarding reading achievement and slightly negative regarding math. The results from more rigorous experimental evaluations are somewhat more positive than those from less rigorous quasi-experiments.

Why are the achievement results from private school choice studies trending less positive lately and diverging so dramatically between reading and math? We can only speculate. The earlier studies focused on voucher pilot projects and small privately funded scholarship programs. It is possible that the achievement gains reported for those early programs could not be sustained under larger-scale initiatives such as the statewide Indiana, Louisiana, and Ohio choice programs. Private school choice might have its strongest positive achievement effects on African American students (Howell et al., 2002), who compose a smaller portion of the recently studied voucher programs than they did of the earlier ones. Competition from vouchers and charter schools may have pressured traditional public schools to improve their educational performance, a claim supported by an increasing amount of evidence (Egalite & Wolf, 2016). The supply of private schools available to students in voucher programs may have decreased in quality, particularly due to widespread closures of Catholic schools (Brinig & Garnett, 2014). Parents may be seeking non-academic outcomes, such as safety or character skills, from the private schools they are accessing through choice (Wolf et al., 2018). Additional research is required to pinpoint which of these developments, or combination of them, explains the recent fall-off in the number of voucher evaluations reporting positive achievement effects.

But what about the divide between the more positive reading impacts and the less positive math findings in recent private school choice evaluations? Again, we cannot say for sure why choice programs appear to be doing better at producing relative reading gains than math improvement. Math is a more heavily sequenced discipline than is reading. It could be that the disruption of switching schools required to exercise private school choice has a stronger and more lasting negative effect on subsequent math achievement than on reading scores. There is a nationwide shortage of quality math teachers that has worsened recently. It might be that private schools, in particular, have difficulty luring talented math teachers to their classrooms because teacher pay tends to be lower in private than in public schools. Finally, it is possible that the private schools in recent voucher studies spend comparatively less instructional time on math but comparatively more instructional time on reading than do the public schools educating students in the study comparison groups.

As choice programs continue to expand, research should seek to answer those questions regarding why school voucher achievement effects are less positive now than before, and less positive in math than in reading. Research also should inform the following policy questions:

- How does the government achieve a balance of regulation and autonomy to ensure choice programs facilitate innovation and creativity whilst protecting the state's coffers from fraud and students from low-quality services?
- What strategies are in place to help parents become better school shoppers for their children?
- What are the fiscal impacts of private school choice policies? Are private schools more productive than public schools in the sense that they produce similar education outcomes at lower cost?
- What about the supply side of school choice (Egalite, 2014; McShane, 2014)? How are policies designed to ensure families have real choices? How can policymakers encourage existing high-quality private schools to expand and new private schools to open?
- Does increased private school choice expand the talent pool of educators and school leaders attracted to teaching? Do approaches to teacher and principal preparation evolve to be more similar or more different across school sectors as school choice expands?

One thing is sure: private school choice in its many forms is here to stay. It behooves us to learn more about the effects of this particular form of parental school choice.

Notes

1 For instance, a student entering ninth grade in a town in which the public schools only serve Kindergarten through eighth grade would qualify for the Town Tuitioning program.
2 The Milwaukee program was expanded to religious schools after a State Supreme Court ruling in 1998. The Montana program remains limited to secular private schools but that restriction is being challenged in court as a violation of the free exercise clause of the U.S. Constitution.

References

Abdulkadiroglu, A., Pathak, P. A., & Walters, C. R. (2018). Free to choose: Can school choice reduce student achievement? *American Economic Journal: Applied Economics*, *10*(1), 175–206.

Anderson, K. & Wolf, P.W. (2017). Evaluating school vouchers: Evidence from a within-study comparison. *EDRE Working Paper No. 2017-10*. Retrieved from https://papers.ssrn.com/sol3/papers.cfm?abstract_id=2952967.

Anrig, G. (2008, April). An idea whose time has gone: Conservatives abandon their support for school vouchers, *Washington Monthly*. Retrieved from http://www.washingtonmonthly.com/features/2008/0804.anrig.html.

Barnard, J., Frangakis, C. E., Hill, J. L., & Rubin, D. B. (2003). Principal stratification approach to broken randomized experiments: A case study of school choice vouchers in New York City. *Journal of the American Statistical Association, 98*(462), 299–311.

Bettinger, E. & Slonim, R. (2006). The effect of educational vouchers on academic and non-academic outcomes: Using experimental economic methods to study a randomized natural experiment. *Journal of Public Economics, 90*: 1625–48.

Bifulco, R. (2012). Can nonexperimental estimates replicate estimates based on random assignment in evaluations of school choice? A within-study comparison. *Journal of Policy Analysis and Management, 31*(3), 729–51.

Bitler, M. P., Domina, T., Penner, E. K., & Hoynes, H. W. (2014). Distributional analysis in educational evaluation: A case study from the New York City voucher program. *Journal of Research on Educational Effectiveness, 8*(3), 419–50.

Black, S. E. (1999). Do better schools matter? Parental valuation of elementary education. *Quarterly Journal of Economics, 114*(2), 577–99.

Brinig, M. F. & Garnett, N. S. (2014). *Lost classroom, lost community: Catholic schools' importance in urban America.* Chicago, IL: University of Chicago Press.

Butcher, J. & Burke, L. M. (2016). *The education debit card II: What Arizona parents purchase with Education Savings Accounts.* Indianapolis, IN: The Friedman Foundation for Educational Choice. Retrieved from http://www.edchoice.org/wp-content/uploads/2016/02/2016-2-The-Education-Debit-Card-II-WEB-1.pdf.

CAPE (2018). Facts and studies. Council for American Private Education. Retrieved from http://www.capenet.org/facts.html.

Chubb, J. E. & Moe, T. M. (1990). *Politics, markets, & America's schools.* Washington, DC: Brookings Institution Press.

Condliffe, B. F., Boyd, M. L., & DeLuca, S. (2015). Stuck in school: How social context shapes school choice for inner-city students. *Teachers College Record, 117*(3): 1–36.

Cook, T. D., Shadish, W. R., & Wong, V. C. (2008). Three conditions under which experiments and observational studies produce comparable causal estimates: New findings from within-study comparisons. *Journal of Policy Analysis and Management, 27*(4), 724–50.

Cowen, J. M. (2008). School choice as a latent variable: Estimating the "complier average causal effect" of vouchers in Charlotte. *Policy Studies Journal, 36*(2), 301–15.

Dynarski, M., Rui, N., Webber, A., Gutmann, B., & Bachmann, M. (2017). *Evaluation of the D.C. Opportunity Scholarship Program: Impacts after one year* (NCEE 2017–4022). Washington, DC: U.S. Department of Education. Retrieved from https://ies.ed.gov/ncee/pubs/20174022/pdf/20174022.pdf.

EdChoice (2017). *The ABCs of school choice.* Indianapolis, IN: EdChoice.

Egalite, A. J. (2014). Choice program design and school supply. In *New and better schools: The supply side of school choice,* edited by M. Q. McShane (pp. 163–84). Lanham, MD: Rowman & Littlefield Publishers, Inc.

Egalite, A. J. (2016). How family background influences student achievement. *Education Next, 16*(2). Retrieved from http://educationnext.org/how-family-background-influences-student-achievement/.

Egalite, A. J. & Wolf, P. J. (2016). A review of the empirical research on school choice. *Peabody Journal of Education, 91*(4), 441–54.

Figlio, D. N. (2011). *Evaluation of the Florida Tax Credit Scholarship Program: Participation, compliance and test scores in 2009–10*. Tallahassee, FL: Florida Department of Education.

Figlio, D. N. & Karbownik, K. (2016). *Evaluation of Ohio's EdChoice Scholarship Program: Selection, Competition, and Performance Effects*. Washington, DC: Thomas B. Fordham Institute. Retrieved from https://edex.s3-us-west-2.amazonaws.com/publication/pdfs/FORDHAM%20Ed%20Choice%20Evaluation%20Report_online%20edition.pdf.

Forster, G. (2016). A win-win solution: The empirical evidence on school choice. Indianapolis, IN: The Friedman Foundation for Educational Choice. Retrieved from http://www.edchoice.org/wp-content/uploads/2016/05/A-Win-Win-Solution-The-Empirical-Evidence-on-School-Choice.pdf.

Fuhrer, R. (2013). Know the facts on parental school choice. *NEA-Alaska President's Blog*. Retrieved from www.neaalaska.org.

Garcia, D. R. (2008). Academic and racial segregation in charter schools: Do parents sort students into specialized charter schools? *Education and Urban Society, 40*(5), 590–612.

Grady, S. & Bielick, S. (2010). *Trends in the Use of School Choice: 1993 to 2007*. Washington DC: U.S. Department of Education.

Greene, J. P. (2001). Vouchers in Charlotte. *Education Next, 1*(2), 55–60.

Greene, J. P. & Marsh, R. H. (2009). *The effect of Milwaukee's Parental Choice Program on student achievement in Milwaukee public schools*. Fayetteville, AR: School Choice Demonstration Project, University of Arkansas.

Greene, J. P., Mills, J. N., & Buck, S. (2010). *The Milwaukee Parental Choice Program's effect on school integration*. Fayetteville, AR: School Choice Demonstration Project, University of Arkansas.

Greene, J. P., Peterson, P. E., & Du, J. (1998). School Choice in Milwaukee: A Randomized Experiment. In *Learning from School Choice*, edited by P. E. Peterson & B. Hassel C. (pp. 335–56). Brookings Institution Press.

Henig, J. R. (1996). The local dynamics of choice: Ethnic preferences and institutional responses. In *Who chooses? Who loses? Culture, institutions, and the unequal effect of school choice*, edited by B. Fuller & R. Elmore F. New York: Teachers College Press.

Howell, W., Wolf, P. J., Campbell, D., & Peterson, P. E. (2002). School vouchers and academic performance: Results from three randomized field trials. *Journal of Policy Analysis and Management, 21*, 191–217.

Jin, H., Barnard, J., & Rubin, D. B. (2010). A modified general location model for noncompliance with missing data: Revisiting the New York City School Choice Scholarship Program using principal stratification. *Journal of Educational and Behavioral Statistics, 35*(2), 154–73.

Krueger, A. & Zhu, P. (2004). Another look at the New York City voucher experiment. *American Behavioral Scientist, 47*(5), 658–98.

Lauder, H. & Hughes, D. (1999). *Trading in futures: Why markets in education don't work*. Berkshire, United Kingdom: Open University Press.

Lubienski, C. A. & Lubienski, S. T. (2013). *The public school advantage: Why public schools outperform private schools*. Chicago, IL: University of Chicago Press.

McClaughry, J. (1987). *Educational choice in Vermont*. Concord, VT: Institute for Liberty and Community.

McShane, M. Q. (Ed.). (2014). *New and better schools: The supply side of school choice*. Lanham, MD: Rowman & Littlefield Publishers, Inc.

Maddaus, J. & Mirochnik, D. A. (1992). Town tuitioning in Maine: Parental choice of secondary schools in rural communities. *Journal of Research in Rural Education, 8*(1), 27–40.

Metcalf, K. K., West, S. D., Legan, N. A., Paul, K. M., & Boone, W. J. (2003). *Evaluation of the Cleveland scholarship and tutoring program: Summary report 1998–2002.* Bloomington, IN: Indiana University.

Mills, J. N. & Wolf, P. J. (2017). The effects of the Louisiana Scholarship Program on student achievement after three years. New Orleans, LA: Education Research Alliance. Retrieved from https://educationresearchalliancenola.org/files/publications/Mills-Wolf-Effects-of-LSP-on-Student-Achievement-After-Three-Years.pdf.

Mosteller, F. & Boruch, R. (2002). *Evidence Matters: Randomized Trials in Education Research,* Washington, DC: Brookings Institution Press.

Peterson, P., Greene, J. P., & Howell, W. (1998). New Findings from the Cleveland Scholarship Program: A Reanalysis of Data from the Indiana University School of Education Evaluation. Cambridge, MA: PEPG. Retrieved from https://sites.hks.harvard.edu/pepg/PDF/Papers/nwclvrpt.pdf.

Peterson, P., Howell, W., Wolf, P. J., & Campbell, D. (2003). School vouchers: Results from randomized experiments. In *The economics of school choice* edited by Caroline M. Hoxby. Chicago, IL: University of Chicago Press (pp. 107–44).

Ravitch, D. (2011, April 13). Miracle schools, vouchers and all that educational flim-flam, *Nieman Watchdog.* Retrieved from http://www.niemanwatchdog.org/index.cfm?fuseaction=ask_this.view&askthisid=503.

Rouse, C. E. (1998). Private school vouchers and student achievement: An evaluation of the Milwaukee Parental Choice Program. *The Quarterly Journal of Economics, 113*(2), 553–602.

Schultz, T., Carney, K., Marcavage, W., Jackson, N., Clements, E., Dauphin, P., & Martinez, K. (2017). *School choice yearbook – 2016–2017.* Washington, DC: American Federation for Children Growth Fund.

Shakeel, M. D., Anderson, K. P., & Wolf, P. J. (2017). The participant effects of private school vouchers across the globe: A meta-analytic and systematic review. *EDRE Working Paper 2016-07.* Retrieved from http://www.uaedreform.org/downloads/2016/05/the-participant-effects-of-private-school-vouchers-across-the-globe-a-meta-analytic-and-systematic-review-2.pdf.

Smith, K. B. & Meier, K. (1995). *The case against school choice: Politics, markets and fools.* New York: Routledge.

Snyder, T. D. & Dillow, S. A. (2015). *Digest of Education Statistics 2013.* Washington DC: U.S. Department of Education.

Stern, S. (2008). School choice isn't enough, *City Journal, 18*(1), 1.

Tiebout, C. M. (1956). A pure theory of local expenditures. *Journal of Political Economy, 64*(5), 416–24.

Waddington, R. J. & Berends, M. (2018). Impact of the Indiana Choice Scholarship Program: Achievement effects for students in the upper elementary and middle school. *Journal of Policy Analysis & Management* (Early View).

Witte, J. F. (1998). The Milwaukee voucher experiment. *Educational Evaluation and Policy Analysis, 20*(4), 229–51.

Witte, J., Carlson, D. E., Cowen, J. M., Fleming, D. J., & Wolf, P. J. (2012). *MPCP Longitudinal Educational Growth Study: Fifth Year Report* (No. 29). Fayetteville, AR: School Choice Demonstration Project. Retrieved from http://www.uaedreform.org/mpcp-longitudinal-educational-growth-study-fifth-year-report/.

Wolf, P. J., Hitt, C., & McShane, M. Q. (2018). Exploring the achievement-attainment disconnect in the effects of school choice programs. Paper presented at the conference "Learning from the Long-Term Effects of School Choice in America," Program on Education Policy and Governance, Kennedy School of Government, Harvard University, Cambridge, MA, April 19, 2018.

Wolf, P. J., Kisida, B., Gutmann, B., Puma, M., Eissa, N., & Rizzo, L. (2013). School vouchers and student outcomes: Experimental evidence from Washington, DC. *Journal of Policy Analysis and Management, 32*(2), 246–70.

5

THE EFFECTS OF CHARTER SCHOOLS ON STUDENT ACHIEVEMENT

Julian R. Betts and Y. Emily Tang

Charter schools are public schools that receive public funds but receive exemptions from parts of states' education codes, allowing them to hire teachers differently and to experiment with alternative curricula and pedagogical approaches. In return for this relative independence, charter schools face a greater risk of being closed than traditional public schools. Every few years when a charter school must apply to the chartering authority for a renewal, that authority can turn down the renewal.

Charter schools represent one of the most important innovations in school management in the United States. The National Alliance for Public Charter Schools (2017) estimates that in the 2016–17 school year a total of 6,900 charter schools, enrolling 3.1 million students, were operating in 42 states as well as the District of Columbia. This represents almost a tripling in enrollment over ten years.

Given that charter schools are intended to improve student learning, in this review chapter, we study the relation between attending a charter school and scores on state-mandated tests in mathematics and reading. The chapter updates and extends prior papers we have written (Betts & Tang 2008, 2011, 2014).[1] We use a method known as meta-analysis to estimate the overall relation between attending charter schools and achievement, and also, crucially, to examine the variation across studies and locations.

Our findings are as follows. On average, for the limited set of charter schools, locations, and years that have been studied to date, charter schools are producing higher achievement gains in math relative to traditional public schools in elementary and middle but not high schools. For reading achievement charter schools on average are producing higher gains in middle schools but not in elementary or high schools. For both math and reading, middle school studies tend to produce the highest effect sizes of all of the grade groupings. The literature shows a large variation in estimated charter school effects across locations, and some studies also show large variations within a given city or state. Later in this chapter, we briefly examine some of the factors related to these differences.

We focus on charter school studies that adopt one of two methods. The first approach involves comparing students who win and lose lotteries to attend charter schools. The second approach, known as value-added modeling, is not experimental, but takes into account a student's past academic achievement, unlike some of the weaker non-experimental approaches.[2]

Only nine papers have used the lottery approach to date, covering a total of 142 charter schools. Non-lottery-based studies that take the value-added approach while also constructing a comparison group against which to benchmark the academic progress of charter school students are far more abundant. In total, the present report includes in its analysis 38 value-added papers that use lottery-based or rigorous value-added approaches, although many of these include estimates for multiple locations or multiple types of charter schools within a given location. This is an increase from 29 papers in our 2014 review. In addition, we updated estimates for five of the studies we cited in 2014, using slightly changed estimates from newly published versions. In our main table that examines estimates for all students in charter schools, across six different grade configurations, we have 182 estimates for reading and 190 for math, up from 120 and 125 in our 2014 analysis. The number of estimates exceeds the number of papers because most studies include estimates for sub-populations of their study area.

Data and Methods

Our study includes all studies of the relation between charter schools and achievement included in Betts and Tang (2014) plus those found in a Google Scholar search for more recent papers. To be included, a study needed to observe achievement at the student level, to control for past student achievement, and to provide the estimated effect, its standard error, and the standard deviation of test scores.[3]

Meta-analysis is a widely used method, especially in the medical literature, of combining estimates from a variety of studies to draw overall conclusions. We use this approach to test whether the average impact of charter schools on achievement is zero, to portray visually the variation across studies, and to estimate the degree to which this is real variation in the effectiveness of charter schools as opposed to statistical noise. Details appear in the appendix of an expanded version of this chapter, available online (Betts & Tang, 2018).

Appendix A shows the set of papers that we included, along with information on the geographic location, the grade- and time-span of the study, and the label we use to identify the study in graphs.

The charter schools studies group schools into a variety of different grade configurations. Accordingly, we characterize charter school outcomes for elementary, middle, and high school levels, and various combinations. The most common of these are studies that combine elementary and middle charter schools into a single analysis. We refer to these studies as "combined elementary/middle" studies. Another popular approach has been to combine elementary, middle, and high schools into a single analysis, which we refer to as an "all" grade span.

There are a number of locations in which multiple charter school effectiveness estimates exist because different authors have studied the same place. Appendix A lists these studies.

We note that the literature on charter schools and achievement continues to grow quickly. The nature of the research is evolving as well. More studies have started to compare outcomes for different groups of students and different types of charter schools. This trend is laudable as it will help us to pinpoint what types of programs, and for which students, charters contribute to academic success. The only downside to this trend is that some papers no longer produce an overall estimate of the effects of charter schools in an area, which makes it harder for readers to get an overall sense of the success of the charter schools in a given area.

Mean Effects and Variations across Studies

We began by obtaining estimates of charter school effects for the main grade spans found often in the literature. As in our previous studies (Betts & Tang, 2011, 2014), our main results in this section, shown in Table 5.1, exclude the results for KIPP charter schools from both the middle school results and the results that combine elementary studies, elementary/middle studies, and middle school studies. (KIPP refers to the Knowledge is Power Program, a charter school operator. The KIPP estimates are often much larger than the estimates in studies that include all charter schools in a given region, and they would assume a disproportionate weight if we included them in the main analysis.) We later perform a meta-analysis of the KIPP studies themselves.

Tables 5.1 and 5.2 show the main results. Table 5.1 shows the results in terms of "effect sizes," that is, the predicted change in a student's achievement measured in terms of the number of standard deviations of achievement. Although this is the normal way of presenting results in education research, many readers may find it more understandable to read the results in terms of predicted changes in percentile rank for a student attending a charter school. Table 5.2 shows the results transformed into percentile rankings.[4]

In Table 5.1, results for each grade span for reading and math appear in the first and second columns respectively. For each grade span, the first number shows the estimated overall effect size. Effect sizes that are statistically significant (at the 5 percent level) are indicated with an asterisk. For elementary schools, the overall estimated effect sizes for reading and math achievement are 0.018 and 0.033, although only the latter estimate is significant at the five

TABLE 5.1 Effect Sizes and Significance from Meta-Analysis, by Grade Span and Subject Area

Grade Span	Reading Tests (# estimates–# locations), % true variation	Math Tests (# estimates–# locations), % true variation
Elementary	0.018 (20–16), 99.0%	0.033* (21–17), 99.0%
Middle	0.054* (23–17), 99.1%	0.097* (24–17), 99.4%
High	0.038 (21–15), 98.4%	0.042 (20–15), 99.2%
Combined Elementary/Middle	0.000 (23–19), 98.6%	-0.018 (28–19), 99.7%
Elementary, Middle, and Combined Elementary/Middle	0.020* (70–28), 98.7%	0.033* (72–29), 99.3%
All	0.012 (25–18), 98.7%	0.023 (25–19), 99.9%

Note: Asterisks indicate effect size significantly different from zero at the 5 percent level or less. The numbers in parentheses indicate the number of estimates included in the associated estimate of effect size and the number of locations. The percentage refers to the I^2 estimate of the percentage of the variation across estimates that reflect true variation in the effect of charter schools, rather than just statistical noise. Thus, for example, in the reading test result for elementary schools "(20–16), 99.0%" indicates 20 estimates covering 16 locations (with two studies each of Los Angeles and San Diego schools, and three studies of New York City area schools), and that 99.0 percent of the variation across estimates in the literature may reflect true variation in the effect of charter schools. As mentioned in the text, we exclude a large number of studies of KIPP schools from the middle school tabulations as the number of studies greatly outweighs the share of these schools in the charter school population, while the effect sizes are also much larger than the average seen in other studies.

TABLE 5.2A Effect Sizes Expressed as Charter Students' Predicted Percentile After One Year, Starting at 50th Percentile, by Grade Span and Subject Area

Grade Span	Reading Tests	Math Tests
Elementary	50.7	51.3*
Middle	52.2*	53.9*
High	51.5	51.7
Combined Elementary/Middle	50.0	49.3
Elementary, Middle, and Combined Elementary/Middle	50.8*	51.3*
All	50.5	50.9

Note: Asterisks indicate effect size significantly different from zero at the 5 percent level or less. The numbers show the predicted test score percentile of a student who started at the 50th percentile, after one year of charter school attendance.

TABLE 5.2B Effect Sizes Expressed as Charter Students' Predicted Percentile After One Year, Starting at 25th Percentile, by Grade Span and Subject Area

Grade Span	Reading Tests	Math Tests
Elementary	25.6	26.1★
Middle	26.7★	28.2★
High	26.2	26.4
Combined Elementary/Middle	25.0	24.4
Elementary, Middle, and Combined Elementary/Middle	25.6★	26.1★
All	25.4	25.7

Note: Asterisks indicate effect size significantly different from zero at the 5 percent level or less. The numbers show the predicted test score percentile of a student who started at the 25th percentile, after one year of charter school attendance.

percent level. The corresponding estimates from Betts & Tang (2014) were 0.020 and 0.045 respectively, and both were significant.

The second number for each grade span shows, in parentheses, the number of estimates contributing to the overall estimate, followed by the number of regions examined in the given studies. For example, in the meta-analysis of reading effects for elementary schools, "(20–16)" indicates that we found and used 20 separate estimates from 16 geographic areas in calculating the overall effect.

The third number presented for each grade span shows an estimate of the percentage of the variation across estimates that reflects true variation in the impact of charter schools, as opposed to variation due to random noise. (This is the I^2 statistic introduced by Higgins et al. (2003)). For both reading and math studies at the elementary level, we estimate that 99 percent of the variation reflects true variations in impact across studies. Clearly, there appear to be important variations in charter school effects across studies and, implicitly, across geographic areas.

For elementary schools, the average effect of charter schools is not statistically significant for reading but is positive and significant for math. For middle schools, we find positive and significant effects of charter schools for both reading and math achievement. For high school studies, neither effect is statistically significant.

A number of studies combine elementary and middle schools and, as shown in the fourth row of Table 5.1, on average there is no significant effect of attending a charter school on reading or math achievement in these studies. It is somewhat unusual to combine elementary and middle schools in this way but perhaps a practical convenience due to the fact that the exact grade in which elementary school students transition to middle school differs by place. In a bid to find a representative portrait of the overall evidence on the impact of charter schools from studies of schools at the elementary, middle, and combined elementary/middle levels, the fifth row of Table 5.1 combines all three of these study approaches. When pooling studies in this way, we find a statistically significant positive average estimated effect size for attending a charter school in these studies for both reading and math.

Finally, some studies include test scores from elementary, middle, and high school grades together in one model. We refer to these as "All" grade span models. The sixth row of Table 5.1 shows that neither the mean effect size in reading nor in math is significant in these studies.

In sum, no significant mean effect size emerges in studies of combined elementary/middle school levels, high school levels, or all grade levels combined. In studies of middle schools only, and combining studies of elementary, middle, and elementary/middle combined levels, a positive and significant effect for both reading and math emerges. Studies at the elementary level have mean positive effects for both math and reading, but only those for math are significant.

How do the estimated effects compare to the estimated impact of other common educational interventions? Focusing on the statistically significant results, the effect sizes for math range between 0.033 and 0.097 among the elementary, middle, and high school grade spans, signifying that after one year of attending charter school a student's test score would increase, relative to those of other students, by 3 to 10 percent of one standard deviation. For the two cases in which the charter effect is significant for reading, the predicted gain is 2 to 5 percent of one standard deviation. Clotfelter, Ladd, and Vigdor (2007) estimate that in North Carolina reducing class size by five students is associated with gains in achievement of 1 to 1.5 percent of a standard deviation.

Another way of gauging the size of the charter school effect sizes is to translate them into how a charter school student's academic ranking is predicted to change over time. Table 5.2 translates the effect sizes in Table 5.1 into a student's predicted percentile after attending a charter school for one year. Table 5.2a makes the assumption that the student starts at the 50th percentile. Table 5.2b assumes the student starts at the 25th percentile. For the latter case the predicted movement in percentile points is very slightly smaller.

With the important exception of middle schools, the predicted gains in achievement from attending a charter school for one year are small, typically 0.5 to one percentile point. These are not huge effects, but if a student stayed in charter schools for four, six or even 12 years cumulatively the predicted effects would be meaningful.

The predicted effects are much bigger for charter schools operating at the middle school level, for both math and reading achievement, and these predicted changes are statistically significant. For reading, depending on whether a student started at the 25th or 50th percentile, a single year in a charter school is predicted to boost a student by 1.7 to 2.2 percentile points. For middle school math, a student is predicted to gain between 3.2 to 3.9 percentile points in a single year depending on the starting point. Over several years, a student's rank is predicted to move up considerably.

Differences in Effect Sizes Across Studies

It is useful to look at the effect sizes of individual studies and how they contribute to the overall estimates shown in Table 5.1. In all cases, almost 100 percent of the variation across studies appears to be true variation, and not just a lack of precision in the estimates. This is as important a finding as the estimates of the average effects. The variation probably reflects both variation in the effectiveness of different charter schools across studies but also in the effectiveness of the traditional public schools against which the research studies compare the charter schools.

Figures 5.1 and 5.2 provide an illustration of the variation in the effect sizes across studies of elementary schools for reading and math respectively. The figures use horizontal lines to indicate the 95 percent confidence interval for each estimate. The rightmost column shows the weight attributed to each study. (The size of each square is proportional to these weights.) The diamond at the bottom of each figure illustrates the overall estimated effect size, with the width of the diamond indicating the 95 percent confidence interval.

The elementary school studies with the largest estimated reading effect size include studies of New York City, Boston, Los Angeles, Michigan, Louisiana, and Chicago. Two studies show negative and significant results: a study by Ni &

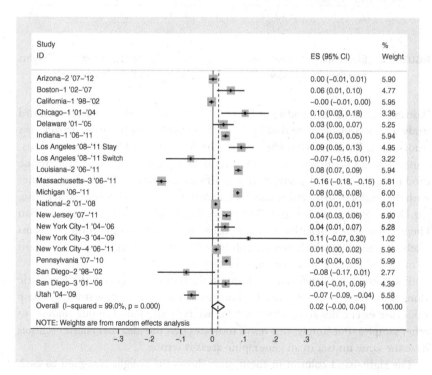

FIGURE 5.1 Elementary School Reading Effect Sizes by Study, Showing Weights Ascribed by Random-Effects Meta-Analysis to Each Study.

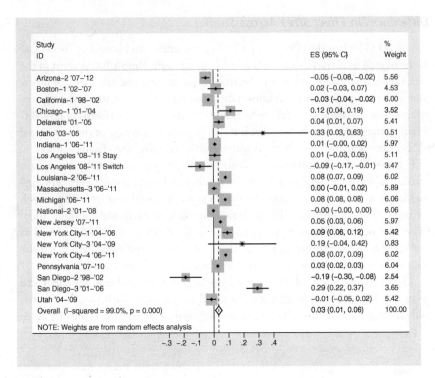

FIGURE 5.2   Elementary School Math Effect Sizes by Study, Showing Weights Ascribed by Random-Effects Meta-Analysis to Each Study.

Rorrer of Utah (2012), and a CREDO (2013a) study of Massachusetts. A third study with a large negative (but in this case not quite significant) coefficient is a study of San Diego charters (Betts et al., 2005). A study of San Diego by Betts, Tang, & Zau (2010) using the same statistical approach but a later time frame produced a positive and, again, nearly significant coefficient. In math, the studies with the largest positive effect sizes for elementary charter schools were in Idaho, San Diego, New York City, and Chicago. (Again, a study of an earlier period in San Diego produced a negative and this time significant counterpoint. It seems likely that San Diego's charter schools have become more effective with regard to math and reading achievement over time.)

The bottom of the left-hand column in the figures reproduces the I^2 statistic along with the p value of a test for homogeneous effects across studies. The p values are essentially zero, which is what we typically found in our analyses of other samples. Put simply, this result indicates that the idea that charter schools have the same impact in all geographic areas is wrong.

The right-hand column in the figures shows the weights assigned to each study when obtaining our overall estimated effect size. Smaller, less precise estimates get less weight than larger, more precise estimates, but because most of the variation is estimated to be "true," for the most part there is not much difference in the weight assigned to the various studies.

Figures 5.3 and 5.4 show the estimated effects in middle school studies for reading and math respectively. For reading, estimates lie in a fairly narrow band centered at just above zero, with roughly two-thirds of estimates being positive. Positive results from Los Angeles (for students staying in newly converted charter schools), Boston, and Massachusetts exhibit the largest effect size in these studies. Figure 5.4 shows that most studies of math achievement produced positive effect sizes, often statistically significant. Again, the biggest outlier is the result from Boston, with a positive effect size about double the size of the next biggest estimate (from New York City).

In our expanded discussion paper (Betts & Tang, 2018) we present and discuss figures depicting the meta-analyses for the five other grade span combinations shown in Table 5.1. Specifics vary by grade span, but a constant feature is the high degree of variation in charter school effects across locations. The figures depicting results for high schools also highlight two recent studies of virtual (online) charter high schools in Indiana and Ohio (Ferrare et al., 2017; Ahn & McEachin, 2017).

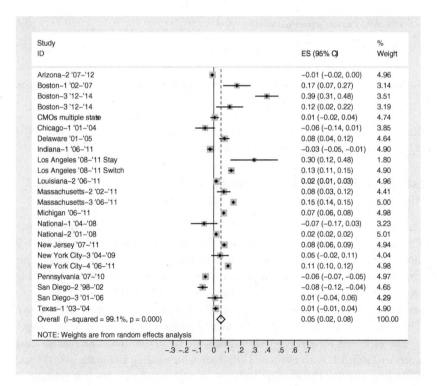

Study ID	ES (95% CI)	% Weight
Arizona–2 '07–'12	–0.01 (–0.02, 0.00)	4.96
Boston–1 '02–'07	0.17 (0.07, 0.27)	3.14
Boston–3 '12–'14	0.39 (0.31, 0.48)	3.51
Boston–3 '12–'14	0.12 (0.02, 0.22)	3.19
CMOs multiple state	0.01 (–0.02, 0.04)	4.74
Chicago–1 '01–'04	–0.06 (–0.14, 0.01)	3.85
Delaware '01–'05	0.08 (0.04, 0.12)	4.64
Indiana–1 '06–'11	–0.03 (–0.05, –0.01)	4.90
Los Angeles '08–'11 Stay	0.30 (0.12, 0.48)	1.80
Los Angeles '08–'11 Switch	0.13 (0.11, 0.15)	4.90
Louisiana–2 '06–'11	0.02 (0.01, 0.03)	4.96
Massachusetts–2 '02–'11	0.08 (0.03, 0.12)	4.41
Massachusetts–3 '06–'11	0.15 (0.14, 0.15)	5.00
Michigan '06–'11	0.07 (0.06, 0.08)	4.98
National–1 '04–'08	–0.07 (–0.17, 0.03)	3.23
National–2 '01–'08	0.02 (0.02, 0.02)	5.01
New Jersey '07–'11	0.08 (0.06, 0.09)	4.94
New York City–3 '04–'09	0.05 (–0.02, 0.11)	4.04
New York City–4 '06–'11	0.11 (0.10, 0.12)	4.98
Pennsylvania '07–'10	–0.06 (–0.07, –0.05)	4.97
San Diego–2 '98–'02	–0.08 (–0.12, –0.04)	4.65
San Diego–3 '01–'06	0.01 (–0.04, 0.06)	4.29
Texas–1 '03–'04	0.01 (–0.01, 0.04)	4.90
Overall (I–squared = 99.1%, p = 0.000)	0.05 (0.02, 0.08)	100.00

NOTE: Weights are from random effects analysis

FIGURE 5.3 Middle School Reading Effect Sizes by Study, Showing Weights Ascribed by Random-Effects Meta-Analysis to Each Study.

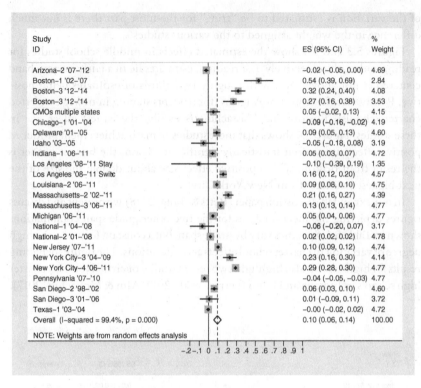

Study ID	ES (95% CI)	% Weight
Arizona–2 '07–'12	–0.02 (–0.05, 0.00)	4.69
Boston–1 '02–'07	0.54 (0.39, 0.69)	2.84
Boston–3 '12–'14	0.32 (0.24, 0.40)	4.08
Boston–3 '12–'14	0.27 (0.16, 0.38)	3.53
CMOs multiple states	0.05 (–0.02, 0.13)	4.15
Chicago–1 '01–'04	–0.09 (–0.16, –0.02)	4.19
Delaware '01–'05	0.09 (0.05, 0.13)	4.60
Idaho '03–'05	–0.05 (–0.18, 0.08)	3.19
Indiana–1 '06–'11	0.05 (0.03, 0.07)	4.72
Los Angeles '08–'11 Stay	–0.10 (–0.39, 0.19)	1.35
Los Angeles '08–'11 Switc	0.16 (0.12, 0.20)	4.57
Louisiana–2 '06–'11	0.09 (0.08, 0.10)	4.75
Massachusetts–2 '02–'11	0.21 (0.16, 0.27)	4.39
Massachusetts–3 '06–'11	0.13 (0.13, 0.14)	4.77
Michigan '06–'11	0.05 (0.04, 0.06)	4.77
National–1 '04–'08	–0.06 (–0.20, 0.07)	3.17
National–2 '01–'08	0.02 (0.02, 0.02)	4.78
New Jersey '07–'11	0.10 (0.09, 0.12)	4.74
New York City–3 '04–'09	0.23 (0.16, 0.30)	4.14
New York City–4 '06–'11	0.29 (0.28, 0.30)	4.77
Pennsylvania '07–'10	–0.04 (–0.05, –0.03)	4.77
San Diego–2 '98–'02	0.06 (0.03, 0.10)	4.60
San Diego–3 '01–'06	0.01 (–0.09, 0.11)	3.72
Texas–1 '03–'04	–0.00 (–0.02, 0.02)	4.72
Overall (I-squared = 99.4%, p = 0.000)	0.10 (0.06, 0.14)	100.00

NOTE: Weights are from random effects analysis

–.2 –.1 0 .1 .2 .3 .4 .5 .6 .7 .8 .9 1

FIGURE 5.4 Middle School Math Effect Sizes by Study, Showing Weights Ascribed by Random-Effects Meta-Analysis to Each Study.

Both studies stand out in the figures for their unusually large and negative estimated effects of virtual charter schools in these states.

Estimated Effects for KIPP Middle Schools Are Far Higher Than for Other Charter Middle Schools

The middle school results presented in Tables 5.1, 5.2a and 5.2b and in Figures 5.3 and 5.4 exclude the many estimates for individual KIPP schools. Table 5.3 shows the results of a meta-analysis that includes only the KIPP schools. This can be thought of as the second meta-analysis of the KIPP literature, following up on the similar analysis in Betts and Tang (2011). KIPP schools appear to have a statistically significant and positive influence on both reading and math achievement, with the effect size for math being twice as large as for reading.[5]

The estimates for KIPP middle schools are far higher than our average estimates in Table 5.1, with estimated effect sizes for reading and math of 0.174 and 0.374 respectively. These effect sizes are enough to move a student initially at the 50th percentile to percentiles 56.9 and 64.6 in a single year of attendance at a KIPP school. These are very large effects, by any standard.

TABLE 5.3 KIPP School Estimates: Effect Sizes and Significance by Grade Span and Subject Area

Grade Span	Reading Tests (# estimates-# locations), % true variation	Math Tests (# estimates-# locations), % true variation
Including Only KIPP Estimates		
Middle	0.174★ (8–5), 85.2%	0.374★ (8–5), 94.2%

Note: Asterisks indicate effect size significantly different from zero at the 5 percent level or less. The numbers in parentheses indicate the number of estimates included in the associated estimate of effect size, and the number of locales, which in the case of KIPP schools is unknown due to the shielding of charter school identities in one study.

Understanding Sources of Variation across Locations, Types of Charters and Types of Students

The earlier results show that most variation across studies is real. Betts and Atkinson (2012) argue that there should not be a single estimate of the gains from school choice, because not only do schools of choice differ in the quality of education they provide, but so do the traditional public schools against which schools of choice compete. A recent paper by Chabrier, Cohodes, and Oreopoulos (2016) shows this latter source of variation clearly, with the estimated impact of charter schools falling sharply as average test scores increase at the traditional public schools that charter applicants would otherwise attend.

Variations across types of charters surely matter too. First, our analysis suggests that charters operating at the middle school level produce larger gains in achievement, relative to traditional public schools, than charters at other grade spans. Second, the literature on KIPP schools, and the broader literature on "No Excuse" charter schools, including the KIPP schools, which feature extended school time, uniforms and parent contracts, suggests that these types of charters consistently outperform traditional public schools. A smaller literature examines "virtual" charter schools, also known as online charter schools. A multi-state report by CREDO (2015) and studies in Indiana and Ohio suggest that on average these schools produce learning gains much below that of traditional public schools. (Our study includes only the latter two results due to a lack of information on standard errors in the first report.)

Results for Student Subgroups

Turning to variations by students, a key question is whether charter schools benefit students from some groups more than others. A warning about the subgroup estimates in this section is that only a subset of studies have performed these analyses, meaning that they may not apply to the locations studied

TABLE 5.4 Effect Sizes for Studies of Selected Subsamples of Student Populations and Significance From Meta-Analysis, by Grade Span and Subject Area

Student Population	Grade Span		
	Combined E/M (# estimates-# locations), % true variation	E, M and Combined E/M (# estimates-# locations), % true variation	All (# estimates-# locations), % true variation
READING TESTS			
Students in Special Education	−0.002 (12–12), 79.9%	−0.002 (12–12), 79.9%	0.025★ (10–10), 82.7%
English Language Learners	0.005 (12–12), 73.5%	0.010 (13–12), 76.5%	0.032 (10–10), 87.7%
Students Eligible for Federal Meal Assistance	0.020★ (16–13), 86.7%	0.021★ (18–15), 84.9%	0.028★ (10–10), 93.8%
MATH TESTS			
Students in Special Education	0.002 (12–12), 79.4%	0.002 (12–12), 79.4%	0.017★ (10–10), 0.0%
English Language Learners	0.027 (12–12), 81.3%	0.027 (13–12), 80.3%	0.015 (10–10), 58.6%
Students Eligible for Federal Meal Assistance	0.013 (16–13), 89.6%	0.023★ (18–15), 90.4%	0.022★ (10–10), 93.1%

Note: Asterisks indicate effect size significantly different from zero at the 5 percent level or less.

nationally. For this reason, comparing the results below to the overall results for the same grade span in Table 5.1 is likely to be misleading. Table 5.4 shows estimated effect sizes from meta-analyses for three at-risk populations: students in special education, English Language Learners (ELLs), and students eligible for federal meal assistance, the last of which is a commonly used proxy for poverty, for grade spans with multiple estimates available.

Results for the three types of at-risk populations are mixed, and difficult to summarize simply. No subpopulation appears to do worse when attending charter schools, but beyond that the impact of charter schools varies by subject and grade span. For students eligible for meal assistance, results are positive and statistically significant for all three grade spans for reading and for two of three grade spans for math.

Table 5.5 shows results from grade spans with multiple studies by race/ethnicity.[6] Interestingly, in most but not all cases, results are negative and significant for both reading and math for White and Asian students. This contrasts with results for Black students, where coefficients are always positive and significant in two cases. For Hispanic students, results are never significant.

TABLE 5.5 Effect Sizes for Studies of Racial/Ethnic Subsamples of Student Populations and Significance From Meta-Analysis, by Grade Span and Subject Area

Race/Ethnicity	Grade Span		
	Combined E/M (# estimates-# locations), % true variation	E, M and Combined E/M (# estimates-# locations), % true variation	All (# estimates-# locations), % true variation
READING TESTS			
White	−0.032★	−0.040★	−0.020★
	(19–14), 97.3%	(22–17), 96.9%	(14–13), 97.5%
Black	0.031★	0.027★	0.006
	(20–14), 93.3%	(23–16), 92.4%	(14–13), 97.2%
Hispanic	−0.021	−0.023	−0.001
	(20–14), 93.3%	(23–16), 88.6%	(14–13), 95.7%
Native American	−0.142	−0.142	−0.054
	(9–9), 95.4%	(9–9), 95.4%	(9–9), 45.8%
Asian	−0.026	−0.033★	−0.051★
	(12–12), 59.4%	(14–13), 61.1%	(10–10), 95%
MATH TESTS			
White	−0.081★	−0.082★	−0.012
	(19–14), 99.0%	(22–16), 98.6%	(14–3), 98.7%
Black	0.021	0.024	0.024
	(20–14), 96.1%	(23–16), 95.6%	(14–13), 98.6%
Hispanic	−0.011	−0.008	0.019
	(20–14), 93.7%	(23–16), 93.5%	(14–13), 98%
Native American	−0.034	−0.034	−0.077★
	(7–7), 67.6%	(7–7), 67.6%	(9–9), 57.9%
Asian	−0.46★	−0.058★	−0.037★
	(12–12), 78.3%	(14–13), 77.8%	(10–10), 64.2%

Note: Asterisks indicate effect size significantly different from zero at the 5 percent level or less.

These results are not necessarily representative of all the geographic locations studied in the literature: the number of locations studied is about one-third to one-half the number of locations studied for the results for all students in Table 5.1. But the results provide at least weak evidence that Black students may gain more than White or Asian students. This could of course reflect the relative effectiveness of traditional public schools available to the various racial/ethnic groups.

Urban Districts and Schools

Table 5.6 shows the results when we focus on studies of urban districts or on individual schools in urban areas. In all but one case the effect sizes are positive

TABLE 5.6 Effect Sizes for Studies of Urban Districts and Schools, by Grade Span and Subject Area

Grade Span	Reading Tests (# estimates-# locations), % true variation	Math Tests (# estimates-# locations), % true variation
Elementary	0.034★ (9–5), 77.8%	0.054★ (9–5), 91.5%
Middle	0.098★ (10–5), 95.2%	0.176★ (10–5), 97.2%
High	0.121★ (8–4), 93.8%	0.132★ (6–3), 92.8%
Combined Elementary/Middle	-0.002 (6–4), 82.6%	0.023★ (6–4), 40.6%)
Elementary, Middle, and Combined Elementary/Middle	0.050★ (25–7), 96.0%	0.102★ (25–7), 98.8%
All	0.019★ (10–7), 21.8%	0.064★ (10–7), 95.9%

Note: Asterisks indicate effect size significantly different from zero at the 5 percent level or less.

and statistically significant. In contrast, in the overall sample (Table 5.1) effects were positive and significant for five of 12 cases. The math and reading effects size estimates are higher in the urban subsample shown in Table 5.6 than in the overall sample shown in Table 5.1 for all cases except reading in the combined elementary/middle school grade span. As in Table 5.1, we continue to exclude KIPP schools from the analysis of urban charter schools, even though KIPP schools typically locate in urban settings. Including them would have increased the effect sizes in Table 5.6 considerably.

There could be multiple reasons for the larger effects in urban settings. One obvious possibility is that charter schools have more value to add in large urban districts if the traditional schools in these areas are underserving their students to a greater extent than are their non-urban counterparts. Angrist et al. (2013) attributes the success of urban charter schools in Massachusetts to the "No Excuses" approach to education, which the authors describe as emphasizing "discipline and comportment, traditional reading and math skills, instruction time, and selective teacher hiring."

Conclusion

When studying charter schools' effect on achievement, one can ask several related questions. First, on *average* are charter schools boosting achievement relative to traditional public schools? Second, are there exceptions where we can find some charters outperforming and others underperforming?

Third, what have social scientists learned about the types of charter schools, the types of students, or the school settings, which can predict the relative effectiveness of charter schools?

On the question of the average overall effect, for no grade span or subject tested did we find a negative average effect of charter schools. For five out of 12 combinations of grades and subject areas, we found a positive and significant overall effect of charter schools on achievement. (For six of the remaining seven cases, the estimated average effect was positive but not statistically significant.) The results are more compelling for math than reading, both in terms of the number of grade spans for which we found significant effects and the magnitude of those significant effects. In cases of significant average effects, students are often predicted to gain about one half to one percentile point per year, but with larger estimates for charter schools at the middle school level.

On the second question, we find considerable variation in effect sizes across studies. Overall, our findings confirm that the impact of the charter sector on student outcomes varies considerably—especially across geographic areas. This likely reflects variation not only in charter schools' effectiveness but also in that of the traditional public schools against which the charters are compared. There is little doubt that charters outperform traditional public schools in some areas and underperform them in others—most of the variation across studies is real and does not reflect statistical "noise."

On the third question, the factors related to charter effectiveness, social scientists are beginning to make some progress. Charter schools in urban areas on average produce strong positive effects, especially in math. Charter schools operating as middle schools produce quite high predicted effects for both math and reading relative to charter schools in other grade spans. Only a fraction of studies break down the charter schools' effects by student characteristics, but the existing papers tentatively suggest that Black students and those receiving federal meal assistance are among the students most likely to benefit from attending a charter school. A number of studies point to preliminary evidence that "No Excuse" charter schools, such as the KIPP schools, produce unusually large gains. Conversely, a handful of recent studies suggests that virtual (online) charter schools are markedly less effective than traditional public schools.

Looking forward, we expect that new studies will continue to appear, and over time some of the above conclusions will evolve as we gain a fuller picture of charter schools' effects. Of the three sets of results, on average effects, the degree of variation in effects, and factors related to variation, the result most likely to stand the test of time is that the relative performance of charter schools and traditional public schools is highly variable. A challenge for the charter school movement will be to ensure going forward that those charters that underperform either improve or, over time, shut down.

Appendix A

Details on the Studies Used in Any of Our Approaches

Authors	Year Published	Name of State or City	First Year of Data	Final Year of Data	Study Label in Meta-Analysis Plots	Grade spans Included in Meta-Analysis of Effect Size
Abdulkadiroglu et al.	2009	Boston	2002	2007	Boston-1 '02-'07	E, M, H
Abdulkadiroglu et al.	2016	Boston, New Orleans	2012	2014		M
			2010	2013	New Orleans '10-'13	EM
Ahn and McEachin	2017	Ohio	2011	2013	Ohio-3 '11-'13 and	EM, virtual and other charters
			2012	2013	Ohio-3 '11-'13, virtual	H, virtual and other charters
Angrist et al.	2012	Boston (1 KIPP school)	2006	2009	kipp-lynn	M
Angrist, Pathak, and Walters	2013	Massachusetts	2002	2011	Massachusetts-2 '02-'11	M
Angrist et al.	2016	Boston	2004	2011	Boston-2 '04-'11	H
Ballou et al.	2006	Idaho	2003	2005	Idaho '03-'05	E, M, H, A
Betts et al.	2005	San Diego	1998	2002	San Diego-2 '98-'02	E, M, H
Betts, Tang, and Zau	2010	San Diego	2001	2006	San Diego-3 '01-'06	E, M, H, A
Bifulco and Ladd	2006	North Carolina	1996	2002	North Carolina-1 '96-'02	EM
Booker et al.	2007	Texas	1995	2002	Texas-2 '95-'02	EM

(continued)

Authors	Year Published	Name of State or City	First Year of Data	Final Year of Data	Study Label in Meta-Analysis Plots	Grade spans Included in Meta-Analysis of Effect Size
Buddin and Zimmer	2003	California	1998	2002	California-1 '98-'02	E
Chingos and West	2015	Arizona	2007	2012	Arizona-2 '07-'12	E, M, H
CREDO	2009	National	2001	2008	National-2 '01-'08	E, M, H
CREDO	2009	Arizona, Arkansas, California, Chicago, Denver, DC, Florida, Georgia, Massachusetts, Minnesota, Missouri, New Mexico, North Carolina, . Ohio, Texas	varies	varies	Arizona-1 '05-'08 Arkansas '04-'08 California-2 '06-'08 Chicago-3 '05-'08 Denver-2 '04-'08 DC '06-'08 Florida-2 '01-'08 Georgia '04-'08 Massachusetts-1 '05-'07 Minnesota '05-'08 Missouri '06-'08 New Mexico '05-'08 North Carolina-2 '03-'07 Ohio-2 '06-'08 Texas-4 '03-'07	EM (9 locations), A (7 locations)
CREDO	2013	Louisiana, Massachusetts, Michigan, New York City	varies	varies	Louisiana-2 '06-'11 Massachusetts-3 '06-'11 Michigan '06-'11 New York City-4 '06-'11	E, M, H, A (LA, MA, NYC), E, M, EM (MI)
CREDO	2012	Indiana, New Jersey	varies	varies	Indiana-1 '06-'11 New Jersey '07-'11	E, M, H, A (IN), E, M, EM (NJ)
CREDO	2011	Pennsylvania	2007	2010	Pennsylvania '07-'10	E, M, H, (EM)
Dobbie and Fryer	2011	NYC (1 school, Promise Academy in Harlem Children's Zone)	2004	2009	New York City-3 '04-'09	E, M

(continued)

Authors	Year Published	Name of State or City	First Year of Data	Final Year of Data	Study Label in Meta-Analysis Plots	Grade spans Included in Meta-Analysis of Effect Size
Dobbie and Fryer	2016	Texas	1996	2004	Texas-5 '96–'04	A
Ferrare, Waddington and Berends	2017	Indiana	2011	2016	Indiana-2 '11–'16 (with indications for school type: CMO, EMO, Independent, Virtual)	EM
Foreman et al.	2017	Anon. state	2013	2014	Anon. state '13–'14	EM
Furgeson et al.	2012	CMOs multiple states	varies	varies	CMOs multiple states	M
Gleason et al.	2010	National (29 schools)	2004	2008	National-3 '04–'08	M
Gronberg and Jansen	2005	Texas	2003	2004	Texas-1 '03–'04	M, H
Hoxby and Murarka	2007	NYC	2004	2006	New York City-1 '04–'06	E
Hoxby, Murarka, and Kang	2009	NYC	2000	2008	New York City-2 '00–'08	EM
Hoxby and Rockoff	2004	Chicago	2001	2004	Chicago-1 '01–'04	E, M
Imberman	2010	Anonymous district	1995	2005	Anon. district '95–'07	A
Ladd Clotfelter and Holbein	2017	North Carolina	2003	2007	North Carolina-3 '03–'07	A
			2008	2011	North Carolina-4 '08–'11	A
McClure et al.	2005	San Diego	2003	2004	San Diego-1 '–03-'04	H
Miron et al.	2007	Delaware	2000	2005	Delaware '01–'05	E, M, H, A
Ni and Rorrer	2012	Utah	2004	2009	Utah '04–'09	E
Nichols and Özek	2010	DC	2001	2009	DC-2 '01–'09	EM

(continued)

Authors	Year Published	Name of State or City	First Year of Data	Final Year of Data	Study Label in Meta-Analysis Plots	Grade spans Included in Meta-Analysis of Effect Size
Nicotera, Mendiburo, and Berends	2011	Indianapolis	2002	2006	Indianapolis '02–'06	A
Nisar	2012	Milwaukee	2006	2009	Milwaukee-2 '06–'09	EM
Sass	2006	Florida	2000	2003	Florida-1 '00–'03	A
Shin, Fuller and Dauter	2017	Los Angeles (separate analyses for movers and stayers)	2008	2011	Los Angeles '08–'11 Switch, Los Angeles '08–'11 Stay	E, M, H
Tuttle et al.	2013	KIPP multiple states	2002	2011	KIPP multiple states '02–'11	M
Witte, Wolf, Carlson, and Dean	2010, 2011, 2012 (average of one year gains from each of four years)	Milwaukee	2007	2011	Milwaukee-3 '07–'11	A
Woodworth et al.	2008	Bay Area (3 KIPP schools)	2003	2005	kipp-bayarea-A, -B and -C	M
Zimmer et al.	2009 (sub-group estimates)2012 (all students)	Chicago, Denver, Milwaukee, Ohio, Philadelphia, San Diego, Texas	varies	varies	Chicago-2 '98–'07, Denver-1 '02–'06 Milwaukee-1 '01–'07 Ohio-1 '05–'08 Philadelphia '03–'07 San Diego-4 '98–'07 Texas-3 '96–'04	EM (3 locations), A (4 locations)

Note: E, M, H, and A stand for analyses of elementary, middle, high schools, and all grades, respectively, and EM stands for combined elementary and middle.

Notes

1 We would like to thank the many researchers who provided supplementary information we needed to incorporate their papers into this or our earlier (2014, 2011, and 2008) literature reviews: Dale Ballou; Richard Buddin; Leesa M. Foreman, Kaitlin Anderson, Gary Ritter, and Patrick Wolf; Caroline Hoxby and Jonah Rockoff; Anna Nicotera and Mark Berends; Macke Raymond; Christopher Reicher and Larry McClure; Tim Gronberg; and Scott Imberman all provided key data we needed for one or more of our analyses.

2 Betts, Tang, and Zau (2010) use data from San Diego and show that models that do not measure individual students' achievement growth produce quite different results from the more sophisticated value-added models, and that the changes in estimated effects of charters are consistent with the idea that the weaker approaches fail to take into account the relatively disadvantaged backgrounds of students who attend charters.

3 In past reviews, we have noted that not all authors follow the norm of including both an estimated effect and either a standard error or t-statistic. This is problematic because without the latter we lack a measure of how precise the estimated effect is, which is key to calculating the study's weight in the meta-analysis. Among new papers since our 2014 work, the main example of papers that lacked standard errors were 10 studies by CREDO of New York, New York City, Texas, Ohio, California, Los Angeles, and an urban study. We requested the standard errors for these studies, but were not able to obtain them.

4 The percentile ranking of a student indicates the number of students out of 100 that the student would score as highly as or higher than. For example, a 99th percentile student scores as highly as or higher than 99 out of 100 students on average, while a 50th percentile student is in the middle of the achievement distribution.

5 The effect sizes for KIPP are materially higher than the effects estimated by Betts and Tang (2011), which were 0.096 and 0.223 respectively. Since our earlier literature review, the preliminary report from a national study (Tuttle et al. 2010) has been replaced by a final report (Tuttle et al. 2013), and we have substituted the single effect size by subject in the later report for the many school-level estimates in the earlier report on the advice of one of the authors (Brian Gill, personal communication, February 2014).

6 The table does not separately show results for studies of E, M, and H grade spans as there are only one or two studies at these grade spans.

References

Abdulkadiroğlu, A., Angrist, J. D., Cohodes, S. R., Dynarski, S. M., Fullerton, J., Kane, T. J., & Pathak, P. A. (2009). *Informing the debate: Comparing Boston's charter, pilot and traditional schools*. Boston, MA: The Boston Foundation.

Abdulkadiroğlu, A., Angrist, J. D., Hull, P. D., & Pathak, P. A. (2016). Charters without lotteries: Testing takeovers in New Orleans and Boston. *American Economic Review, 106*(7), 1878–920.

Ahn, J. & McEachin, A. (2017). Student enrollment patterns and achievement in Ohio's online charter Schools. *Educational Researcher, 46*(1), 44–57. Retrieved from https://doi.org/10.3102/0013189X17692999.

Angrist, J. D., Cohodes, S. R., Dynarski, S. M., Pathak, P. A., & Walters, C. R. (2016). Stand and deliver: Effects of Boston's charter high schools on college preparation, entry, and choice. *Journal of Labor Economics, 34*(2), 275–318.

Angrist, J. D., Dynarski, S. M., Kane, T. J., Pathak, P. A., & Walters, C. R. (2012). Who benefits from KIPP? *Journal of Policy Analysis and Management, 31*(4), 837–60.

Angrist, J. D., Pathak, P. A., & Walters, C. R. (2013). Explaining charter school effectiveness. *American Economic Journal: Applied Economics, 5*, 1–27.

Ballou, D., Teasley, B., & Zeidner, T. (2006). *Charter Schools in Idaho* (Paper prepared for the National Conference on Charter School Research, National Center on

School Choice). Nashville, TN: Vanderbilt University. Retrieved from http://www. vanderbilt.edu/schoolchoice/conference/papers/Ballouetal_2006-DRAFT.pdf.

Betts, J. R. & Tang, Y. E. (2008). *Value-added and experimental studies of the effect of charter schools on student achievement: A literature review.* Seattle, WA: National Charter School Research Project, Center on Reinventing Public Education.

Betts, J. R. & Tang, Y. E. (2011). *The effect of charter schools on student achievement: A meta-analysis of the literature.* Seattle, WA: National Charter School Research Project, Center on Reinventing Public Education.

Betts, J. R. & Tang, Y. E. (2014). *A meta-analysis of the literature on the effect of charter schools on student achievement.* Bothell, WA: Center on Reinventing Public Education. Retrieved from http://www.crpe.org/sites/default/files/CRPE_meta-analysis_ charter-schools-effect-student-achievement_workingpaper.pdf.

Betts, J. R. & Tang, Y. E. (2018). *A meta-analysis of the effect of charter schools on student achievement.* San Diego Education Research Alliance. Retrieved from sandera.ucsd. edu at https://sandera.ucsd.edu/research-and-publications/DISC%20PAPER%20 Betts%20Tang%20Charter%20Lit%20Review%202018%2001.pdf.

Betts, J. R., Rice, L. A., Zau, A. C., Tang, Y. E., & Koedel, C. R. (2005). *Does school choice work? Effects on student integration and achievement.* San Francisco: Public Policy Institute of California.

Betts, J. R., Tang, Y. E., & Zau, A. C. (2010). Madness in the method? A critical analysis of popular methods of estimating the effect of charter schools on student achievement. In *Taking measure of charter schools: Better assessments, better policymaking, better schools,* edited by J. R. Betts & P. T. Hill. Lanham, MD: Rowman & Littlefield.

Bifulco, R. & Ladd, H. F. (2006). The impacts of charter schools on student achievement: Evidence from North Carolina. *Education Finance and Policy, 1,* 50–90.

Booker, K., Gilpatric, S., Gronberg, T., & Jansen, D. (2007). The impact of charter school attendance on student performance. *Journal of Public Economics, 91,* 5–6.

Buddin, R. & Zimmer, R. (2003). Appendix C: Academic outcomes. In *Charter school operations and performance: Evidence from California.* Santa Monica, CA: RAND Corporation.

Chabrier, J., Cohodes, S. R., & Oreopoulos, P. (2016). What can we learn from charter school lotteries? *Journal of Economic Perspectives, 30*(5), 57–84.

Chingos, M. M. & West, M. R. (2015). The uneven performance of Arizona's charter schools. *Educational Evaluation and Policy Analysis, 37*(1), 120–34.

Clotfelter, C. T., Ladd, H. F., & Vigdor, J. L. (2007). *How and why do teacher credentials matter for student achievement?* Cambridge, MA: National Bureau of Economic Research. Retrieved from http://www.nber.org/papers/w12828.

CREDO. (2009). *Multiple choice: Charter school performance in 16 states.* Stanford, CA: CREDO. Retrieved from http://credo.stanford.edu.

CREDO. (2011). *Charter school performance in Pennsylvania.* Stanford, CA: CREDO. Retrieved from http://credo.stanford.edu.

CREDO. (2012a). *Charter school performance in Indiana.* Stanford, CA: CREDO. Retrieved from http://credo.stanford.edu.

CREDO. (2012b). *Charter school performance in New Jersey.* Stanford, CA: CREDO. Retrieved from http://credo.stanford.edu.

CREDO. (2013a). *Charter school performance in Louisiana.* Stanford, CA: CREDO. Retrieved from http://credo.stanford.edu.

CREDO. (2013b). *Charter school performance in Massachusetts.* Stanford, CA: CREDO. Retrieved from http://credo.stanford.edu.

CREDO. (2013c). *Charter school performance in Michigan.* Stanford, CA: CREDO. Retrieved from http://credo.stanford.edu.

CREDO. (2013d). *Charter school performance in New York City.* Stanford, CA: CREDO. Retrieved from http://credo.stanford.edu.

CREDO. (2015). *Online charter school study.* Stanford, CA: CREDO.

Dobbie, W. & Fryer Jr, R. G. (2011). Are high-quality schools enough to increase achievement among the poor? Evidence from the Harlem Children's Zone. *American Economic Journal: Applied Economics, 3*(3), 158–87.

Dobbie, W. S. & Fryer Jr, R. G. (2016). *Charter schools and labor market outcomes.* Cambridge, MA: National Bureau of Economic Research.

Ferrare, J. J., Waddington, J. R., & Berends, M. (2017). *Virtual illusion: Longitudinal effects of charter school types on student achievement in Indiana.* Center for Research on Educational Opportunity, Notre Dame University. Notre Dame, IN.

Foreman, L. M., Anderson, K. P., Ritter, G. W., & Wolf, P. J. (2017). Using "broken" lotteries to check the validity of charter school evaluations using matching designs. *Educational Policy.*

Furgeson, J., Gill, B., Haimson, J., Killewald, A., McCullough, M., Nichols-Barrer, I., … Lake, & R. (2012). *Charter-school management organizations: Diverse strategies and diverse student impacts.* Princeton, NJ & Seattle, WA: Mathematica Policy Research and Center for Reinventing Public Education.

Gleason, P., Clark, M., Tuttle, C. C., & Dwoyer, E. (2010). *"The evaluation of charter school impacts: Final report." NCEE 2010–4029.* Washington, DC: National Center for Education Evaluation and Regional Assistance, Institute of Education Sciences, U.S. Department of Education.

Gronberg, T. J. & Jansen, D. W. (2005). *Texas charter schools: An assessment in 2005.* Austin: Texas: Public Policy Foundation. Retrieved from http://www.texaspolicy. com/pdf/2005-09-charterschools-rr.pdf.

Higgins, J., Thompson, S. G., Deeks, J. J., & Altman, D. G. (2003). Measuring inconsistency in meta-analyses. *British Medical Journal* 327(7414), 557–60.

Hoxby, C. M. & Murarka, S. (2007). *New York city's charter schools overall report.* Cambridge, MA: New. Retrieved from http://users.nber.org/.

Hoxby, C. M. & Rockoff, J. E. (2004). *The impact of charter schools on student achievement. Unpublished paper.* Cambridge, MA: New. Retrieved from http://www.rand.org/ content/dam/rand/www/external/labor/seminars/adp/pdfs/2005hoxby.pdf.

Hoxby, C. M., Murarka, S., & Kang, J. (2009). *How New York city's charter schools affect achievement.* Cambridge, MA: New. Retrieved from http://users.nber.org/.

Imberman, S. A. (2010). Achievement and behavior in charter schools: Drawing a more complete picture. *The Review of Economics and Statistics, 93*(2), 416–35.

Ladd, H. F., Clotfelter, C. T., & Holbein, J. B. (2017). The growing segmentation of the charter school sector in North Carolina. *Education Finance and Policy, 12*(4), 536–63.

McClure, L., Strick, B., Jacob-Almeida, R., & Reicher, C. (2005). *The Preuss School at UCSD: School characteristics and students' achievement.* University of California, San Diego, The Center for Research on Educational Equity, Assessment and Teaching Excellence. Retrieved from http://create.ucsd.edu/Research_Evaluation/PreussReportDecember 2005.pdf.

Miron, G., Cullen, A., Applegate, B., & Farrell, P. (2007). *Evaluation of the Delaware charter school reform: Year one report.* Kalamazoo, MI: The Evaluation Center, Western Michigan University. Retrieved from http://www.doe.k12.de.us/files/pdf/sbe_decseval.pdf.

National Alliance for Public Charter Schools. (2017). *Estimated charter public school enrollment, 2016–17*. Retrieved from https://www.publiccharters.org/sites/default/files/migrated/wp-content/uploads/2017/01/EER_Report_V5.pdf.

Ni, Y. & Rorrer, A. K. (2012). Twice considered: Charter schools and student achievement in Utah. *Economics of Education Review, 31*(5), 835–49.

Nichols, A. & Özek, U. (2010). *Public school choice and student achievement in the district of Columbia* (Working Paper 53). Washington, DC: National Center for Analysis of Longitudinal Data. Retrieved from http://www.edweek.org/media/publicschoolchoiceandstudentachievement-calder.pdf.

Nicotera, A., Mendiburo, M., & Berends, M. (2011). Charter school effects in Indianapolis. In *School Choice and School Improvement*, edited by M. Berends, M. Cannata, & E. B. Goldring (pp. 35–50). Cambridge, MA: Harvard Education Press.

Nisar, H. (2012). Do charter schools improve student achievement? New York: national center for the study of privatization in education. Retrieved from http://www.ncspe.org/publications_files/OP216.pdf.

Sass, T. R. (2006). Charter schools and student achievement in Florida. *Education Finance and Policy, 1*(1), 91–122.

Shin, H. J., Fuller, B., & Dauter, L. (2017). Heterogeneous effects of charter schools: Unpacking family selection and achievement growth in Los Angeles. *Journal of School Choice, 11*(1), 60–94.

Tuttle, C. C., Gill, B., Gleason, P., Knechtel, V., Nichols-Barrer, I., & Resch, A. (2013). *KIPP middle schools: Impacts on achievement and other outcomes. Final report*. Washington, DC: Mathematica Policy Research.

Tuttle, C. C., Teh, B., Nichols-Barrer, I., Gill, B. P., & Gleason, P. (2010). *Student characteristics and achievement in 22 KIPP middle schools*. Washington, DC: Mathematica Policy Research.

Witte, J. F., Wolf, P. J., Carlson, D., & Dean, A. (2012). *Milwaukee independent charter schools study: Final report on four-year achievement gains* (SCDP Evaluation Report #31). Fayetteville, AR: School Choice Demonstration Project. Retrieved from http://www.uaedreform.org/milwaukee-parental-choice-program-evaluation/.

Witte, J. F., Wolf, P. J., Dean, A., & Carlson, D. (2010). *Milwaukee independent charter schools study: Report on one year of student growth* (SCDP Evaluation Report #21). Fayetteville, AR: School Choice Demonstration Project. Retrieved from http://www.uaedreform.org/downloads/2011/03/report-21-milwaukee-independent-charter-schools-study-report-on-one-year-of-student-growth-2010-2011-update-and-policy-options.pdf.

Witte, J. F., Wolf, P. J., Dean, A., & Carlson, D. (2011). *Milwaukee independent charter schools study: Report on two- and three-year achievement gains* (SCDP Evaluation Report #21). Fayetteville, AR: School Choice Demonstration Project. Retrieved from http://files.eric.ed.gov/fulltext/ED518594.pdf.

Woodworth, K. R., David, J. L., Guha, R., Wang, H., & Lopez-Torkos, A. (2008). *San Francisco Bay area KIPP schools: A study of early implementation and achievement: Final report*. Menlo Park, CA: SRI International.

Zimmer, R., Gill, B., Booker, K., Lavertu, S., Sass, T. R., & Witte, J. (2009). *Charter schools in eight states: Effects on achievement, attainment, integration, and competition*. Santa Monica, CA: Rand.

Zimmer, R., Gill, B., Booker, K., Lavertu, S., & Witte, J. (2012). Examining charter student achievement effects across seven states. *Economics of Education Review, Special Issue: Charter Schools, 31*(2), 213–24.

6

INNOVATION IN CHARTER SCHOOLS

An Exploratory Analysis

Mark Berends, Roberto V. Peñaloza,
Marisa Cannata, and Ellen B. Goldring

With few exceptions, much of the research on school choice has neglected school structure and processes as they relate not only to student outcomes but the three key aspects of schools that the choice movement intends to improve—autonomy, innovation, and accountability (see Austin & Berends, in press; Berends, 2015; Gill et al., 2007; Lubienski, 2003, Oberfield, 2017).[1] Central to advocates' argument for choice is that these aspects of reform will produce changes in organizational innovations that promote curriculum, instruction, and learning, which in turn will lead to better student outcomes (Chubb & Moe, 1990; Walberg & Bast, 2003). As Lubienski (2003) states, "choice, competition, and innovation are cast as the necessary vehicles for advancing academic outcomes" (p. 397). Moreover, the argument goes, practices and conditions related to autonomy, innovation, and accountability will differ across schools (and school types), thus responding to parental and community preferences and further promoting student achievement (Walberg, 2011). According to Chubb and Moe (1990, p. 67), choice schools

> operate in a very different institutional setting distinguished by the basic features of markets—decentralization, competition, and choice—and their organizations should be expected to bear a very different stamp as a result. They should tend to possess the autonomy, clarity of mission, strong leadership, teacher professionalism, and team cooperation that public schools want but except under very fortunate circumstances are unlikely to have.

Some hold that school choice can bring about "creative destruction," borrowing from Joseph Schumpeter, who in the 1940s argued that entrepreneurs relied on radically new technologies—whether more effective, more efficient, or both—to promote economic progress and replace older technologies (Walberg, 2011;

Schumpeter, 1942). As the theory goes, such privatization and increased choice will lead to better outcomes, lower costs, and greater satisfaction of employees, parents, and students. According to Walberg (2011, p. 73), "market-based consumer-driven school choice seems the best hope for creative destruction of new technologies, the expansion of choice, competition, and diversity for substantial, sustained achievement improvement." Chubb and Moe (1990, p. 217) hold a similar position:

> The whole point of a thoroughgoing system of choice is to free the schools from ... disabling constraints by sweeping away the old institutions and replacing them with new ones. Taken seriously, choice is not a system-preserving reform. It is a revolutionary reform that introduces a new system of public education.

Notwithstanding these foundational claims of school choice advocates, research supporting or refuting the idea that school choice leads to more innovative instructional practices is limited (for reviews see Austin & Berends, in press; Berends, 2015; also see Lubienski, 2003; Mavrogordato, Chapter 8; Oberfield, 2017; Preston et al., 2012; Gleason, Chapter 11).

Even the definition of innovation is varied. Central to market theorists' argument for school choice is that charter school autonomy and accountability will produce organizational innovations that promote new organizational structures and processes that lead to changes in instructional practices, which in turn will lead to better student outcomes (Chubb & Moe, 1990; Walberg & Bast, 2003). However, innovation has been operationalized by researchers in different ways (see Berends, 2015). What one considers innovative may be standard or conventional practice to another. Some claim that charter schools in and of themselves constitute an innovation because of their governance structure and autonomy (Center for Education Reform, 2008; U.S. Department of Education, 2004, 2008). Others define innovation as simply the ability to hire their own teachers. Still others see it as the ability to implement comprehensive designs that aim to change the teaching staff, professional development, and the organization of time, curriculum, and instruction, either at the local level or in partnership with an external non-profit charter management organization (CMO) or for-profit educational management organization (EMO). This latter innovation in schools may be developed locally at the building level or in partnership with an external provider, such as KIPP, Expeditionary Learning, Green Dot, National Heritage Academies, or many other external providers.

Although there are several ways to define innovation (see Berends, 2015; Preston et al., 2012; Wohlstetter et al., 2013), in this chapter we draw on Lubienski's (2003) conceptualization of innovation that distinguishes between "*educational* changes (practices regarding curricular content and instructional strategies with immediate impact at the classroom-level) and *administrative* changes (organizational-level practices and structural designs that do not directly affect classroom techniques or content) (pp. 404–5, emphasis in original). Here we focus mostly on the *educational* practices in charter and traditional public schools. School effectiveness research indicates that the aspects of schooling closest to students (i.e., teaching, instruction, and curriculum) have the greatest impact on student learning (Gamoran et al., 1995; Newman & Associates, 1996; Newmann et al., 2000; Newmann & Wehlage, 1995).

Thus, we are interested primarily in innovations related to changing the core technology of schools—classrooms and the teaching and learning that occurs within them. Although informative, the notion of *educational changes* from Lubienski as helping define innovation needs more conceptual elaboration. In this chapter, we look at educational innovations of several types including those that emphasize values as being part of the curriculum, teacher development of instructional materials, innovative instructional strategies and student evaluation, extended learning time, instructional grouping of students, instructional organization of teachers, and school policy strategies aimed at student engagement. Although some of these aspects are closer to the instructional core of classrooms than others (e.g., innovative instructional strategies vs. school policies about uniforms), it is important to examine these types of educational changes for deepening our theoretical and empirical understanding of innovation among different types of schools.

For example, some schools of choice have emphasized the need for values and morals being a part of the regular curriculum. For example, in their study of Catholic schools, Bryk et al. (1993) take an in-depth examination of school structure and instructional processes of seven Catholic high schools. Their quantitative results are consistent with previous studies that find a Catholic school advantage in terms of student achievement (Coleman & Hoffer, 1987). Their qualitative analysis also provides some insight into how Catholic schools are organized to promote higher academic achievement. Traditional public schools have drawn lessons from this Catholic school literature to emphasize strong school mission statements and values being integrated throughout the curriculum (Goldring & Berends, 2009; Hallinan, 2005; Hill, Foster & Gendler, 1990; Sizer & Sizer, 1999).

In addition, some schools have altered conventional instructional designs to emphasize alternative instructional grouping arrangements. Because research has shown that students placed in high ability groups tend to learn at a greater rate than students placed in low groups—contributing to greater inequality in achievement scores (for reviews see Gamoran, 2010; Gamoran & Berends, 1987; Gamoran & Hallinan, 1995; Oakes et al., 1992; for charter schools see Berends & Donaldson, 2016)—some have argued for detracking and alternative grouping arrangements (Welner & Oakes, 2000; Wheelock, 1992). Some of the innovations around alternative grouping arrangements include flexible schedules, "looping" (where teachers progress with the same group of students across grade levels), or used multi-grade or mixed-age grouping (see examples in Glennan et al., 2004).

Despite these examples and the number of additional educational innovations that have been suggested, we know little about how these types of educational innovations (Lubienski, 2003) are distributed across charter and traditional public schools. In the sections that follow, we outline our sample design and methods. We then explore the differences in our measures across school types, and we end the paper with a discussion of possible next steps for further research.

Data and Methods

The data we use for this chapter were part of a larger research project conducted by the National Center on School Choice at Vanderbilt University that aimed to open up the "black box" of charter and traditional public schools. Unpacking this "black box" furthers understanding of differences among these school types, such as curriculum, instruction, and organizational conditions that promote achievement (Berends et al., 2010).

Making charter-traditional public school comparisons is a challenging task if researchers want to examine schools across a variety of contexts in a cost-effective manner. Our approach was to collaborate with the Northwest Evaluation Association (NWEA), a non-profit testing organization that partnered at the time of the study with more than 4,300 districts and 12,300 schools in 50 states to provide computer-based, vertically equated assessments in mathematics, reading, and English/language arts. Taking advantage of the NWEA partnerships with large numbers of charter and traditional public schools, we constructed a matched sample to administer teacher and principal surveys in the 2007–08 school year to link to student achievement gains (for technical details see Berends & Donaldson, 2016; Cannata & Engel, 2012; Cannata & Peñaloza, 2012; Cravens et al., 2012; Goff et al., 2012).

Traditional public schools were matched to charters in two stages. At the first stage, we used the Common Core of Data (CCD) of the National Center for Education Statistics to identify the best match for schools. For schools to match, they had to be located in the same state and the closest possible traditional public school (TPS) to the charter public school (CPS) in terms of geographic distance, grade range served, racial-ethnic composition, socioeconomic status, and size. Distance was a crucial criterion because we wanted the CPS and the matched TPS to reflect the choice of schools that families and students had in the same geographic area. Thus, we restricted matches to within 20 miles to ensure matched schools would be within the same choice set for parents; 79 percent of the matched schools were within 15 miles of each other. We wanted to model choice with *reasonable* comparisons—a critical condition of examining any potential differences between school types, according to market theory. This is also consistent with a study that found matched comparison groups based on geographically defined criteria (rather than across states) produced estimates closer to randomized experiments (Cook et al., 2008).

For the matching process, we did not use propensity score matching because the different models we tested produced inconsistent matches, and we wanted a method by which we could weigh certain matching variables (e.g., distance between schools) differentially. Instead, we constructed an overall difference index, which measured the difference between the CPS and the TPS in terms of racial/ethnic composition, socioeconomic status, and school size.[2] The index gave equal weight to racial/ethnic composition and socioeconomic status differences and much lower weight to school size differences. An index value of zero indicated a perfect match. Then, we sorted the school pairs by distance brackets and the index and selected the pair with the smallest index and the greatest tested grade overlap within the closest distance bracket.[3]

The second stage of the matching process involved obtaining school participation in the teacher and principal survey. Once charter schools agreed to participate, we then approached the best-matched traditional public school (and its district) to participate in the study. All participating schools submitted teacher rosters, and those teachers filled out confidential, online surveys. Schools are in the sample if they agreed to participate and at least one teacher completed a survey. The school participation rates were 52 percent and 36 percent for charter and traditional public schools, respectively. Our final sample consisted of 59 traditional public schools and 59 charter schools, 22 of which were affiliated with either an EMO or CMO.[4] The questionnaire completion rates for teachers were 80 percent for the charter schools and 72.5 percent for the traditional public schools. Missing data were imputed using a multiple imputation procedure.[5]

We compared our sample of charter and traditional public schools to a subset of the 2008–09 CCD, using the population of schools in the six states: Colorado, Delaware, Indiana, Michigan, Minnesota, and Ohio. Based on CCD characteristics, the sample charter schools are generally similar to charter schools in the selected states in terms of racial/ethnic composition, school percentage of students who qualify for free and reduced lunch, and student-teacher ratios. One notable difference is that the charter schools in our sample are larger in size, on average, compared with charter schools in the sampled states. For traditional public schools, sampled traditional public schools served slightly different student populations than traditional public schools in the six states. In the sample, Black students comprised 28 percent of schools, compared to 13 percent for traditional public schools in the six states, and roughly 53 percent of students in sampled schools qualified for free and reduced lunch, compared with 41 percent for schools in the sampled states. Although the schools are similar to the general population of schools in the six states, any differences between the schools in the matched sample are controlled for in the multivariate analyses that follow. See Tables 6.1 and 6.2 for CCD and sample comparisons.

TABLE 6.1 Means and Standard Deviations for Charter Schools by Analytic Sample vs. CCD Subset of Schools in Sampled States

School Measures	Sample	CCD
Percentage of American Indian Students	0.589 (0.627)	1.509 (8.185)★
Percentage of Asian Students	3.592 (6.596)	3.022 (10.796)
Percentage of Hispanic Students	7.561 (10.804)	8.639 (16.715)
Percentage of Black Students	36.411 (35.201)	42.560 (39.817)
Percentage of White Students	51.847 (33.140)	44.270 (37.366)
Percent of Free / Reduced Lunch Students	52.773 (28.092)	54.215 (34.991)
Student to Teacher Ratio	16.626 (4.187)	18.136 (13.723)
Number of Students per Grade	57.573 (24.144)	45.440 (42.485)★
Student Enrollment	499.720 (238.726)	311.245 (433.693)★

Note: N_{SAMPLE}=25; N_{CCD}=986.

★ $p \leq 0.05$.

Variables

Innovation Measures

After pre-testing and a pilot of our surveys, we aimed to expand our measures of innovation since innovation is an important buzzword in the educational landscape of school choice, yet often not well defined (see Berends et al., 2010; Goldring & Cravens, 2008). Because we were primarily interested in measures of innovation that may have predictive validity for student achievement gains, we reviewed the literature at the time on educational innovation, comprehensive school reforms, and school choice reforms, and charter school organizations (e.g., Aladjem & Borman, 2006; Berends et al., 2002; Berends et al., 2009; Borman et al., 2003; Gill et al., 2007; Lee & Smith, 1995; Lubienski, 2003; U.S. Department

TABLE 6.2 Means and Standard Deviations for Traditional Public Schools by Analytic Sample vs. CCD Subset of Schools in Sampled States

School Measures	Sample	CCD
Percentage of American Indian Students	1.227 (1.714)	1.116 (5.309)
Percentage of Asian Students	4.344 (6.614)	2.257 (4.301)
Percentage of Hispanic Students	10.100 (13.882)	8.273 (14.887)
Percentage of Black Students	28.187 (29.958)	13.011 (23.457)★
Percentage of White Students	56.142 (35.500)	75.344 (28.078)★
Percent of Free / Reduced Lunch Students	53.260 (24.209)	41.289 (25.336)★
Student to Teacher Ratio	16.773 (2.376)	16.697 (8.531)
Number of Students per Grade	100.116 (78.935)	113.665 (113.491)
Student Enrollment	464.074 (200.792)	475.025 (370.174)

Note: N_{SAMPLE}=27; N_{CCD}=11,962.

★ $p \leq 0.05$.

of Education, 2004). This literature review included peer-reviewed journal articles, books, reports, as well as information on various websites of school reforms for various types of schools, whether choice schools or traditional public (e.g., KIPP, Green-Dot, National Heritage Academies, Expeditionary Learning).

Of course, in developing a survey of this nature, not all types of innovations can be included. To help focus our survey research efforts, we concentrated on those educational innovations that school reformers have argued change the core technology of school (curriculum and instruction) in ways that promote student achievement growth, such as use of instructional time (extended day, summer and weekends), curriculum strategies (project based, community-linked, direct instruction), and additional requirements for students and families (community service, school uniforms, homework contracts). For some of these, the empirical research is non-existent or extremely limited, but we included them in our surveys because policymakers and school reformers emphasize their relevance.[6]

Our surveys of teachers and principals asked a series of yes-no questions. On the teacher survey, we asked to report about instructional innovations, such as a value-based curriculum, innovations in developing instructional materials, different types of instructional strategies, and alternative student evaluation. We asked principals to report about whether or not their schools used different types of innovations that involved extended learning time, the organization of classroom instruction for students, the structuring of teacher teams and interaction, and school policies that required students and/or families to commit to certain activities (school uniforms, volunteering, sign a home/school contract).

When examining these various innovation items, because none of them had previously been developed for use in scales, we began by trying to conceptualize scales in terms of constructivist approaches to learning or direct instruction approaches to learning. We then examined scale properties but found that none of the items we thought would hold together in a single scale did (DeVellis, 2017). We then conducted several exploratory factor analyses at the teacher and principal level, but virtually none of these data-driven analyses resulted in factors that had conceptual or substantive meaning.

We also considered whether we might create an index for the number of innovations in a school to capture whether some schools are more innovative than others (e.g., Berends & King, 1994; Berends & Zottola, 2009). That is, we considered whether adding up the "yes" responses to these items to create an index might be a way to capture innovation. However, it is difficult to hypothesize that the greater the number of innovations, the higher the gains in achievement would be. Just because some schools are doing more innovations, does not necessarily imply that they would be better schools. Many schools that implement innovations do so not for the sheer number but are selective in intentionally implementing a specific set of reforms to improve student achievement (Glennan et al., 2004).

Because of these prior analyses, we made the decision for this chapter to examine the descriptive analyses of the innovation measures individually across charter and traditional public schools, and we also disaggregate the overall charter sector into independent charter and affiliated charter schools (EMO or CMOs). Findings account for teacher clustering within schools.

Results

In what follows, we report the descriptive results for our innovation measures by school type (traditional public [TPS] and charter schools ([CPS] broken down further into independent and affiliated) as reported at the classroom level by teachers and the school level as reported by principals. The results reported here are not causal but exploratory, intended to promote further reflection and research.

Instructional Innovations Reported by Teachers

There are several innovation items at the classroom level that differ by school type, whether considering a values-based curriculum, instructional materials, instructional strategies, or student evaluation. Table 6.3 reports these results for traditional and charter public schools.

Values-Based Curriculum

When compared with traditional public school teachers (TPS), Table 6.3 reveals that charter school teachers (CPS) are more likely to report that morals, values, and virtues are a regular part of their curriculum. About 85 percent of CPS teachers compared with 75 percent of TPS teachers report that morals, values and virtues are a regular part of the curriculum, with 82 percent of independent charter teachers and 91 percent of affiliated charter school teachers reporting so.

Instructional Materials

Teachers in charter schools are more likely to report that they rely less on published instructional materials and more on instructional materials they develop themselves compared with TPS teachers. Fifty-seven percent of both groups of CPS teachers report that they (and/or other teachers in their school) developed the primary instructional materials for instruction. By contrast, 59 percent of TPS teachers report that their primary instructional materials are published textbooks and workbooks, compared with 52 percent of CPS teachers.

Instructional Strategies

When examining instructional strategies across teachers in different school types, there are several significant contrasts that suggest that CPS teachers more frequently use innovative instructional strategies than their TPS counterparts.

TABLE 6.3 Proportion of TPS and CPS Teachers Reporting Classroom Innovations

	TPS	Charter	Independent Charter	Affiliated Charter
Values-Based Curriculum	0.753	0.847*	0.816*	0.913*
Morals, values, and virtues are a regular part of my curriculum	(0.431)	(0.360)	(0.388)	(0.282)
Instructional Materials	0.587	0.518*	0.480*	0.598
My primary instructional materials are textbooks, workbooks, and other published materials	(0.493)	(0.500)	(0.500)	(0.491)
My primary instructional materials were developed by myself or other teachers in this school	0.475	0.566*	0.577*	0.540*
	(0.500)	(0.496)	(0.494)	(0.499)
Instructional Strategies	0.445	0.508*	0.529*	0.464
Student work is focused around long-term investigations of compelling questions (e.g., learning expeditions)	(0.497)	(0.500)	(0.500)	(0.500)
All of my students have individual or personalized education plans	0.170	0.198	0.215*	0.163
	(0.376)	(0.399)	(0.411)	(0.370)
My students set the pace of my instruction	0.753	0.779	0.779	0.779
	(0.431)	(0.415)	(0.416)	(0.416)
My lessons are tightly structured (e.g., direct instruction)	0.544	0.477*	0.432*	0.571
	(0.498)	(0.500)	(0.496)	(0.496)
I use cooperative learning strategies where students earn group rewards for mastery of academic skill	0.564	0.620*	0.622*	0.615
	(0.496)	(0.486)	(0.485)	(0.487)
My students use their communities as sites of learning and investigation	0.450	0.569*	0.592*	0.520*
	(0.498)	(0.495)	(0.492)	(0.500)
My instructional methods focus on complex/real-life projects that provide students with authentic learning experiences	0.563	0.646*	0.673*	0.590
	(0.496)	(0.478)	(0.470)	(0.493)
My students collaborate with outside experts over the Internet	0.078	0.109*	0.132*	0.060
	(0.269)	(0.312)	(0.339)	(0.237)
In my classroom, learning is primarily based around students asking questions and investigating solutions	0.358	0.417*	0.454*	0.340
	(0.480)	(0.493)	(0.498)	(0.475)
My instruction is primarily focused around activity or work centers in my classroom	0.468	0.470	0.496	0.415
	(0.499)	(0.499)	(0.500)	(0.493)
I use instructional methods that involve all five senses in learning	0.730	0.760	0.746	0.791*
	(0.444)	(0.427)	(0.436)	(0.407)
Student Evaluation	0.169	0.249*	0.283*	0.176
All of my students are evaluated using portfolios	(0.375)	(0.433)	(0.451)	(0.381)
My curriculum emphasizes preparing students for standardized tests	0.438	0.402	0.357*	0.496
	(0.496)	(0.491)	(0.480)	(0.501)
N	1,300	1,015	689	326

(*) An asterisk indicates a statistically significant difference in means between charter types and traditional public schools (TPS) at the 5 percent level. Results are shown for all charters and charters broken down into independent and affiliated. The data are binary responses (1=Yes, 0=No) to questionnaire items reported by the schools' teachers, so the means are proportions of 1 responses. N shows the number of reporting teachers who are in 59 TPS and 59 charters (48 independent and 11 affiliated). Results combine five multiple imputations per teacher when needed.

Of the 11 items used as indicators for innovative instructional strategies, seven of 11 are statistically significant when comparing CPS vs. TPS teachers.

When comparing the significant differences between CPS to TPS teachers, we find:

- 51 percent of CPS teachers compared with 45 percent of TPS teachers indicate that student work is focused on long-term investigations and compelling questions.
- 48 percent of CPS teachers report that their lessons were tightly structured (e.g., direct instruction [arguably, a less innovative practice]) compared with 54 percent of TPS teachers.
- 62 percent of CPS teachers report that they use cooperative learning strategies where students earn group rewards for mastery of academic skill compared with 56 percent of TPS teachers.
- Compared with 45 percent of TPS teachers, 57 percent of CPS teachers report that their students used their communities as sites of learning and investigation.
- 65 percent of CPS teachers and 56 percent of TPS say their instructional methods focus on complex or real-life projects providing authentic learning experiences to students.
- 11 percent of CPS compared with 8 percent of TPS teachers have their students collaborate with outside experts over the internet.
- 42 percent of CPS teachers report that their instruction is primarily focused around students asking questions and investigating solutions compared with 36 percent of TPS teachers.

Student Evaluation

Because some educational reform innovations have emphasized the use of portfolios to monitor student progress throughout their schooling (Meier, 1995; Sizer & Sizer, 1999), we examine this innovative assessment approach in CPS and TPS. Although schools under *No Child Left Behind* prepared their students to take a standardized, high-stakes accountability test (Hamilton et al, 2007; Kortez, 2017), some schools may innovate by relying on portfolios.

We asked teachers about whether or not all their students were evaluated with portfolios. Compared with TPS teachers, CPS teachers were more likely to rely on more innovative assessment of students with portfolios, even though overall this type of assessment did not appear commonplace. Twenty-five percent of CPS teachers said that all their students were evaluated using portfolios compared with 17 percent of TPS teachers.

Among these differences between CPS and TPS teachers, it is important to note the differences between independent and affiliated charter school teachers. In terms of morals, values, and virtues being a regular part of the curriculum, 82 percent of the independent and 91 percent of affiliated CPS teachers report this is the case compared with 75 percent of TPS teachers. Both types of charter school teachers also significantly differ from TPS teachers when reporting about self-developed curricular materials. Independent CPS teachers appear to be driving the significant differences compared with TPS teachers when considering the innovative instructional strategies and portfolio assessment indicators.

Classroom Innovations Reported by Principals

Based on principal surveys, we found that there are several innovation items that differ by school type (see Table 6.4). For principals, the innovative dimensions of the instructional core that we consider include extended learning time, instructional grouping, the organization of teachers for instruction, and innovative school policies.

Extended Learning Time

When examining the indicators of extended learning time, we do not find statistically significant variation between CPS and TPS principals. A number of CPS and TPS schools offer voluntary before-school, after-school, or weekend tutorial or instructional programs (83 percent of TPS and 90 percent of CPS).

Instructional Grouping

All of the indicators for instructional grouping differ between CPS and TPS principals. With the exception of one indicator, the results suggest that CPS principals report more innovation than TPS principals. If flexible class scheduling is considered innovative, CPS are less innovative than TPS. Sixteen percent of CPS principals report that class schedules are flexible compared with 46 percent of TPS principals.

For the other indicators of instructional grouping we find:

- 48 percent of CPS principals report use of block scheduling compared with 16 percent of TPS principals. Both the independent and affiliated CPS principals significantly differ from TPS principals.
- 42 percent of CPS principals and 18 percent of TPS principals report that in core subjects, classrooms are multi-grade or mixed-age.
- 62 percent of CPS principals said that arts are integrated throughout the curriculum compared with 39 percent of TPS principals.
- These latter two overall findings appear to be due to affiliated charter school principals reporting more innovation than TPS principals.

Instructional Organization of Teachers

Turning to measures of how schools organize teachers for instructional purposes, we find few significant differences between CPS and TPS principals. The school types

TABLE 6.4 Proportion of TPS and CPS Principals Reporting Classroom Innovations

	TPS	Charter	Independent Charter	Affiliated Charter
Extended Learning Time	0.129	0.193	0.204	0.145
We provide mandatory before-school, after-school, or weekend tutorial instructional programs for students	(0.338)	(0.398)	(0.407)	(0.371)
We offer voluntary before-school, after-school, or weekend tutorial or instructional programs	0.831 (0.378)	0.898 (0.305)	0.875 (0.334)	1.000 (0.000)
Instructional Grouping	0.458	0.163★	0.129★	0.309
Our class schedules are flexible: today's class periods may be longer/shorter than tomorrow's	(0.503)	(0.372)	(0.339)	(0.485)
We use block scheduling	0.159 (0.369)	0.475★ (0.504)	0.438★ (0.502)	0.636★ (0.505)
In core subjects, our classrooms are multi-grade or mixed-age	0.176 (0.384)	0.417★ (0.497)	0.488★ (0.505)	0.109 (0.328)
We integrate the arts throughout the curriculum (e.g., arts are not just in separate courses)	0.386 (0.491)	0.620★ (0.490)	0.663★ (0.478)	0.436 (0.521)
Instructional Organization of Teachers	0.356	0.295	0.300	0.273
Our teachers work in teams of two or more in the same class at the same time	(0.483)	(0.460)	(0.463)	(0.467)
We have interdisciplinary teams of teachers who share the same students	0.631 (0.487)	0.725 (0.451)	0.667 (0.477)	0.982★ (0.142)
Teacher teams have common planning times	0.776 (0.421)	0.769 (0.425)	0.738 (0.445)	0.909 (0.302)
Our teachers visit other schools for observations	0.600 (0.494)	0.492 (0.504)	0.496 (0.505)	0.473 (0.524)
N	59	59	48	11

(★) An asterisk indicates a statistically significant difference in means between charter types and Traditional Public Schools (TPS) at the 5 percent level. Results are shown for all charters and charters broken down into independent and affiliated. The data are binary responses (1=Yes, 0=No) to questionnaire items reported by the schools' principals, so the means are proportions of 1 responses. N shows the number of reporting principals (or schools). Results combine five multiple imputations per principal when needed.

do not significantly differ when we consider teacher teams, interdisciplinary teacher teams sharing students, teacher teams having common planning times, or teachers visiting other schools for observations. The one exception to this pattern is that 98 percent of affiliated CPS principals report that the school has interdisciplinary teacher teams who share the same students compared with 63 percent of TPS principals.

Innovative School Policy Strategies Reported by Principals

On the principal surveys, we also asked whether schools made additional requirements of students and their families, such as whether community service was mandatory, school uniforms were required, parents had to volunteer in the schools or sign a home-school contract. Table 6.5 shows the results for CPS and TPS principal reports.

CPS principals were much more likely to report that these additional requirements were in place in their schools compared with TPS principals. Specifically,

- 37 percent of CPS principals reported that community service was mandatory for students compared with 10 percent of TPS principals.
- 56 percent of the CPS principals compared with 25 percent of TPS principals said that school uniforms were required.
- 41 percent of CPS principals and 3 percent of TPS principals reported that parents were required to volunteer at the school.
- Compared with 35 percent of TPS principals, 64 percent of CPS principals responded that parents were required to sign a home-school contract.

Future Research

We should be cautious about drawing conclusions and making policy recommendations based on the exploratory results in this chapter. Even so, the descriptive results suggest that there are important differences between charter schools

TABLE 6.5 Proportion of TPS and CPS Principals Reporting Innovative School Policy Strategies

	TPS	Charter	Independent Charter	Affiliated Charter
Community service is mandatory for all students in some grade levels	0.102 (0.305)	0.369★ (0.487)	0.396★ (0.494)	0.255 (0.457)
We have school uniforms or a standardized dress code	0.251 (0.437)	0.556★ (0.501)	0.563★ (0.501)	0.527 (0.524)
We require parents to volunteer at the school	0.027 (0.164)	0.407★ (0.495)	0.396★ (0.494)	0.455★ (0.522)
We require each parent to sign a home/school contract	0.349 (0.481)	0.644★ (0.483)	0.625★ (0.489)	0.727★ (0.467)
N	59	59	48	11

(★) An asterisk indicates a statistically significant difference in means between charter types and Traditional Public Schools (TPS) at the 5 percent level. Results are shown for all charters and charters broken down into independent and affiliated. The data are binary responses (1=Yes, 0=No) to questionnaire items reported by the schools' principals, so the means are proportions of 1 responses. N shows the number of reporting principals (or schools). Results combine five multiple imputations per principal when needed.

and traditional public schools when comparing educational innovations at the core technology of classrooms. Some of these differences are not only statistically significant but also quite large. For example, charter schools of choice tend to add additional requirements for students and parents whether that is requiring school uniforms, parent volunteering in the school, or having students participate in community service. The magnitude of differences between charter and traditional public schools for these items ranged from 28 to 38 percentage points.

In addition, at the classroom and school levels, charter schools were more likely to report innovative educational practices than traditional public schools. These findings suggest that research examining specific innovative practices of schools and classrooms provides a promising avenue to understanding differences among different school choice options.

The differences among the innovation indicators in this chapter shows some promise for exploring the variability of achievement effects comparing CPS and TPS (Austin & Berends, in press; Berends, 2015; Betts & Tang, Chapter 4). Our future research hopes to examine how innovation indicators moderate and mediate the CPS effects on student achievement in mathematics and reading.

Although further research is necessary in terms of establishing a connection between innovation measures and achievement gains, the findings of this chapter suggest that schools and classrooms do differ in their educational innovative practices. Yet, innovation for innovation's sake is not the goal of those who advocate for school choice reform. It is the connection to achievement and other student outcomes that is key. Although the findings here are exploratory, the impact of school choice reform on innovation and achievement is likely to be more complicated and nuanced than what the indicators in this chapter portray. Moving forward researchers and policymakers should attend to how these connections between innovation and student outcomes vary among different social contexts.

Notes

1 This chapter was supported by the National Center on School Choice, which was funded by a grant from the US Department of Education's Institute of Education Sciences (IES) (R305A040043). All opinions expressed in this paper represent those of the authors and not necessarily the institutions with which they are affiliated or the US Department of Education. All errors in this paper are solely the responsibility of the authors.

2 The formula for the Overall Difference Index was: 0.48*(socioeconomic difference) + 0.48*(racial/ethnic composition difference) + 0.04*(school size difference). Socioeconomic status difference was calculated by taking the absolute value of the difference in percentage of students qualifying for free and reduced lunch in a given matched school pair—school a (charter school) and school b (traditional public school). The difference in racial-ethnic composition was calculated in a similar way, calculating the summed difference in percentage American Indian, Asian, Hispanic, Black and White students between matched schools. Finally, school size was calculated by taking the absolute value of the difference of students per grade between school a and school b, dividing by the number of students per grade in school a (again, the charter school in the pair) and multiplying the result by 100.

Matches reflect schools with the smallest index scores and the greatest tested grade overlap within the closest geographical distance.

3 There were 61 matches in our sample. Due to differences in grade configurations between charter and traditional public schools, there were cases where we had more than one match for a charter school to match all the grade levels in the school. For instance, a K–8 charter could be matched to both an elementary (K–5) and a middle (6–8) traditional public school. Some traditional public schools were also used as matches for more than one charter school. Nearly 20 percent of these matches were located within five miles of each other; about 45 percent were located within 10 miles of each other; and approximately 79 percent were located within 15 or fewer miles of one another.

4 One large EMO represents 18.6 percent of all charter schools (11 of 59) and 50 percent of the affiliated charter schools (11 of 22).

5 We examined the missing and non-missing values for the selected variables before imputing. For the teacher file, there was always at least one teacher per school with a non-missing value for each one of the variables considered. The variables that had the greatest proportion of missing values overall and per school type (i.e. charter and traditional) were also identified. For the teacher file, practically all variables had missing-value proportions below 5 percent, suggesting that imputation would have little effect on analysis results. Because no patterns in missing data emerged, we operated under the assumption that the data were normally distributed and the missing data are Missing at Random (MAR). With both files having non-monotonous patterns of missing data, the Markov Chain Monte Carlo (MCMC) imputation method with a single chain and a non-informative prior was used to create five imputations.

6 After we developed the survey items, we shared them with our project monitor and staff at the U.S. Department of Education's Institute of Education Sciences to receive additional feedback to focus the surveys.

References

Aladjem, D. K. & Borman, K. M. (2006). *Examining comprehensive school reform.* Washington, DC: Urban Institute Press.

Austin, M. & Berends, M. (In Press). School choice and learning opportunities. In *Handbook of the Sociology of Education in the 21st Century*, edited by B. Schneider. New York: Springer.

Berends, M. (2015). Sociology and school choice: What we know after two decades of charter schools. *Annual Review of Sociology, 41*(15), 159–80. Retrieved from http://www.annualreviews.org/doi/pdf/10.1146/annurev-soc-073014-112340.

Berends, M. & Donaldson, K. (2016). Does the organization of instruction differ in charter schools? Ability grouping and students' mathematics gains. *Teachers College Record, 118*(11), 1–38.

Berends, M. & King, M. B. (1994). A description of restructuring in nationally nominated schools: The legacy of the iron cage? *Educational Policy, 8*(1), 28–50.

Berends, M. & Zottola, G. (2009). A primer on survey methods. In *Research essentials: An introduction to deigns and practices*, edited by S. D. Lapan & M. L. Quartaroli (pp. 79–101). San Francisco, CA: Jossey-Bass.

Berends, M., Bodilly, S., & Kirby, S. N. (2002). *Facing the challenges of whole-school reform: New American Schools after a decade.* Santa Monica, CA: RAND.

Berends, M., Goldring, E., Stein, M., & Cravens, X. (2010). Instructional conditions in charter schools and students' mathematics achievement gains. *American Journal of Education,* 116(3), 303–35.

Berends, M. Springer, M. G., Ballou, D., & Walberg, H. J. (Eds.) (2009). *Handbook of research on school choice.* New York: Routledge.

Borman, G. D., Hewes, G. M., Overman, L. T., & Brown, S. (2003). Comprehensive school reform and achievement: A meta-analysis. *Review of Educational Research, 73,* 125–30.

Bryk, A. S., Lee, V. E., & Holland, P. B. (1993). *Catholic schools and the common good.* Cambridge, MA: Harvard University Press.

Cannata, M. & Engel, M. (2012). Does charter status determine preferences? Comparing the hiring preferences of charter and traditional public school principals. *Education Finance and Policy, 7*(4), 455–88.

Cannata, M. & Peñaloza, R.V. (2012). Who are charter school teachers? Comparing teacher characteristics, job choices, and job preferences. *Education Policy Analysis Archives, 20*(29), 1–21.

Center for Education Reform. (2008). *America's attitudes toward charter schools.* Washington, DC: Author.

Chubb, J. & Moe, T. (1990). *Politics markets & America's schools.* Washington, DC: Brookings.

Coleman, J. S. & Hoffer, T. (1987). *Public and private high schools: The impact of communities.* New York: Basic Books, Inc.

Cook, T. D., Shadish, W. R., & Wong, V. C. (2008). Three conditions under which experiments and observational studies produce comparable causal estimates: New findings from within-study comparisons. *Journal of Policy Analysis and Management, 27*(4), 724–50.

Cravens, X., Goldring, E., & Peñaloza, R. V. (2012). Leadership practice in the context of U.S. school choice reform. *Leadership and Policy in Schools, 11*(4), 452–76.

DeVellis, R. F. (2017). *Scale development: Theory and applications, 4th edition.* Los Angeles, CA: Sage Publications.

Gamoran, A. (2010). Tracking and inequality: new directions for research and practice. In *The Routledge International handbook of the sociology of education,* edited by M. W. Apple, S. J. Ball, & L. A. Gandin (pp. 213–28). London: Routledge.

Gamoran, A. & Berends, M. (1987). The effects of stratification in secondary schools: Synthesis of survey and ethnographic research. *Review of Educational Research, 57,* 415–35.

Gamoran, A. & Hallinan, M. T. (1995). Tracking students for instruction: Consequences and implications for school restructuring. In *Restructuring schools: Promising practices and policies,* edited by M. T. Hallinan (pp. 113–31). New York: Plenum Press.

Gamoran, A., Nystrand, M., Berends, M., & LePore, P. (1995). An organizational analysis of the effects of ability grouping. *American Educational Research Journal, 24,* 687–715.

Goldring, E. & Cravens, X. (2008). Teachers' academic focus on learning in charter and traditional public schools. In *Charter school outcomes,* edited by M. Berends, M. G. Springer, & H. J. Walberg (pp. 39–60). New York: Taylor & Francis.

Gill, B. P., Timpane, P. M., Ross, K. E., Brewer, D. J., & Booker, K. (2007). *Rhetoric versus reality: What we know and what we need to know about vouchers and charter schools.* Santa Monica, CA: RAND.

Glennan, T. K., Bodilly, S. J., Galegher, J. R., & Kerr, K. A. (2004). *Expanding the reach of education reforms: Perspectives from leaders in the scale-up of educational interventions.* Santa Monica, CA: RAND.

Goff, P. T., Mavrogordato, M., & Goldring, E. B. (2012). Instructional leadership in charter schools: Is there an organizational effect or are leadership practices the result of faculty characteristics and preferences? *Leadership and Policy in Schools, 11*(1), 1–25.

Goldring, E. & Berends, M. (2009). *Leading with data: Pathways to improve your schools.* Thousand Oaks, CA: Corwin Press.

Hallinan, M. T. (2005). The normative culture of school and student socialization. In *Social organization of schooling,* edited by L. Hedges & B. Schneider (pp. 129–46). New York: Russell Sage.

Hamilton, L. S., Stecher, B. M., Marsh, J. A., McCombs, J. S., Robyn, A., Russell, J. L., Naftel, S., & Barney, H. (2007). *Standards-based accountability under No Child Left Behind.* Santa Monica, CA: RAND.

Hill, P. T., Foster, G. E., & Gendler, T. (1990). *High schools with character.* Santa Monica, CA: RAND.

Koretz, D. (2017). *The testing charade: Pretending to make schools better.* Chicago, IL: University of Chicago Press.

Lee, V. E. & Smith, J. B. (1995). Effects of high school restructuring and size on early gains in achievement and engagement. *Sociology of Education, 68*(4), 241–70.

Lubienski, C. (2003). Innovation in education markets: Theory and evidence on the impact of competition and choice in charter schools. *American Educational Research Journal, 40*(2), 395–443.

Meier, D., (1995). *The power of their ideas: Lessons for America from a small school in Harlem.* Boston, MA: Beacon Press.

Newmann, F. M. & Associates. (1996). *Authentic achievement: Restructuring schools for intellectual quality.* San Francisco, CA: Jossey-Bass.

Newmann, F. M. & Wehlage, G. (1995). *Successful school restructuring: A report to the public and educators by the Center on Organization and Restructuring of Schools.* Alexandria, VA: Association for Supervision and Curriculum Development; Reston, VA: National Association for Secondary School Principals.

Newmann, F. M., King, M. B., & Youngs, P. (2000). Professional development that addresses school capacity: Lessons from urban elementary schools. *American Journal of Education, 108*(4), 259–99.

Oakes, J., Gamoran, A., Page, R. N. (1992). Curriculum differentiation: Opportunities, outcomes, and meanings. In *Handbook of research on curriculum*, edited by P.W. Jackson (pp. 570–608). New York: Macmillan.

Oberfield, Z. W. (2017). *Are charter schools different? Public education, teachers, and the charter school debate.* Cambridge, MA: Harvard Education Press.

Preston, C., Goldring, E., Berends, M., & Cannata, M. (2012) School innovation in district context: Comparison of traditional public schools and charter schools. *Economics of Education Review, 31*, 318–30.

Sizer, T. R. & Sizer, N. F. (1999). *The students are watching: Schools and the moral contract.* Boston, MA: Beacon Press.

U.S. Department of Education. (2004). *Successful charter schools.* Washington, DC: U.S. Department of Education, Office of Innovation and Improvement.

U.S. Department of Education. (2008). *A commitment to quality: National charter school policy forum report.* Washington, DC: U.S. Department of Education, Office of Innovation and Improvement.

Walberg, H. J. (2011). *Tests, testing, and genuine school reform.* Stanford, CA: Hoover Institution Press.

Walberg, H. J. & Bast, J. L. (2003). *Education and capitalism: How overcoming our fear of markets and economics can improve America's schools.* Stanford, CA: Hoover Institution Press.

Welner, K. G. & Oakes, J. (2000). *Navigating the politics of detracking: Leadership strategies.* Arlington Heights, IL: SkyLight Professional Development.

Wheelock, A. (1992). *Crossing the tracks: How "untracking" can save America's schools.* New York: The New Press.

Wohlstetter, P., Smith, J., & Farell, C. C. (2013). *Choices and challenges: Charter school performance in perspective.* Cambridge: Harvard Education Press.

7

REDEFINING WHAT IT MEANS TO BE A TEACHER

An Examination of Teacher Autonomy and Innovation in Indianapolis Charter Schools

Madeline Mavrogordato

By definition, charter schools are given considerable autonomy from the bureaucracy that school choice proponents argue has plagued traditional public school districts and inhibited educational progress for many years.[1] Charter school supporters believe this autonomy will spur positive educational innovation that would otherwise be stifled (e.g., Chubb & Moe, 1990; Finn & Gau, 1998). One aspect in which this autonomy is evident is in the realm of organizational conditions. School organizational conditions might be configured differently under school choice reforms such as charter schools (Hausman & Goldring, 2001). Many charter schools are exempt from regulations that apply to their traditional public school counterparts. For example, charter schools are free to develop their own instructional focus and curriculum, create their own academic calendar and recruit specific personnel who they believe would best serve the needs of their students. This organizational independence and decentralization in charter schools may also be reflected in the greater autonomy possessed by teachers.

Given the critical role teachers play in shaping student outcomes (e.g., Clotfelter, Ladd, & Vigdor, 2007; Goldhaber, 2007; Harris, 2011; Rivkin, Hanushek, & Kain, 2005) the potential for charter schools to improve education for students arguably hinges on whether the autonomy afforded to charter schools reaches teachers and allows them to implement innovative practices in their classrooms. Teachers, as "street-level bureaucrats" (Lipsky, 1980), often lack sufficient resources to implement policy in a way that meets the ambitious expectations of policymakers. Instead, they may adopt practices that are practical within their context and reflect the constraints they face. Although policymakers intend for charter schools to reflect innovative teaching practices, teachers in these schools may instead employ more standard practices due to limited resources, time, technology, skills, or knowledge. Thus, teachers are in a position to profoundly influence the policy outcomes of charter schools (e.g., Marsh & Odden, 1991; McDonnell, 1991; Werts & Brewer, 2015).

Research Questions

Using qualitative data from interviews with 33 teachers across two case study charter schools, this chapter explores the extent to which the claims about charter schools' autonomy and innovation are reflected in the work teachers do. Specifically, this chapter investigates the following research questions:

1. What roles and responsibilities do teachers have in charter schools? Do these roles reflect teacher autonomy and innovation?
2. How does the school context inform teacher autonomy and innovation?

Theoretical Claims for Autonomy and Innovation in Charter Schools

Charter school advocates argue that schools will improve when they are permitted to operate outside of entrenched bureaucracies that inhibit educational reform efforts (Loveless & Field, 2009). These supporters believe that the market-based approaches that allow for competition between schools will lead to innovative practices (Carnoy et al., 2005; Chubb & Moe, 1990; Finn et al., 2000; Gawlik, 2007). The underlying assumption is that the competition introduced by school choice "undercuts bureaucratic political control of public education [and] provides educators in schools of choice the opportunity and motivation to experiment with new organizational and instructional strategies for improving student achievement" (Berends et al., 2010, p. 306). As such, charter schools have the potential to serve as "laboratories of innovation" (Loveless & Field, 2009, p. 101).

Market theory also suggests that charter schools will be driven to constantly strive to improve in order to respond to parents' preferences and continuously attract students (Friedman, 1962). Following the supply and demand assumption implicit in market theory, it is possible that charter schools will seek to distinguish themselves by redesigning core elements of the schooling experience in an effort to gain a competitive advantage. Recognizing the central role that teachers play in student learning, it follows that the roles and responsibilities of teachers in charter schools may be redefined as a result of competitive pressures.

However, critics of charter schools argue that there is an underlying and persistent pattern of institutionalized guidelines that not only defines the key actions of schools but legitimizes them as well (Berends, 2015; Berends et al., 2010; Bidwell & Kassarda, 1980). Included in these rules of schooling are elements such as the presence of a school principal and certified teachers, the use of curricular materials such as textbooks for instruction, and students being grouped into age-based classes that are taught by an individual teacher (Berends et al., 2010). Not only is it particularly challenging to reformulate these institutionalized aspects of schooling, but doing so may also cause parents to question the quality of a school because its elements are largely unrecognized and unfamiliar. As such, institutional theorists assert that despite reduced regulation, charter schools will ultimately reflect institutional isomorphism and adopt traditional elements of education that signal that their organization is a legitimate institution of education (Bidwell & Dreeben, 2006; Elmore, 2007; Meyer & Rowan, 1992; Scott & Davis, 2007). Thus, changes in the area of teaching may be minimal or non-existent.

Although the research base surrounding charter schools has grown substantially, it is unclear whether charter schools have prompted innovation as market theory would suggest, or if the practices occurring within charter schools mirror those occurring in traditional public schools, as institutional theory would imply. The limited literature that explores organizational practices of charter schools (reviewed below) is mixed. This is not surprising considering the inherent autonomy charter school operators possess; it makes sense that the variety of organizational strategies reflects the freedom afforded to charter schools. Some schools may opt to break from tradition while others may largely embrace institutionalized schooling norms. For example, as shown in the previous chapter in this volume, some charter schools may simply require students to wear uniforms while others implement "comprehensive school instructional designs that aim to change the teaching staff, their professional development, [and] the organization of instructional time, curriculum and instruction" (Berends et al., 2018). This chapter adds to the research base by utilizing market and institutional lenses to examine how the conditions of autonomy and innovation play out in charter school teachers' roles.

Defining Innovation in Charter Schools

A primary argument for charter schools pertains to the notion that teacher autonomy will spur innovative teaching practices in the classroom and will encourage teachers to assume new roles outside the classroom. In fact, most charter school laws include the desire to "facilitate innovative teaching" (Malloy & Wohlstetter, 2003, p. 220). Innovation is valued because it is seen as a means of improving student achievement. As Lubienski (2003) notes, "choice, competition, and innovation are cast as the necessary vehicles for advancing academic outcomes" (p. 397).

Lubienski (2003) conceptualizes innovation in terms of "*educational* changes, (practices regarding curricular content and instructional strategies with immediate impact at the classroom-level), and *administrative* changes (organizational-level practices and structural designs that do not directly affect classroom techniques or content)" (p. 404–5, emphasis in original). Research on school effectiveness suggests that the components of schooling that are most closely related to students— such as teaching, instruction, and curriculum—are most likely to affect student learning outcomes (Berends et al., 2010; Gamoran et al.,1995; Gleason, 2018;

Newmann et al., 2000). As such, this investigation of autonomy and innovation focuses on teachers, who are the managers of this "core technology of schools" where educational changes may occur (Berends & Zottola, 2009, p. 9).

More recent research asserts that innovation in charter schools must be defined in context. Preston et al. (2012) define innovation "in terms of a practice's relative prevalence in a local district context" (p. 318). In other words, a charter school practice is considered innovative if the traditional public schools in its local school district are not employing that practice. Thus, a given practice may be considered innovative in one context while it is non-innovative in another context.

Prior Research on Teacher Autonomy and Innovation in Charter Schools

The limited extent empirical research provides some evidence that charter schools exhibit higher levels of autonomy and innovation in certain aspects of schooling. Bifulco and Ladd (2005) found higher levels of school autonomy with regard to school programs and policies in charter schools. In other words, school administrators report that key players within the school, such as teachers and principals, have more influence over decisions surrounding areas such as establishing performance standards, determining the curriculum, deciding on the content of professional development, and setting discipline policies than their peers at traditional public schools. Teachers in charter schools also report greater influence over academic standards and curriculum compared to their counterparts in traditional public schools (Christensen & Lake, 2007; Podgursky, 2008).

Using data collected from surveys completed by 2,108 charter school teachers and 2,872 traditional public school teachers, Berends and colleagues (2018) examined teacher reports of innovative instructional strategies (e.g., long-term student investigations, students setting the pace of instruction, tightly structured lessons, etc.) and innovative student evaluation (e.g., portfolios). They found that teachers in choice schools differed from traditional public school teachers in statistically meaningful ways, but that differences were five percentage points or less.

While innovative teaching practices have been detected in some studies, others suggest that charter schools are surprisingly similar to traditional public schools. Gross and Pochop (2008) found that charter schools adopt novel instructional models such as block scheduling and team teaching infrequently, but instead rely on reduced class size and extended learning time (due to longer school days and stretched school years). While these modifications are certainly noteworthy, it is unclear whether or not these changes have prompted teachers' roles and responsibilities to shift. Moreover, Preston et al. (2012) find that charter schools are somewhat more innovative in the areas of parental involvement and teacher tenure when compared to their traditional public school counterparts in the same context, but overall conclude that charter schools are not more innovative than traditional public schools.

The scant literature on teacher autonomy and innovation in charter schools largely relies on data collected through surveys of teachers and principals. This type of data allows for relatively straightforward comparisons of autonomy and innovation between traditional public and charter schools, but it does not allow for the in-depth exploration of how educational context and conditions inform innovation or the lack thereof. Despite the proliferation of charter schools and the multitude of studies that attempt to quantitatively measure the differences between traditional public schools and charter schools, there has been little research that gets inside the black box and seeks to better understand whether teachers' roles and responsibilities are constructed differently in charter schools.

Research Methods

Site Selection

This study is based on a purposeful sample of two case study schools selected from the 16 charter schools all located within the geographic boundaries of Indiana's most populous traditional public school district, Indianapolis Public Schools, during the 2008–09 school year. Many charter school advocates consider the Indiana charter law to be one of the "strongest" or most "friendly" to the creation of charter schools (Center for Education Reform, 2008). The "strong" designation stems from provisions in the charter law that provide for multiple authorizers, funding formulas on par with traditional public schools, and the presence of automatic waivers from state and district regulations and policies. The specific charter school law that applies to the schools in this study is unique in that it is the only law in the United States that has given a mayor the power to authorize charter schools (Smrekar, 2009). The first mayoral charter schools opened in the 2002–03 school year with approximately 500 students. By the 2006–07 school year a total of 16 charter schools had been approved, serving approximately 4,000 K–12th grade students (Read, 2008). Nearly all of the charter schools in this city were authorized by the mayor and overseen by the Mayor's Office. Thus, the variation in autonomy and innovation is most likely being prompted by school-level decisions rather than variation in end goals set by different authorizers or oversight metrics.

An effort was made to include contrasting schools in the study to capture variability in the roles teachers may play in the charter school context. The research team considered academic achievement records, student demographics, grade distribution, school size, type of charter school (independently operated or operated by a charter management organization), Adequate Yearly Progress (AYP) ratings, and responses to prior student and parent surveys that were conducted that measured levels of student engagement and parent involvement and satisfaction.

Case Study #1: King Academy.[2] King Academy, an independent college preparatory charter school founded in the mid-2000s, sits in a predominantly low-income neighborhood in Indianapolis. King Academy serves approximately 400 students,

95 percent of whom are African American, in grades 6–12. It continues to be led by the founder, an individual who is deeply committed to the school's mission of preparing traditionally underserved students to excel in a selective four-year college setting.

The building provides an immediate signal to passersby that this school is atypical. In fact, those unfamiliar with King Academy may not even realize that the building is a school because the structure was originally built to house a supermarket. The facility is boxy and windowless, and there is limited green space because the building is still surrounded by the expansive parking lot that served grocery store patrons. From the outside, the building is neat and tidy, but stark, sterile and intimidating. Upon stepping through the automatic sliding glass doors into the lobby, college acceptance letters for the senior class are prominently displayed in frames above wooden benches on one wall. The school crest and King Academy's motto, "Scientia Est Virtus" (Knowledge Is Strength), are emblazoned across another wall. The halls are strikingly quiet as students wearing sweater vests with the King Academy logo, khakis, and plaid kilts switch classes; students are not permitted to socialize during transitions, but are instead expected to be "quiet and purposeful" as they make their way to their next class (King Academy Teacher Handbook, 2008). The general tone is structured, serious, and studious.

All students are provided with an accelerated curriculum that pushes students to perform well above grade level. An attitude of high expectations is pervasive. Students are expected to maintain an 80 percent average in all coursework; those who do not do so attend mandatory two-hour tutorials four days each week and are prohibited from participating in any extracurricular activities, such as sports. Students who consistently perform below grade level are demoted to a lower grade level until academic performance improves.

King Academy one of the top charter schools in the city in terms of academic achievement rankings. In the year following data collection, this school earned a National Blue Ribbon Award. Staff proudly share that every member of the first graduating class (2008) was admitted to at least one four-year college. Despite these accolades, King Academy has been criticized for being overly rigid and strict in terms of disciplinary expectations and too lofty in their academic expectations of students. These unrealistic expectations may prompt students to transfer elsewhere, particularly in high school. While every member of the first graduating class was accepted to college, the entire class consisted of only 12 students.

Case Study #2: Davis Community Charter School. Davis Community Charter School is a small independent school located in a historic African American neighborhood with close ties to an enduring community non-profit organization. It is relatively small compared to most schools in Indianapolis, serving 235 students in kindergarten through sixth grade. Approximately 99 percent of the students are African American. During the 2008–09 school year, more than 80 percent of students qualified for free or reduced price lunch. Many of the students live in the neighborhood immediately surrounding the school, but a handful of students also come from more affluent areas such as the suburbs surrounding the city. One staff member explained that parents of students from outside the neighborhood feel that their children have positive African American role models at the school and that their "children can learn how to be both professional *and* Black" in this setting, which can be a challenge in suburban schools that have few minority students. The administration and faculty at Davis encourage students to be proud of their heritage; every school day starts not only with the Pledge of Allegiance, but the Black National Anthem as well.

Davis shares its cramped facility with a public library; preschool; daycare; a family service center, which provides assistance to secure employment, pay rent, obtain transportation and food, etc.; and a child support center that accepts cash payments for child support cases. Upon entering the building, visitors and parents are received by a receptionist who sits behind a glass window directing traffic. In order to get access to the school's main office, the receptionist must buzz parents in.

The research team was interested in exploring teacher autonomy and innovation at this Davis Community Charter School, particularly because this school met AYP from when they initially opened until 2007, but they did not meet AYP in 2008. Conversations with district officials and staff from the Mayor's Office indicated that this school is known for their focus on academics and student success as well as its strong ties to the surrounding community.

Data Sources and Procedures

Each week-long on-site visit during the 2008–09 school year included semi-structured interviews with administrators, faculty, staff, volunteers and a sample of parents. Because this paper centers on teacher autonomy and innovation, the focus is on teacher interviews. We were able to interview most classroom teachers at King Academy (21 out of 23 teachers) and all of the teachers at Davis Community Charter School (12 out of 12). Interview questions focused on such themes as teaching and learning, assessments, resources, decision-making and governance, and parent engagement. Appendix A contains additional information on the distribution of interviewees at each case study school, and Appendix B provides relevant excerpts of the teacher interview protocol.

Members of the research team also wrote field notes describing the interviews and observations. In between interviews, members of the team sat in on classes. In addition, the research team also collected documents for analysis, including school newsletters, lesson plans, curricular guides, salary schedules, teacher handbooks, and parent contracts. For this analysis, particular attention was paid to documentation that pertains to teachers and teaching.

Analytic Strategy

This study employs pattern coding to investigate patterns of thought, action, and behavior among teachers (Fetterman, 1989; Yin, 2009). Initial analysis focused on fully understanding each participant's responses. I did this by carefully rereading the interview transcripts from each school and thinking about them in relation to one another in an effort to see how they fit together as one case study.

I established a baseline *a priori* frame derived from the relevant sections of the interview guide and applied this during my first round of coding the data. I coded interview transcripts according to general descriptive categories derived from the theoretical framework and the literature review using the constant comparative method (Patton, 2001). This portion of the coding process was guided by the concepts unpacked from the theoretical framework linked to the research questions and interview protocols (e.g., teaching and learning philosophy, expectations of and demands on teachers, classroom autonomy, etc.).

As I coded, new categories and themes emerged, and they were added to the framework (Miles & Huberman, 1994). I used this strategy of coding and thematic analysis in which the data are coded into discrete categories (nodes) to reveal patterns among the interviewees. Repeated analyses of the interview transcripts allowed for more fine-grained coding to take place within each of the baseline nodes, and additional nodes emerged and were added to the analysis framework. Thus, this process was both iterative and theory-driven, and reflected inductive and deductive analysis (Strauss & Corbin, 1990).

Research Findings

Research Question #1: What roles and responsibilities do teachers have in charter schools? Do these roles reflect teacher autonomy and innovation?

At both schools, teachers were keenly focused on instruction and student learning. While teachers emphasized that instruction is driven largely by state standards, teachers expressed that they have quite a bit of autonomy in how and when they teach particular standards. Several teachers expressed that this was part of what drew them to teach in a charter school. A first-year teacher explained that he chose King because, "we can use our own teaching methods and stuff like that. There is a little more freedom at charter schools as far as the way you teach." Ms. Holliday, a second-grade teacher who had been teaching at King for six years said she has "a lot of freedom to get creative, to go outside of the curriculum and bring things in and bring people in." Teachers also appreciated the flexibility with lesson timing, and they stressed that their administrators do not fixate on sticking to a rigid instructional schedule, but instead they focus on whether or not important content is being taught so that students can understand it. One teacher at King, Ms. Briar, contrasted this with the experience of a friend of hers at a nearby traditional public school: "He was telling me that he got written up because he was running 30 minutes behind on his lesson and the principal did a pop-in inspection … I couldn't imagine that ever happening here."

Teachers at both sites also emphasize that being creative in how they teach is not just allowed, but that it is something that is valued at their schools. Ms. Jonah, a King teacher explained, "We're left … to be creative, and in fact, I think to a certain extent, [the administrators] actually encourage creativity … I'm pleased with that." Ms. Grover, at Davis, sees the ability to adapt in the classroom as a requirement to work at the school:

> You have to be flexible. To teach at this particular charter school, you have to be flexible because you have to be able to change as your students change. You can't just say, "I'm going to teach it this way, and that is the only way I'm going to teach it" because that is not how these children learn. That is not how any children learn. You have to be flexible.

While the content is largely determined by the state standards, teachers report having some degree of autonomy in both of these charter school settings.

While teachers at King and Davis indicated they had similar autonomy as instructors, teachers indicated differing levels of autonomy in some of their other roles: disciplinarian, documentation manager, and curriculum designer.

Disciplinarian. In most schools, teachers are encouraged to manage behavior issues within the classroom, and only students with severe behavioral infractions are sent out of the classroom. This is certainly true at Davis, where teachers deal with most issues surrounding student discipline by designing and implementing a classroom management plan. Ms. Holliday explained that her discipline plan is "up to me," while Ms. Briar indicated that she has "a lot of freedom" when it comes to student discipline. Consequently, teachers have different ways of managing student behavior. Many Davis teachers, particularly novice faculty, are left somewhat confused by this lack of a school-wide discipline policy. Ms. Hooper, a third-grade teacher, explained that she, "borrowed [my behavior management system] from my own kids' classrooms. I have three kids and I would walk into their classrooms and see what their teachers were doing. I didn't have anything else really to go on." Ms. Jonah, expressed that Davis "probably has [a discipline policy] written down, but it is not the one that we follow … so I just try to handle everything in my room." Part of being an educator at Davis includes designing and implementing a student discipline system.

Conversely, teachers at King Academy are largely exempt from the disciplinarian role. Whereas in most schools teachers discipline students in the classroom and only send students out of the classroom when more severe infractions occur, at King the slightest infraction resulted in a student being removed from the classroom and sent to the main office. Examples included coming to class without a pencil, having incomplete homework, or forgetting to wear a belt. King's principal, Mr. West, justified this policy saying, "we sweat the small stuff" in an effort to prevent more severe disciplinary infractions. The fact that teachers were expected to send students out of the classroom to have someone else deal with discipline even for minor issues set the tone that the classroom is for learning and the teachers' job is to teach. As sixth-grade teacher Ms. Jerry explained, she was interested in working at King because of

> how orderly everything was supposed to be ... and disciplined, and that just really attracted me because in my previous experience, those are some of the major issues that I've had. It was hard to teach because you have people throwing things across the room ... so having that type of orderly classroom drew me 'cause it makes it a whole lot easier.

Ms. Smith, a ninth-grade science teacher echoed this sentiment:

> that's one thing I noticed when I came here for my interview. The students are engaged ... you might have a little bit of talking while the teacher's talking, but not any major horseplay ... those kids are focused because the amount of rigor is so high they know if they do not pay attention that they're the ones that are going to be hurt in the long run.

Ms. Meyer, one of King's sixth-grade teachers, also had a sibling who is a student at the school. She wholeheartedly supported the discipline policy because she had seen how her sister benefited from it: "I feel like there isn't anything that's going to be allowed to distract her from the learning process here, and she's pushed to be her absolute best."

These quotes suggest that the strict disciplinary policies enacted at King Academy helped to set the tone of academic rigor and made it clear that teachers were expected to focus on teaching and push students to excel academically rather than getting bogged down by issues surrounding student discipline.

Documentation Manager

Although issues surrounding discipline were generally not the responsibility of educators at King, the teachers there had an immense amount of mandatory documentation responsibilities to manage. Teachers prepared and submitted various documents to the administration for review on a weekly basis. These documents included class syllabi, parent contact logs, and class reports with weekly grades. They also managed individual student portfolios. As King's music teacher, Mr. Harris, indicated:

> We have to keep all of our kids' work in folders, copies of all our kids' work. So, I have a file folder on every single one of my kids, in my room, with all of their work that they've completed this year. Anything they've written ... so having to keep all that filed, and I have 90 students this semester

At Davis, documentation was rarely collected and reviewed by the administration. Teachers explained that they are expected to write weekly lesson plans, but that they do not submit them for review. Ms. Jones, the principal, explained the logic behind this policy:

> One thing that I noticed when I was teaching, some people can write excellent lesson plans, beautiful lesson plans. But if you are not executing those lesson plans, they are nothing. So to me, I can look at a lesson plan to see what they are doing, but my biggest thing is the observation, seeing it. Being able to see it because people don't realize that you can walk into a classroom and sit there for 20 minutes and you can tell right off if the teacher is planning or if they are going on a whim.

Multiple teachers at Davis confirmed that the principal is in fact in each classroom between one and three times monthly conducting teacher observations and modeling lessons. Doing so allowed Ms. Williams to monitor instruction and academic progress without asking teachers to submit a multitude of paperwork.

Curriculum Designer

Autonomy is reflected in the contrasting ways that teachers at both schools approached designing the curriculum. At King, teachers indicated that they were responsible for designing their own pacing guide and writing large chunks of the curriculum based on state standards. For example, Ms. Meyer, one of the sixth-grade teachers, commented:

> Our sixth grade leader is phenomenal. She has belted out this curriculum all year. I mean, last summer she put [it] together for the entire year. Anytime there needs to be an adjustment made, she goes back to the computer, she fixes it, gets it back to us.

The eighth-grade science teacher explained that he determines what he teaches, how he teaches and when he teaches it, "because actually I wrote the curriculum for physics." Even the music teacher, Mr. Harris, spends time creating curriculum maps for his students, which differs significantly from his experience at a nearby traditional public school where he "was not required to turn in any lesson plan in the past four years."

Teachers at Davis do some curriculum design, but not nearly as much as their peers at King. This difference may be attributable to the fact that teachers at Davis possess textbooks for all of their subjects. Rather than taking a tremendous amount of time to design an actual curriculum, teachers at Davis tweaked the curriculum that is laid out in their textbooks or supplemented it. As one teacher explained:

> [Our math curriculum] meets every single standard for first-grade math. And then [our language arts curriculum], the only thing it is missing that we already know about has to do with writing, and we need to focus a bit more on poetry and those kinds of things because we also noticed that as our kids are getting older, they will have to read a poem and interpret what that poem means on the [state standardized test].

Additionally, teachers recognized that one math curriculum was not working for their students, so they worked with the administration to select a new curriculum and purchase new textbooks to better fit the needs of their students.

Research Question #2: How does school context inform teacher autonomy and innovation?

As charter schools, King Academy and Davis Community Charter School were both provided with some degree of autonomy. The administration at both schools indicated that their authorizer, the mayor, tended not to interfere with their operations. This autonomy is evident in the variation displayed in these two case study charter schools.

Two patterns emerge that relate to teacher autonomy and innovation at King and Davis. First, school leadership, particularly that of the principal, appears to shape the amount of autonomy teachers in these charter schools possess. Second, at times teachers enacted innovative practices unintentionally as a way of improvising when they lacked resources.

Teacher Autonomy and School Leadership

Literature on charter schools suggests that teachers will benefit from a reduced bureaucracy and will have the freedom to be innovative in their classrooms. In fact, teachers at both schools cited "less bureaucracy" and "more freedom" as reasons they were interested in teaching at a charter school. However, in practice, teacher autonomy was determined by the school principal. At King, Principal West required teachers to adhere to a set of uniform policies and procedures. For example, all teachers had to follow the same discipline policies and hand in the same in-depth documentation at the end of every week. All teachers were required to provide students with feedback on at least three assignments weekly.

Much of the autonomy that could have "trickled down" to teachers at King Academy was instead absorbed by the principal. Mr. West was relentlessly focused on the mission of his school, which resulted in a highly structured environment not only for students but teachers as well. He explained:

> It's non-negotiable [the school mission]. We're not going to create a second diploma track. We're not going to have a self-sustaining middle program that's separate that allows us to say, "Well, some of you are going to early college, and some of you need to find a different high school to go to." We're going to have that outcome for every kid. It helps us to really draw a line in the sand about what we're doing, how serious we are about it.

This intense focus on mission translated to a highly standardized, rigid working environment for teachers, which does in fact reflect innovation, but not at the teacher-level.

The situation at Davis was quite different. Teachers possess the freedom to make decisions in a variety of areas, such as instruction, student discipline, and how (or whether or not) they provide extended support to students. One of the reasons that teachers have this autonomy is because the administration permits it. As Ms. Gordon explained:

> [Principal Jones] came in and did a hands-on demonstration, not just came in and told me what to do, she came and sat down and worked with my students so I could see how you run a guided reading group. She has been very helpful in getting some one-on-one time with small group time with my students, so that they are getting instruction from her ... She is hands-on when needed [but she is] not a micromanager at all.

Teachers seemed to greatly appreciate Ms. Jones' willingness to help when they express a need but leave them to make many of the decisions about instructional methods in the classroom, the order in which they cover academic standards, and whether or not they team-teach with their grade-level counterpart.

Voluntary Innovation or Involuntary Improvisation

The second theme that emerged from case study data suggests that teachers may implement what they define to be innovative practices for two distinct reasons, one voluntary and the other involuntary. The first is *voluntary innovation*: new ideas and practices that organically emerge when teachers have the freedom and resources necessary to be creative in their practice. The second is *involuntary improvisation*: new ideas and practices that only occur because teachers are forced to overcome a barrier or resource constraint.

At King Academy, teachers lacked textbooks in many subject areas because the administration had chosen not to allocate resources to purchase them all at once but instead purchase different subject area textbooks for different grade levels over time. Without textbooks for certain subject areas, teachers found themselves driving curriculum design at their school, which may seem innovative, but it was simply having to improvise in a less than favorable situation. The teachers at King were not voluntary curriculum designers; they were begrudgingly forced to assume this role or otherwise they would not have a means of teaching state standards. As sixth-grade teacher Ms. Jerry explained:

> I have gone and researched and pulled together materials, so when we studied Rome, we made copies of things from maybe four or five different sources, and pulled those together and then created guided reading notes from those, whereas if we had a textbook with a teacher's manual, and all that other stuff … that's all there for you.

The reason that they did not possess textbooks for a number of subject areas is not because of a school philosophy suggesting that creating their own curriculum is more advantageous; rather, it was simply because resources were not set aside to purchase textbooks. Ms. Jerry explained that "certain years, certain grades get books for things, so like seventh grade has science textbooks, but sixth grade doesn't. So sixth grade and seventh grade have grammar books that we've had for two or three years, sixth grade has math books, seventh grade needs math books." While on the surface it appears that teachers generating the curriculum is a valued innovation, it is really a time-consuming improvisation until textbooks can be purchased for all subject areas and grades.

This can be contrasted with the voluntary curricular innovation that occurred at Davis. Teachers at Davis explained that they had adequate baseline curricular resources, including textbooks for all subject areas. They used textbooks as a guide for their standards-based instruction but explained that they had the freedom to innovate by altering the lessons to fit the needs of their students, adjust their pacing based on weekly assessments, and supplement the text with additional resources and materials.

Teachers at Davis also had additional resources at their disposal that provided them with the freedom to be more innovative in the classroom. In particular, the administration provided teachers with the time to plan. This time allowed teachers to conduct home visits, and plan and execute events such as a "Harvest Festival" and field days to reinforce standards being taught in the classroom. In an effort to raise awareness about childhood obesity, Ms. March, the gym teacher at Davis, planned a curriculum culminating in a neighborhood walkathon for students, faculty, and parents on one Saturday. Because teachers were afforded time to plan and given autonomy by the administration, they were free to generate innovative ideas and carry them out.

One Davis teacher, Ms. Holliday, believed that this freedom may have developed over time:

> I think teachers being able to voice what they need over the years a lot more, being able to kind of mold the school, put your little touches in as

to where you think [the school] should go. Everybody's going in the same direction, towards the same goal, but I think over the years, teachers now are able to really put more opinions into it, and that's nice.

In essence, because Davis was one of the oldest charter schools in this area, and because the school existed as a private institution beforehand, the school had the opportunity to develop capacity in a number of its teachers, which in this case seems to provide teachers with more autonomy.

Discussion

The case studies of King Academy and Davis Community Charter School provide an interesting snapshot of charter schools in one setting. What is immediately apparent is how different the two schools were, which suggests that the authorizer, the city mayor, allowed schools the autonomy to implement their own models. However, these two case studies also illustrate that much of the autonomy provided to the leaders of these schools did not necessarily reach the teachers who work within them, raising important questions about the potential for charter schools to redefine the roles and responsibilities of teachers. At King Academy, the principal's unwavering focus on the school's college preparatory mission resulted in highly structured policies surrounding teaching, instruction, and discipline, which appeared to restrict teachers' autonomy, thereby reducing the chances of teacher-driven innovation.

Moreover, teachers in case study schools made an important distinction between voluntary innovation, which occurs when new practices emerge in response to autonomy, and involuntary improvisation, which happens when teachers must act as street-level bureaucrats to devise solutions in response to resource constraints or challenging circumstances. When teachers are forced to improvise, it may result in practices that may be viewed as innovative (e.g., teacher-designed curriculum) but that teachers see as inferior to traditional, well-established practices.

It is important to note that the qualitative case study design used in this study allowed for the distinctions between voluntary innovation and involuntary improvisation to emerge from the data. Had we administered a survey, we may very well have labeled teacher-generated curriculum at King as innovative because the traditional public schools in the surrounding local school district were not employing that practice (Preston et al., 2012). Instead, our in-depth interviews with many educators allowed us to take a more nuanced look at teachers' practices and distinguish between when teachers innovated in response to autonomy or improvised in response to resource constraints. The next generation of research on school choice must employ methods that allow researchers to see inside the black box of charter schools and answer questions about the potential for charter schools to reshape education, particularly for underserved students and in under-resourced environments. Qualitative and mixed methods designs will be critical in this next phase of research.

This chapter explores the extent to which the claims about charter schools' autonomy and innovation are reflected in the work teachers do. The promise of charter schools hinges on whether they can utilize the autonomy they are granted to alter the core technology of schools, teaching, and learning. Thus, whether the autonomy charter schools possess filters down to teachers providing the conditions that allow for innovation in classrooms is critical.

Appendix A

Table 1 Interviews Conducted at Case Study Schools

		Case Study Schools	
	Interviewee	*King Academy Charter School*	*Davis Community Charter School*
Interviews	Teachers	5 sixth grade	2 kindergarten
		3 seventh grade	2 first grade
		4 eighth grade	2 second grade
		4 ninth/tenth grade	2 third grade
		2 eleventh/twelfth grade	2 fourth grade
		1 music	1 fifth grade
		1 special services	1 sixth grade
		1 Title I	
	Administrators	1 principal	1 director of education
		1 assistant principal	1 assistant director of
		1 academic dean	education
		1 dean of the early college	1 director of finance
		1 associate dean of the early college	
		1 director of development	
		1 counselor	
	Support Staff	None interviewed	1 administrative assistant
			1 nurse
			1 police officer
			1 kindergarten teacher aide
			1 receptionist
	Volunteers	None interviewed	1 tutor
	TOTAL	**28 interviews**	**21 interviews**

Appendix B

Relevant Excerpts of Teacher Interview Protocol

Professional Background, Choosing this School

1. Where (what school) did you start your teaching career? What year was that?
2. How long have you been teaching at this school?
3. What did you know about charter schools *in general* when you came here?

4. What did you know about this school *in particular*?
5. Why did you want to teach here, at this particular school?

Teaching and Learning Environment

1. When I walk through the school, will I observe anything different or unique? In other words, will I know this is a charter school? How?
2. How would you describe the teaching (and learning) philosophy here? What did the charter school founders have in mind originally? (later, ask about changes)
3. How similar or different is this school from a traditional public school in terms of curriculum and instruction (and the organization of teaching and learning)?
4. Can you describe the expectations and demands on teachers at this school? Probe for the source of these demands (principal, board, parents, charter authorizer).
5. Do these expectations differ from a traditional public school or private school? Examples?
6. How are curricular goals and specific instructional content determined? In other words who decides what you teach and when you teach it?
7. How would you describe any degrees of "freedom" or "autonomy" to do what you want to do when it comes to *what* you actually teach, and *how* you teach?
8. What about issues surrounding student discipline? Who determines those? How much discretion do you have?
9. To what degree, if any, does the charter school model shape your curriculum and your instruction? Can you give me some examples?
10. How do your students' academic abilities influence your pacing and other instructional strategies/issues? Can you provide me with some examples?

Assessment

1. How do you assess student learning here? Then what happens with this information (links between data and instructional strategies)?
2. Are these assessment systems adequate? In other words, how would you assess your assessment systems?
3. How do assessments shape your instruction?

Resources

1. To what degree are you and your colleagues able to share resources or collaborate at all? When? Are there arrangements (half days, longer days, subs) to support these collaborations?
2. As a teacher at this charter school, do you have additional financial or material resources at your disposal?

3. Does your school partner with any universities, libraries, museums, or corporations? Do you gain any additional resources from these partnerships?
4. How would you describe the academic supports for students here (tutoring, mentoring, instructional assistants, reading/math coaches, parent volunteers)?
5. Describe the types of professional development that you have participated in while you've been teaching at this school.
6. How were these professional development activities connected, if at all, to the curricular and/or instructional goals of your school?

Decision-Making/Governance

1. How would you describe the way in which decisions are made at this school?
2. Do teachers have formal leadership roles? Informal?
3. What types of decisions are teachers involved in?
4. What role does the teachers' union play at the school? What are some key priority issues for the union?
5. Are you satisfied (or surprised) with the role teachers play in governance and decision-making?

Concluding Teacher Questions

1. How has this school changed since you first began teaching here (e.g. students, faculty, academic rigor and focus, level of resources and supports)?
2. What are your biggest challenges as a teacher at this school?
3. What has been the biggest surprise teaching here?

Notes

1 This chapter is supported by the National Center on School Choice, which is funded by a grant from IES (R305A040043). All opinions expressed in this paper represent those of the author and not necessarily the institutions with which they are affiliated or the U.S. Department of Education. All errors in this paper are solely the responsibility of the authors. For more information, please visit the Center website at www.vanderbilt. edu/schoolchoice/. In addition, funding for Madeline Mavrogordato was provided by a grant from the US Department of Education's Institute of Education Sciences (IES) to Vanderbilt's ExpERT program for doctoral training (R305B080025). This work was supported in part by funds from the Education Policy Center at Michigan State University. I am grateful to my colleagues at the National Center on School Choice, in particular, Mark Berends, Marisa Cannata, Ellen B. Goldring, Claire Smrekar, Xiu Cravens and Jason Huff for their collaboration and support. I also wish to recognize and thank the anonymous participants in our study for taking the time to be interviewed.
2 All school and person names included in this manuscript are pseudonyms.

References

Berends, M. & Zottola, G. (2009). Social perspectives on school choice. In *Handbook of research on school choice*, edited by M. Berends, M. G. Springer, D. Ballou & H. J. Walberg. Mahwah, NJ: Lawrence Erlbaum Associates/Taylor and Francis Group.

Berends, M. (2015). Sociology and school choice: What we know after two decades of charter schools. *Annual Review of Sociology, 41*, 159–80.

Berends, M., Goldring, E., Stein, M. & Cravens, X. (2010). Instructional conditions in charter schools and students' mathematics achievement gains. *American Journal of Education, 116*, 303–35.

Berends, M., Peñaloza, R.V., Cannata, M.A. & Goldring, E. B. (2018). Innovation & charter schools. In *School choice at the crossroads: Research perspectives*, edited by Berends, M., Waddington, R. J., & Schoenig, J. (pp. 96–106) New York: Routledge.

Bidwell, C. & Dreeben, R. (2006). Public and private education: Conceptualizing the distinction. In *School sector and student outcomes*, edited by M. T. Hallinan (pp. 9–37). Notre Dame, IN: University of Notre Dame Press.

Bidwell, C. & Kasarda, J. (1980). Conceptualizing and measuring the effects of school and schooling. *American Journal of Education, 88*, 401–30.

Bifulco, R. & Ladd, H. (2005). Results from the Tar Heel State: Older students did better when in regular public schools. *Education Next, 5*(4), 7.

Carnoy, M., Jacobsen, R., Mishel, L. & Rothstein, R. (2005). *The charter school dustup: Examining the evidence on enrollment and achievement.* New York: Teachers College Press.

Center for Education Reform. (2008). *Charter school laws across the states: Rankings and scorecard 2008.* Washington, DC: Center for Education Reform.

Christensen, J. & Lake, R. J. (2007). The national charter school landscape in 2007, in *Hopes, fears and reality: A balanced look at American charter schools in 2007*, edited by Lake, R. J. Seattle, WA: Center on Reinventing Public Education.

Chubb, J. E. & Moe, T. M. (1990). *Politics, markets and America's schools.* Washington, DC: The Brookings Institution.

Clotfelter, C. T., Ladd, H. F. & Vigdor, J. L. (2007). Teacher credentials and student achievement: Longitudinal analysis with student fixed effects. *Economics of Education Review, 26*(6), 673–82.

Elmore, R. (2007). *School reform from the inside out: Policy, practice, and performance.* Boston, MA: Harvard Education Press.

Fetterman, D. (1989). *Ethnography.* Thousand Oaks, CA: Sage.

Finn, C. & Gau, R. (1998). New ways of education. *The Public Interest, 130*, 79–92.

Finn, C., Manno, B., & Vanourek, G. (2000). *Charter schools in action: Renewing public education.* Princeton, HJ: Princeton University Press.

Friedman, M. (1962). *Capitalism and freedom.* Chicago, IL: University of Chicago Press.

Gamoran, A., Nystrand, M., Berends, M. & LePore, P. (1995). An organizational analysis of the effects of ability grouping. *American Educational Research Journal, 24*, 687–715.

Gawlik, M. (2007). Beyond the charter schoolhouse door: Teacher-perceived autonomy. *Education and Urban Society, 39*(4), 524.

Gleason, P. M. (2018). What's the secret ingredient? Search for policies and practices that make charter schools successful. In *School choice at the crossroads: Research perspectives*, edited by Berends, M., Waddington, R. J. & Schoenig, J. (pp. 187–205). New York: Routledge

Goldhaber, D. (2007). Everyone's doing it, but what does teacher testing tell us about teacher effectiveness? *Journal of Human Resources, 42*(4), 765–94.

Gross, B. & Pochop, K. M. (2008) How charter schools organize for instruction. In *Hopes, fears, & reality: A balanced look at charter schools in 2008*, edited by R. Lake. National Charter School Research Project. Seattle, WA: Center on Reinventing Public Education.

Harris, D. N. (2011). *Value-added measures in education: What every educator needs to know.* Cambridge, MA: Harvard Education Press.

Hausman, C. & Goldring, E. (2001). Sustaining teacher commitment: The role of professional communities. *Peabody journal of education, 76*(2), 30–51.

Lipsky, M. (1980). *Street-level bureaucracy: Dilemmas of the individual in public services.* New York, NY: Russell Sage.

Loveless, T. & Field, K. (2009). Perspectives on charter schools. In *Handbook of research on school choice*, edited by M. Berends, M. G. Springer, D., Ballou & H. J. Walberg. Mahwah, NJ: Lawrence Erlbaum Associates/Taylor and Francis Group.

Lubienski, C. (2003). Innovation in education markets: Theory and evidence on the impact of competition and choice in charter schools. *American Educational Research Journal, 40*(2), 395.

McDonnell, L. M. (1991). Ideas and values in implementation analysis: The case of teacher policy. In *Policy implementation*, edited by A. R. Odden (pp. 241–58). Albany, NY: The State University of New York Press.

Malloy, C. & Wohlstetter, P. (2003). Working conditions in charter schools: What's the appeal for teachers? *Education and Urban Society, 35*(2), 219.

Marsh, D. D. & Odden, A. R. (1991). Implementation of the California mathematics and science curriculum and frameworks. In *Policy implementation*, edited by A. R. Odden (pp. 219–40). Albany, NY: The State University of New York Press.

Meyer, J. W. & Rowan, B. (1992). The structure of educational organizations. In *Organizational environments: Ritual and rationality*, edited by J. W. Meyer & W. R. Scott. Beverly Hills, CA: Sage Publications.

Miles, M. B. & Huberman, A. M. (1994). *Qualitative data analysis.* Thousand Oaks, CA: Sage.

Newmann, F., King, B, & Youngs, P. (2000). Professional development that addresses school capacity: Lessons from urban elementary schools. *American Journal of Education, 108*(4), 259–99.

Patton, M. (2001). *Qualitative research and evaluation methods.* Thousand Oaks, CA: SAGE.

Podgursky, M. (2008). Teams versus bureaucracies: Personnel policy, wage-setting, and teacher quality in traditional public, charter, and private schools. In *Charter School Outcomes*, edited by M. Berends, M. G. Springer, & H. J. Walberg (pp. 61–79). New York: Lawrence Erlbaum Associates.

Preston, C., Goldring, E., Berends, M. & Cannata, M. (2012). School innovation in district context: Comparing traditional public schools and charter schools. *Economics of Education Review, 31*(2), 318–30.

Read, T. (2008). Early investment jump-starts change: Lessons from the Annie E. Casey Foundation's strategic support of Indianapolis Mayor Bart Peterson's charter initiative. Retrieved from http://www.innovations.harvard.edu/cache/documents/859/85901.pdf.

Rivkin, S. G., Hanushek, E. A. & Kain, J. F. (2005). Teachers, schools, and academic achievement. *Econometrica, 73*(2), 417–58.

Scott, W. & Davis, G. (2007). *Organizations and organizing: Rational, natural and open system perspectives.* Englewood Cliffs: Prentice Hall.

Smrekar, C. (October 2009). Taking charge of choice: How charter school policy contexts matter. Presented at the National Center on School Choice Second National Invitational Conference. School Choice and School Improvement: Research in State, District, and Community Contexts. Nashville, TN.

Strauss, A. & Corbin, J. (1990). Basics of qualitative research: Techniques and procedures for developing grounded theory. Thousand Oaks, CA: Sage.

Werts, A. B. & Brewer, C. A. (2015). Reframing the study of policy implementation: Lived experience as politics. *Educational Policy, 29*, 206–29.

Yin, R. K. (2009). *Case study research: Design and methods* (Vol. 5). Thousand Oaks, CA: Sage.

8

TAKING CHARGE OF CHOICE

The Case and Implications of Mayoral
Charter Control

Claire Smrekar and Madeline Mavrogordato

In 2001, Indiana became the 38th state to pass a charter school law, ending a seven-year debate that had rumbled through the hearing rooms and hallways of the Indiana General Assembly. Just five years later, charter schools numbered 36 in the state, with a total enrollment of 10,000 students, including almost 4,000 in Indianapolis alone (Office of the Mayor, 2007). The rapid growth of Indiana's charter schools and the debate that preceded passage of the law are commonplace features in the political landscape of school choice in the U.S. The distinguishing feature in Indiana—the one-of-a-kind element when this charter school law was enacted[1]—relates to the set of eligible chartering authorities. The law stipulated only three in the state: local school boards, public state universities, and *the mayor of Indianapolis*. From the passage of the law in 2001, until his unexpected defeat following a second term in 2008, Mayor Bart Peterson of Indianapolis—a Democrat—authorized 16 charter schools and closed one financially troubled one. The two-term Republican mayor who followed Peterson, Greg Ballard, more than doubled the number of mayor-authorized Indianapolis charter schools to 39 by 2016, while closing several that were failing.[2] Today, Indianapolis mayor-sponsored charter schools number 35, enroll over 14,000 students (one-third of the district's public school population) and continue to be authorized and overseen through the Mayor's Office of Educational Innovation (OEI).[3]

This chapter explores how charter school politics are nested within a larger framework of interest group politics and idiosyncratic social and political contexts (Kirst, 2007). The focus centers on examining the political and educational values of public and non-public organizations, state officials, and local actors. How did these stable (and shifting) coalitions form? How did these groups coalesce to produce the nation's first mayoral chartering authority? What are the implications of this "mayoral charge" for choice policy, innovation diffusion, and civic capacity in Indianapolis? Against the backdrop of the vast variability of charter school laws and charter school performance (Gill et al., 2001; Lake & Hill, 2006), the Indianapolis context provides a distinctive yet informative political and cultural canvas to explore charter school policy formulation.

Conceptual Framework: Public Policymaking Process

Mayoral Control, Influence, and Impact

This chapter examines the origins and implications of this unique mayoral function in charter school authorization and accountability against the backdrop of urban school politics in which mayors play increasingly pivotal and powerful roles (Henig & Rich, 2004; Kirst, 2003; Viteritti, 2009a; Wong et al., 2007).

Recent research focuses on the formal structures that expand mayoral authority over city schools, including mayoral selection of school board members (versus ward or city-wide election), the appointment of a school's chief/chancellor/CEO, and the shift from managerial to advisory board functions (Viteritti, 2008). A myriad of questions are raised (and answered) regarding the consequences of mayoral control in a comprehensive empirical analysis of mayor-managed (or "integrated governance") urban school districts and traditionally managed (elected school board) counterparts (Wong et al., 2007). The authors focus upon outputs related to governance (evaluated in terms of financial operations), productivity (assessed in terms of student performance), human capital (appraised in terms of teacher and administrator characteristics), and public confidence (measured by public opinion and awareness). Wong et al. (2007) suggest that expanded mayoral influence and control over public schools contributes to "streamlined governance, an alignment of political incentives, a politics of partnership, and a reallocation of resources to their most efficient use" (p. 95). While the research purposes and scope of data analyses in the work conducted by Wong and colleagues (2007) offer a far more expansive examination than is undertaken here, some pertinent parallels add perspective to this project. This study of Indianapolis mayoral charter school authority responds to the need for case-study level analysis of mayoral control (see Alsbury, 2009), with specific focus upon mayoral authority in charter school policy and the associated claims of increased program transparency and accountability. This project also adds analytical insights to arguments made regarding growth in institution-building and strategic partnerships associated with mayoral control (see Wong et al., 2007). The second part of the chapter explores the implications of the Mayor's Office of Charter Schools on the city's capacity to move forward with public education reforms, undergirded by new alliances, expanded trans-institutional trust, and external interest and investment (Author, 2009).

In sum, unlike the mayoral "take-over" analyses of urban education reforms in Philadelphia (Bulkley, 2007), Chicago (Shipps, 2006; Shipps, 2009), Baltimore (Orr, 1999), New York (Hemphill, 2009; Viteritti, 2009b), Boston (Portz &

Schwartz, 2009) and other cities, this chapter focuses on the "advocacy coalitions" (Sabatier & Jenkins-Smith, 1999) and policy streams (Kingdon, 1995) that made Indianapolis the first—and only—city with *independent* mayoral control over charter school authorization and accountability. The unique contribution here is the intersection of charter school politics with mayoral control of urban schools. As the Obama Administration and the Secretary of Education urge mayors to take greater responsibility for improving school performance (Quaid, 2009), this chapter makes a timely contribution to the debate regarding the appropriate role and scope of authority of these city leaders in public education.

Policy Streams

This study is nested in a policy research tradition that focuses upon policy formulation and change (Lindblom, 1968). Specifically, the interest rests with the political contexts, problems, and preconditions that facilitate charter school policy *formulation*, rather than the structural reforms, school-level innovations and student *outcomes* associated with charter school policy (see Fuller, 2000; Lubienski, 2004).

The Indiana charter school law was passed following seven years of sustained effort and investment by an array of public and non-public stakeholders, or what Sabatier and Jenkins-Smith (1999) refer to as an "advocacy coalition." How (and why) did the policy landscape change to secure passage of the IN charter school law? This project applies Kingdon's (1995) three-part model of the public policymaking process to unpack the pivot points ("windows of opportunity") that converged to produce this landmark charter school law. The model includes three integral parts or process "streams"—the problem stream, policy stream, and political stream (Kingdon, 1995) (for alternative theory see Scott et al., chapter 12).

Problem stream

This stage underscores the conditions that anchor subsequent (and simultaneous) concerted action and policy development. Informal and formal communication processes play a critical role, creating the policy networks that establish the channels of information and influence. As Mintrom (2000) notes, members of the policy networks, including elected officials, interest group representatives, national advocacy groups, philanthropists, foundation officers, university researchers, and business leaders, cross public and non-public roles. During this phase, a central problem emerges as the focus of attention (problem identification), constituting legislative or governmental action. A "policy entrepreneur" who translates the problem to a policy solution sets the agenda.

Policy stream

Policy solutions emerge through a process of debate, discussion, and reformulation. The policy entrepreneur navigates the political changes and organizational innovation necessary for action during this phase when coalitions are built around collective action. In Indiana, Senator Teresa Lubbers, the long-time chair of the Senate Education Committee, played this central role with skill and influence.

Political stream

The political process is dynamic, involving changes in executive and legislative control by different political parties, new elections that bring new mayors with different political philosophies to office, triggering new agenda setting. The change in the Office of Mayor following the election in 1999 produced monumental change and momentum—all in the direction of the "middle ground" sought by the coalition built by Senator Lubbers and other members of the charter school policy network. In Mayor Bart Peterson, Indianapolis citizens transformed the political tilt and trajectory of education and urban reform.

Civic Capacity

In one of the most thorough set of analyses and detailed applications of urban politics, Stone et al. (2001) identify the conditions that give rise to education reform. The authors refer to "greater civic capacity" (p. 12) as the foundation for comprehensive public policies that result in material change and improved outcomes. Civic capacity enables "a community to come together to address its problems" (p. 12) over a sustained period of time. Civic capacity involves linking integral structures and processes across disparate entities—formal (public, governmental, institutional) and informal (private, inter-personal) relationships among key stakeholders, common understandings and trust, and an interest in engaging in collective action for a set of shared, mediated goals (Stone et al., 2001). This scaffolding supports the framework for moving forward with decisive and collective action toward solving public problems—in education, housing, community redevelopment, and other social policies. Civic capacity, then, constitutes a *pre*-requisite for policy reform and change.

In this study, findings indicate that civic capacity expanded in *response* to the convergence of the policy streams (Kingdon, 1995) related to the formulation of charter school policy and passage of the IN charter school law. The analyses suggest that civic capacity coalesced measurably following charter school policy implementation and the establishment of the Mayor's Office of Charter Schools. Mayor Peterson's efforts to elevate public accountability and program transparency established Indianapolis as a strategic template for national urban education reform initiatives. The capacity to change the direction of education policy in Indianapolis was constituted by a public demonstration of collective action, inter-institutional trust, and investment from partners (e.g., national foundations) external to the formal governance structures in the city.

Methods

This qualitative case study of Indiana charter school policy development involved purposeful sampling (Glaser & Strauss, 1967). Interviews were conducted with key "advocacy coalition" (Sabatier & Jenkins-Smith, 1999) members across public and non-public entities, including: two former Indianapolis mayors, state legislators and members of the governor's legislative staff, members of the former and current mayors' staff, urban school superintendents (reps from the Indiana Urban Schools Association), urban school board members, teacher union representatives, business groups and business leaders (including the CEO of Eli Lilly), foundation officers (Annie E. Casey Foundation), philanthropists, university leaders and education researchers (Ball State University and the University of Indianapolis), parent group representatives, national charter school advocacy group representatives, local charter school technical assistance group representatives, editorial writers for the *Indianapolis Star*, local civil rights leaders (e.g., Indianapolis NAACP), community activists, and leaders of faith-based groups in the three largest urban districts in the state. The interviewees were selected purposively based on professional roles (e.g., legislative committee chair) and reported participation (via news reports and official IN state government reports) in the charter school law adoption process in Indiana. Some interviewees were selected based on interviews with key informants, using "snowball" sampling. A total of 34 interviews were conducted with key stakeholders during the time period of February 2008 to March 2008.

We utilized a semi-structured interview protocol, asking participants to address questions linked to our conceptual framework on policy adoption and formulation (see Kingdon, 1995). Questions were clustered under categories related to policy networks, policy innovation and diffusion, politics of charter schools, charter school authorization and mayoral control and urban education. See appendix for interview protocol. All interviews were audiotaped, with participants' permission, and transcribed verbatim. Each interview lasted one hour on average, although interview length varied.

Documents were analyzed for descriptive evidence of the nature of governing coalitions and their members' educational/political values related to charter school policy; these documents include: transcripts from legislative hearings on charter schools from 1994–2001, press releases from the offices of state legislative leaders and the mayor of Indianapolis, transcripts of campaign speeches from the mayor (1999–2001), editorials and articles published in local media, including the *Indianapolis Star*, and press releases from the state teachers' union and urban superintendents' association.

Pattern coding was used to discern patterns of thought, action, and behavior among interview subjects (Fetterman, 1989; Yin, 1989). Accordingly, interview transcripts and documents were coded and summarized according to general descriptive categories derived from the conceptual framework, using the constant comparative method (Patton, 2001). This process was both iterative and theory-driven and reflected inductive and deductive analysis (Strauss & Corbin, 1990). Our coding process was guided by the key themes in the data and the concepts unpacked from the theoretical frameworks linked to our project questions and interview protocols (e.g., charter school law adoption, charter school politics, and mayoral control of schools). The final coding template involved procedures that were guided and open, with codes that are categorical and thematic. Following the coding, converging pieces of information from interview transcripts, field notes, and document analyses were arranged according to broad themes and categories. In sum, we used methodological procedures designed to produce a reliable and valid qualitative report, including an examination of countervailing evidence, constant comparative method, and iterative coding (Patton, 2001).

Results

Politics of Charter School Policy: Case of Indianapolis

"Window of Opportunity"

Charter school policies mark a convergence of national, state, and local political contexts that are complex, characterized by clusters of coalitions and active policy network members (Bulkley, 2005; Kirst, 2007). This case study of the adoption and impact of Indiana's charter school law provides an instructive illustration of the public policymaking process against the canvas of these connected political contexts. Following Kingdon's model (1995), policy changes emerge when three streams—problem, policy, and political—come together to create a "window of opportunity." Changes in local and state leadership, a fiscal crisis, a massive program failure, or creeping incrementalism may help trigger an opportunity. The tipping point—whether or not an opportunity translates to policy change—requires political leadership or a policy entrepreneur. The policy entrepreneur manages the policy network by anchoring the new agenda to a well-defined set of problems and solutions. As Kingdon (1995) explains:

> But their defining characteristic, much as in the case of a business entrepreneur, is their willingness to invest their resources—time, energy, reputation, and sometimes money—in the hope of a future return.
>
> *(p. 122)*

In sum, the problem definition stage sets the agenda for a particular set of policy responses. In Indianapolis, the city's education and economic "problems" were easily identifiable, though the "solutions" remained highly contested across political contexts and policy communities. What were the problems? How did "political streams" galvanize policy networks toward the charter school "solution?"

Paddling Upstream

According to an analysis of state education and economic development reports, and a set of interviews with elected state and local (Indianapolis) officials, business leaders, interest groups, philanthropists, foundation officers, and state agency officials, Indiana's problems were associated with two inter-related sectors: education and economic development. Indianapolis, the state's largest city with a population of more than six million (U.S. Census Bureau, 2000), amplified some of the state's most critical economic conditions—declining economic activity and vitality marked by a steady outflow of corporate interests from the city to the suburban communities, coupled with plant closings and a steady decline in manufacturing (Indianapolis Private Industry Council, 2004). These economic issues were matched by a set of negative education indicators: one of the lowest high school graduation rates in the nation (31 percent) in the Indianapolis Public Schools (IPS) (Swanson, 2008), and a large and persistent achievement gap between White and African American students in the district (Indiana Department of Education, 2009). These conditions were fueling a precipitous population decline in the city (and school district) of Indianapolis that began in the late 1980s.

Officials interviewed for this project noted a cultural tilt and tradition in public education and other government services that tended to exacerbate these documented problems. These issues included excessive rules and regulations and an absence of public accountability and responsiveness. How did these problems open the window of opportunity and set the agenda for charter school policy after more than seven years of failed efforts to pass a charter school bill?

The Streams Converge: Problems, Policies and Politics

By 2001, the battle to win charter school approval in Indiana had been fought for seven years by Senator Teresa Lubbers, a former public school educator, and the reining influential Republican chair of the Senate Education Committee. Lubbers, widely regarded as the "mother of the movement" toward expanded school choice in Indiana, had worked over the years to cultivate a policy network of other elected Republican members of the Senate and House, the Indiana and Indianapolis Chambers of Commerce, and local foundations (Friedman Foundation) and think tanks (Hudson Institute) with a long history and well-established toe-hold in public education, school choice (notably, including tax credits and vouchers), and conservative Republican political circles. She held legislative hearings on the problems of low high school graduation rates, large and persistent achievement gaps, and the lack of public confidence in the Indianapolis public schools. She defined the problems and outlined the solutions, in committee hearings, public speeches, and meetings with members of the growing school choice policy network in Indianapolis. Lubbers embraced policy values with broad appeal as she set the agenda:

> The idea of freedom with accountability was to me like as American as you could get. We are going to treat teachers as professionals. We are going to cut you free of a lot of these rules and regulations that may not be tied to

student learning and in exchange, we are going to hold you accountable for what you do. So I think the whole idea of innovation, the idea of serving different populations ...

In the late 1990s, Senator Lubbers joined forces with well-organized, energized forces within the Indianapolis Chamber of Commerce and national organizations and leading advocates in the expanding charter school movement, including Jeanne Allen and the Center for Education Reform (CER), and the National Association of Charter School Authorizers (NACSA). A local philanthropist (who later founded one of the first mayor-authorized Indianapolis charter schools), and other prominent business officials with links to the IN governor's office, played lead roles. The policy network was fully formed when Senator Earline Rogers, a Democrat from the economically hard-hit and educationally low-performing northern Indiana city of Gary, joined Lubbers in supporting the charter school effort. Rogers, a former school teacher and member of the American Federation of Teachers union, was instrumental in moving some reticent Democratic legislators from stiff opposition to all expanded forms of school choice, to what emerged as "middle ground" on the school choice policy agenda—charter schools. Rogers joined Lubbers and examined other strong state charter school laws as a model for the IN law. In large part, she viewed charter schools as the solution to problems in the current public education system:

> I absolutely believed in the concept of having incubators of learning where people could experiment—that was something that I thought was attractive. When I was teaching, there were some barriers there and I would have liked to have gone outside some of those barriers, but couldn't because of the bureaucracy. I basically wanted to make certain that we could get a law that everybody could agree to and give that opportunity for experimentation to teachers or to other groups who felt that there were some needs that a particular community had.

Kingdon (1995) suggests that policy entrepreneurs move policies forward by seizing upon the "windows of opportunity" presented by the convergence of problem, policy, and political streams. How did the entrepreneur—Lubbers—provide the pivot point for school choice policy formulation and more specifically, charter school adoption? By 1999, Lubbers was building the momentum that would link a set of public problems to a set of policy solutions found in the charter school movement. As Mintrom (2000) explains:

> Among the activities that policy entrepreneurs engage in, the most important include identifying problems, networking in policy circles, shaping the terms of policy debates, and building coalitions to support policy change.
>
> *(p. 57)*

During data collection for this project, numerous elected officials and interest group leaders described a culture of insularity and incremental policymaking in Indiana. Many officials noted that these traditions made education change challenging, and created some disconnections to the policy networks formed around the agenda of school reform and charter school adoption. As Senator Lubbers observed:

> People will say that Missouri is the "Show-Me" state, but I think our state has a bit of that, especially when it comes to education. People are a little reticent to embrace a new idea as the newest and greatest until they really have some reason to think it is a good, new idea.

Lubbers needed to divert other (political) streams to a particular choice policy. She concluded that charter schools were the solution to the problems that state—and the state capital (Indianapolis)—were working to solve. Charter schools would emerge in the late 1990s as the middle ground to the decades-old debate in the state capitol on school vouchers as a policy solution—a position advocated by the Republican mayor of Indianapolis, some Republican legislators, influential Indiana business leaders, and scholars at the Indianapolis-based Friedman Foundation and the Hudson Institute. In 1999, the election of the first Democratic mayor in Indianapolis in 32 years provided a new advocacy coalition—this one tilted toward charter schools as *the* policy solution to the problem of poor-performing public schools.

Peterson's immediate predecessor, Stephen Goldsmith, the Republican mayor of Indianapolis from 1991–99, advocated private out-sourcing and public-private competition to ensure greater innovation, accountability, and efficiency in city government. Sharp ideological differences and entrenched political battles with teacher unions, school superintendents in the city of Indianapolis, and Democrats in the city and state legislatures characterized his tenure as mayor. Goldsmith supported the idea of charter schools but argued that the teacher unions, particularly in Indianapolis, would prevent passage of a strong law, something he favored. As Goldsmith framed the dilemma:

> It would be such a weak law it could take all of the oomph out of the choice movement, without accomplishing anything for the kids. I just didn't feel like even if I could get a strong law, we'd get enough charters to reach a tipping point.

Goldsmith pursued a policy of structural change through competitive pressures. He sought to fracture and then eliminate what he perceived as costly, bureaucratic monopolies throughout city government, and replace government-provided programs with privatized services. He sought market-based reforms in education as well, including publicly financed vouchers for private schools and tuition tax credits to defray the cost of parochial school tuition in the city. Goldsmith cultivated strong policy networks with the conservative Friedman Foundation and the Hudson Institute to bolster his beliefs in the efficiency and productivity of private providers. Goldsmith argued that charter schools could create "competitive pressures" on traditional public schools if enough "strong" charter schools could be approved. He summed up his position on charter schools in a recent interview for this project:

> What I was trying to do was change the system. I viewed the charters, innovative charters as important in and of themselves, but more important as a way to exert structural impact on the rest of the system ... that is why I used competition in the city government because it changed all of the government, not just the stuff that was outsourced, all the rest of it.

During the 1999 campaign for Indianapolis mayor and throughout the first nine months of his administration, Bart Peterson sought a middle ground between two polarizing positions staked out by various political constituencies: privatization, vouchers, and market-based reforms sought by Mayor Goldsmith (and the Hudson Institute, members of the business community), and the outright rejection of any public school choice policies (including charter schools), advocated by most of the Democratic caucus in the Indiana state legislature. In an interview for this project, Peterson noted this political climate raised particular challenges—and imperatives—for a vastly different direction in education policy:

> The city government, the media, the business community – all had been working for close to a decade to change the schools. I felt that the environment was very antagonistic. I felt that if we couldn't find something that, not necessarily initially, but eventually might lead to consensus, that we would never have permanent change.

In the interview for this project, Peterson identified a related *problem* in need of policy *solutions* to those articulated by the charter school policy network led by Senator Lubbers. As noted earlier, these problems involved low student performance, measured by the low high school graduation rates in Indianapolis Public Schools. The issues were linked to a lack of accountability and innovation in the education system. These policy network members focused upon the "logical" (Miron & Nelson, 2002) and widely promoted changes triggered by charter school reforms, including teacher autonomy and improved student achievement. Peterson's view of the city's problems transcended classrooms and high school corridors. He shared his more expansive perspective of mayoral involvement in education problems and policies:

> The reasons why a lot of mayors look to get involved in education is not just because they see how important it is for the lives of children and their future, but how many other issues and problems in our major urban

community are connected with bad education. Excuse me, there is also population decline associated with the perception and reality of poor schools. So if you believe that a city has to retain its population in order to be strong, in order to do all the things you want to do, you have to figure out a way to keep people in the city, and the people are going to vote with their feet.

While successive Republican and Democratic Indiana governors supported the concept of charter schools, none were as vocal or specific about support for charter schools as Indianapolis Mayor Peterson. Peterson vowed to work with state legislative leaders to get a strong charter school law passed during the 2001 legislative session. He coupled his strong support for charter schools with a specific endorsement for an expanded mayoral role in public education as a charter school authorizer. His position was punctuated by a major speech outlining his education policy priorities in his State of the City Address, on February 22, 2001:

A mayor is uniquely positioned to tap into the community resources necessary to make charter schools thrive. A sponsor must evaluate charter school proposals and hold the schools accountable for their performance ... a mayor is accountable to the public for all decisions and the decisions I might make as a charter school sponsor would be no exception.

The Mayoral Charge in School Choice Policy

This expanded and exclusive role for Mayor Peterson—a Democratic—had been developed with Senator Lubbers and other members of the policy network over the previous months, and inserted in a bill that failed in late 2000. Peterson laid the groundwork for his key role as authorizer early—first during the campaign in 1999 as a vocal proponent of a *strong* charter school bill, and later in his major public speeches. But more importantly, Lubbers and other members of the policy network—including the Indianapolis Chamber of Commerce, the Hudson Institute, and philanthropist Chrystal DeHaan (who was funding a separate foundation to provide technical expertise on charter school legislation)—viewed IPS as the major obstacle to charter school *implementation*. "Strong" charter school laws rated by Center for Education Reform (CER) include a wide range and type of authorizers (e.g., universities) in addition to local school boards. CER and the National Association of Charter School Authorizers (NACSA) underscored this point with the charter school policy community led by Lubbers. The traditionally strong ties between local Democratic leaders, elected school board members in IPS, and teacher unions were a central matter of interest and concern as the charter school bill evolved. In an effort to avoid appearing radical, policy network members noted that naming a mayor as an authorizer was not new in 2001: The Wisconsin legislature granted the Milwaukee mayor specific authorizing authority in 1998, though the authority is more restricted—subordinate to a separate, independent Milwaukee board that forwards recommendations to the mayor. The Indiana law flipped this formal authority arrangement, making the mayor of Indianapolis the first mayor with *independent charter school* authorizing power in the U.S. In an interview for this project, Peterson underscored the rationale and significance of this unique approach:

> I think this is where Senator Lubbers was visionary and correct—that you are less likely to get the kind of charter community that you are looking for if you only leave it to school districts to do the chartering. So who the authorizers are is key and then of course she is the one that came up with the innovation of getting the mayor of Indianapolis a charter, which was not something that I had even thought of before.

The match between policy problems (low graduation rates, lack of accountability, population decline in the city) and solutions (innovation and accountability via charter schools) culminated in a final negotiation with the teachers union in Indiana. In exchange for restored collective bargaining rights for Indianapolis district teachers (suspended by legislation urged by Mayor Goldsmith and passed with Republican majorities in both chambers in 1995), and other provisions designed to provide a "level playing field" for charter schools and traditional public schools, House Democrats joined the Republican-led coalition in the Indiana Senate and passed the Indiana charter school law in 2001.

Mayor's Office of Charter Schools: The One Best System?

Granted legislative authority to authorize charter schools in IPS and the surrounding 10 school districts in the city limits of Indianapolis, Mayor Bart Peterson and his chief aide, David Harris, set out to "create the best system." Central to Peterson's efforts was the argument he had embraced along the way to charter school law adoption: the quality of charter schools was ultimately tied to the quality, rigor, and integrity of the authorization process. The new Mayor's Office charter school review process set out to establish a set of central organizing principles: scrutiny, technical assistance, ongoing evaluation, and transparency. The new Mayor's Office on Charter Schools collected information from leading scholars, consulted with charter school authorizing experts across the U.S., and examined "best practices" across an array of urban school districts. Simultaneously, the mayor and his team cultivated an inter-institutional infrastructure of political and financial support. Under the new law, the mayor's recommendations for charters had to be approved by one other governmental entity—the 29 members of the City Council in Indianapolis, a majority Democratic body. By Executive Order, Peterson created the seven-member Mayor's Charter Schools Advisory Board and named prominent local educators, business leaders, and university scholars to serve. The board was charged with formal review responsibilities and for making recommendations to the mayor on all charter school applications. The Mayor's Charter Schools Advisory Board added credibility, expertise, and transparency to the process. Additionally, these steps stitched together the elements for gaining public support across the political spectrum—both advocates and skeptics of school choice. Notably, all 16 of the mayor's recommendations for charter school passed with what became a routine 29–0 vote of council support.

System of Support (Inputs)

With generous financial support from the Annie E. Casey Foundation, the mayor first established a process to promote the development of strong charter school models and applications. Interested individuals and organizations had immediate access to an array of technical assistance and material resources. These support structures were particularly critical for local, independent (non-affiliated) charter school operators who lacked a broader network from which to seek assistance and expertise. The support mechanisms focused upon administrative and instructional inputs for successful charter school management, such as adequate staffing and budgeting, concrete curricular materials and programs, aligned assessment systems, strong board oversight, and sustained leadership capacity.

Monitoring Mechanisms (Outputs)

The mayor's charter program included an extensive accountability and reporting procedure for all approved charter schools that emphasized early diagnosis of program weaknesses, and provided guidance for corrective action. These efforts led to the development of the Charter School Performance Framework, designed to foster ongoing school improvement and high student achievement. The Charter School Accountability Handbook gave charter school operators detailed guidance and direction and was a centerpiece of the mayor's promise of accountability. The Mayor's Office established an annual progress report that included specific academic, demographic, fiscal, and parent and staff evaluation data on every charter school. A grant from the Lilly Endowment supported a research and evaluation component, including "expert site visits" by independent evaluation experts at the University of Indianapolis.

Engine for Innovation and Expanded Civic Capacity

The charter school initiative, coupled with the mayoral team's growing reputation for high performance and accountability, attracted new interest from the Gates Foundation in 2003, culminating in a large grant to foster a small schools initiative in Indianapolis. In 2006, the Mayor's Office on Charter Schools was recognized by Harvard University's Kennedy School of Government for innovation in government. The charter school authorizing program was singled out for its "rigor, transparency, and results" (Harvard University, 2006). By 2008, the Mayor's Office on Charter Schools had become an incubator for new civic capacity in the city, culminating in the creation of Mind Trust, a non-profit organization headed by the mayor's former charter school team. Notable education initiatives were soon attracted to the potential assets and documented expertise represented at Mind Trust, which quickly established a Venture Fund to "recruit top education reform programs to Indianapolis" (The Mind Trust, 2011a). Today, Mind Trust partners include Teach for America, College Summit, and The New Teachers Project. The Venture Fund has invested more than $5 million in these and other new initiatives pegged to the organization's goals to "incubate and invest" (The Mind Trust, 2011b).

Our findings suggest that the mayor's charter school program created the scaffolding for expanded civic capacity in Indianapolis. These elements include new trans-institutional partnerships (e.g., Gates Foundation, University of Indianapolis, Teach for America), new mobilization of community interests focused on public education, and an expanded expertise and human capital within the city government and non-profit organizations. These developments represent the *potential* for achieving some of the promises of charter school reform through a new and novel approach to charter school authorization—one that identifies the office of the mayor as the *specialist* in fostering and managing school choice.

Discussion

Competition and New Conceptualizations

Part of the promise of charter school proponents in Indiana and elsewhere rests with the premise that innovation diffusion, increased student achievement (from competitive pressures), and heightened accountability will flow across both charter systems and traditional public schools. To counter competitive pressures and in an effort to differentiate itself from the charter school program, the IPS has embraced a strategy that highlights IPS magnet schools as explicitly *different*—in design and curricular focus—from the rest. Most notably evident in the district's annual report, press releases, and public presentations, district leaders have repeatedly referred to magnet schools as the "jewels in the IPS crown," including but not limited to a new Law & Public Policy magnet, and an expanded collaboration with the KIPP charter organization. The superintendent's webpage notes that IPS offers "the broadest range of innovative option programs in Indiana." Still, the district acknowledges the persistent challenges it faces—measured by declining enrollment, low graduation rates, and overall poor academic performance (IPS State of the District Annual Report, 2009).

As the number of charter schools expands (24 schools by 2012), the Indiana charter school law remains an important case study that illuminates the potential role mayors can play in charter school promotion and management. More specifically, this case extends the framework for charter school authorizing from support and monitoring to an incubation and trans-institutional model.

Reconceptualizing the Mayoral Role in Education Reform

As urban school districts struggle to meet federal standards specified in the *No Child Left Behind* (NCLB) *Act*, some mayors have responded to these external pressures by playing a more active role in local public education reform. As Crowson and Goldring (2009) note, this "new localism" reflects an emerging paradox that situates federal mandates on one axis and local decision-making on the other, creating a unique pivot point for political leaders. In some cities, mayors have taken complete control of local schools—a controversial and politically risky move that typically involves the mayoral appointment of a new school "czar" with complete governing and decision-making authority in the district. The Indianapolis case provides an alternative platform for mayors—one that is arguably more tenable and manageable than assuming responsibility for an underperforming school system.

Mayor Peterson moved to a platform a half-step outside the traditional public school system. His Office of Charter Schools developed a formula for school reform that laid the structural and political groundwork for new schools. The mayor's monitoring mechanisms emphasized transparency, rigor, and capacity-building. The mayor authorized only a few schools each year—evaluated as among the very best—and built support systems and oversight capacity incrementally. Through this process, Peterson transformed the mayoral role in education from one of a relatively removed "policy generalist" (Wong & Sunderman, 2007) to an involved, informed and invested policy *specialist*. In this role of policy specialist, Peterson was equipped to drive educational innovation and expand civic capacity.

Reframing the Role of Authorizers

Charter school authorizers play a critical "intermediary" role, translating state policy into charter school realities (Bulkley, 1999, p. 695), yet research attention has largely centered on the schools themselves and their operators (Finn & Hill, 2006). Scholars have emphasized the importance of identifying core authorizing practices that promote student achievement (Finn & Hill, 2006; Gau, 2006) and performance accountability (Bulkley, 2001; Vergari, 2000). These authorization models specify itemized support and monitoring checklists, which underscore concrete, easily observable characteristics. This implies that establishing a successful school merely requires a list of ingredients (inputs) and an evaluation of the end product (outputs). The support items identify tasks such as using data, hiring skilled personnel and providing adequate resources. The monitoring mechanisms center on reporting student performance, reviewing admissions and attendance information, and examining fiscal health (Figure 8.1). The case of Indianapolis illustrates that the roles and responsibilities of charter authorizers may be more complex and layered than the existing literature suggests, extending beyond charter schools and spilling over to the broader policy environment. Rather than subscribing to a checklist authorization process, the Mayor's Office of Charter

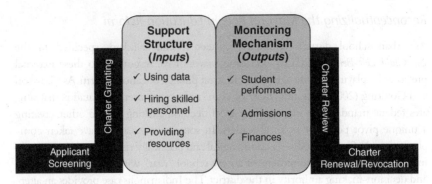

FIGURE 8.1 Traditional Role of Charter School Authorizers.

Schools implemented a capacity-building *system*. The promotional, developmental, and instructional support structures reflect a greater degree of involvement in the details of policymaking and practice. Similarly, the monitoring mechanisms adopted in Indianapolis shifted into a higher gear, stressing analytical, diagnostic, directive, and corrective actions (Figure 8.2).

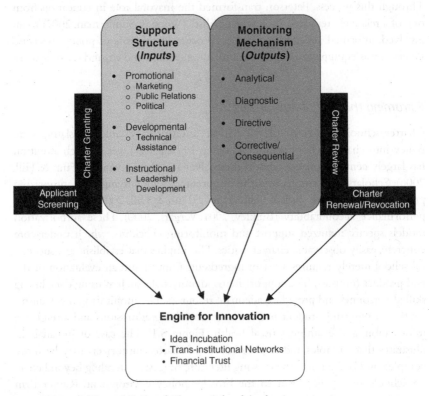

FIGURE 8.2 Reframed Role of Charter School Authorizers.

The case of the Indianapolis mayor indicates that authorizers can embrace a multifaceted role in which the traditional functions that authorizers fulfill are amplified and extended. In addition to the support and monitoring roles, the mayor created an engine for innovation that drove a policy shift in the city and strengthened civic capacity. The Mayor's Office of Charter Schools has acted as an incubator for educational transformation that has rippled across the broader policy context in Indianapolis. This trans-institutional innovation has attracted public attention and private support from well-established, highly regarded funding agencies. The case of Indianapolis prompts policymakers to think more deeply about innovation and charter schools, where innovation extends beyond the classroom, hallway and school building and has the *potential* to affect civic capacity system- and city-wide.

Notes

1 In 2011, the Indiana General Assembly created a new, independent, statewide authorizer, the Indiana Charter School Board (ICSB), as a way of increasing the number of charter schools throughout the state. The General Assembly also added non-profit colleges and universities that offer four-year degree programs to the approved authorizer list. The ICSB tends to authorize national charter *networks* that are designed to establish multiple charter *schools* throughout the state; in contrast, the Mayor's Office of Education Innovation tends to award charters to independent, locally founded and operated charter schools.

2 On the whole, Indianapolis charter schools (the vast majority of which are mayor-authorized) outperform the traditional public schools operated by the Indianapolis Public Schools (IPS) district, though these charter schools serve a slightly poorer population: 81 percent of students enrolled in these charter schools qualify for free or subsidized meals compared to 71 percent in IPS schools. According to the 2015 report, *Urban Charter School Study on 41 Regions,* published by the Center for Research on Educational Outcomes (CREDO) at Stanford University, Indianapolis is among six urban regions whose traditional public schools (TPS) and charter schools combined produce "large region-wide achievement deficits relative to their state's average achievement in math and reading, but within the region have high quality charter sectors compared to their region's local TPS."

3 The Indiana Charter School Board—an independent statewide body—has authorized and currently oversees seven charter schools in Indianapolis and 15 others statewide, for a total of 22. According to the Center for Education Reform, 93 charter schools were operating (including online schools) across the state of Indiana in 2017, with more than a third of that total operating in Indianapolis.

References

Alsbury, T. (2009, June 25). Mayoral takeover cools the crucible of democracy. *Teachers College Record, Invited Commentary.* Retrieved from http://www.tcrecord.org/content. asp?contentid=15697.

Bulkley, K. (1999). Charter school authorizers: A new governance mechanism? *Educational Policy, 13*(5), 674.

Bulkley, K. (2001). Educational performance and charter school authorizers: The accountability bind. *Education Policy Analysis Archives, 9*(37).

Bulkley, K. (2005). Understanding the charter school concept in legislation. *International Journal of Qualitative Studies in Education, 18*, 527–54.

Bulkley, K. E. (2007) Bringing the private into the public: Changing the rules of the game and new regime politics in Philadelphia public education. *Educational Policy, 21*(1), 155–84.

Crowson, R. L. & Goldring, E. (2009). The new localism: Re-examining issues of neighborhood and community in public education. *Yearbook of the National Society for the Study of Education, 108*(1), 1–24.

Fetterman, D. (1989). *Ethnography.* Thousand Oaks, CA: Sage.

Finn, C. E. & Hill, P. (2006). Authorizing: The missing link. In *Charter schools against the odds*, edited by P.T. Hill (pp. 103–26). Stanford, CA: Hoover Press.

Fuller, B. (2000). The public square, big or small? Charter schools in political context. In *Inside charter schools: The paradox of radical decentralization*, edited by B. Fuller (pp. 12–65). Cambridge, MA: Harvard University Press.

Gau, R. (2006). *Trends in charter school authorizing.* Washington, DC: Thomas B. Fordham Foundation & Institute.

Gill, B., Timpane, P., Ross, K., & Brewer, D. (2001). Rhetoric versus reality: What we know and what we need to know about vouchers and charter schools. Santa Monica, CA: RAND.

Glaser, B. G. & Strauss, A. L. (1967). *The discovery of grounded theory: Strategies for qualitative research.* Piscataway, NJ: Aldine Transaction.

Harvard University (2006). Mayor's charter schools initiative: 2006 winner City of Indianapolis, Indiana. Retrieved from http://www.innovations.harvard.edu/awards. html?id=48911.

Hemphill, C. (2009). Parent power and mayoral control: Parent and community involvement in New York City schools. In *When mayors take charge: School governance in the city*, edited by J. P.Viteritti (pp. 187–205). Washington, DC: Brookings Institution Press.

Henig, J. & Rich, W. (2004). *Mayors in the middle: Politics, race, and mayoral control of urban schools.* Princeton, NJ: Princeton University Press.

Indiana Department of Education. (2009). Indianapolis Public Schools overview. Retrieved from http://compass.doe.in.gov/compass/Dashboard.aspx?view=CORP&val=5385& desc=Indianapolis+Public+Schools.

Indianapolis Private Industry Council. (2004). State of the workforce. Indianapolis, IN: Indianapolis Private Industry Council.

Kingdon, J. (1995). *Agendas, alternatives, and public policies.* New York: Addison Wesley.

Kirst, M. (2003). Mayoral influence, new regimes, and public school governance. *Yearbook of the National Society for the Study of Education, 102*(1), 192–218.

Kirst, M. (2007). Politics of charter schools: Competing national advocacy coalitions meet local politics. *Peabody Journal of Education, 82*(2 & 3).

Lake, R. & Hill, P. (2006). *Hopes, fears, & reality: A balanced look at American charter schools in 2006.* Seattle, WA: University of Washington-National Charter School Research Project.

Lindblom, C. E. (1968). *The policy-making process.* Englewood Cliffs, NJ: Prentice Hall.

Lubienski, C. (2004). Charter school innovation in theory and practice. In *Taking account of charter schools: What's happened and what's next?* edited by K. Bulkley & P.Wohlstetter (pp. 72–92). New York: Teachers College Press.

Mintrom, M. (2000). *Policy entrepreneurs and school choice.* Washington, DC: Georgetown Press.

Miron, G. & Nelson, C. (2002). *What's public about charter schools? Lessons learned about choice and accountability.* Thousand Oaks, CA: Corwin Press.

Office of the Mayor (2007). *2007 accountability report on mayor-sponsored charter schools.* Indianapolis, IN: City of Indianapolis.

Orr, M. (1999). *Black social capital: The politics of school reform in Baltimore, 1986-1998.* Lawrence, KS: University of Kansas Press.

Patton, M. (2001). *Qualitative research and evaluation methods.* Thousand Oaks, CA: Sage.

Portz, J. & Schwartz, R. (2009). Governing the Boston public schools: Lessons in mayoral control. In *When mayors take charge: School governance in the city,* edited by J. P. Viteritti (pp. 91–116). Washington, DC: Brookings Institution Press.

Quaid, L. (2009, March 31). Education Secretary: Mayors need control of urban schools. Associated Press.

Sabatier, P. & Jenkins-Smith, H. (1999). The advocacy coalition framework: An assessment. In *Theories of the policy process,* edited by P. Sebatier (pp. 117–66). Boulder, CO: Westview Press.

Shipps, D. (2006). *School reform, Chicago style: Chicago: 1880–2000.* Lawrence, KS: University of Kansas Press.

Shipps, D. (2009). Updating tradition: The institutional underpinnings of modern mayoral control in Chicago's public schools. In *When mayors take charge: School governance in the city,* edited by J. P. Viteritti (pp. 117–47). Washington, DC: Brookings Institution Press.

Strauss, A. L. & Corbin, J. (1990). *Basics of qualitative research: Grounded theory procedures and techniques* (Vol. 1). Thousand Oaks, CA: Sage.

Stone, C., Henig, J., Jones, B., & Pierannunzi, C. (2001). *Building civic capacity: The new politics of urban school reform.* Lawrence, KS: University Press of Kansas.

Swanson, C. (2008). *Cities in crisis: A special analytic report on high school graduation.* Bethesda, MD: EPE Research Center.

The Mind Trust (2011a). About the venture fund. Retrieved from http://themindtrust. org/fund/aboutFund.aspx.

The Mind Trust (2011b). Mission and vision. Retrieved from http://www.themindtrust. org/about/mission.aspx.

U.S. Census Bureau (2000). State and county quick facts: Indiana. Retrieved from http:// quickfacts.census.gov/qfd/states/18000.html.

Vergari, S. (2000). The regulatory styles of statewide charter school authorizers: Arizona, Massachusetts, and Michigan. *Educational Administration Quarterly, 36*(5), 730.

Viteritti, J. P. (2008, March 11). The education mayor: Improving America's schools [Review of the book *The education mayor: Improving America's schools*]. Teachers College Record. Retrieved from http://www.tcrecord.org/content.asp?contentid=15094.

Viteritti, J. P. (2009a). *When mayors take charge: School governance in the city.* Washington, DC: Brookings Institution Press.

Viteritti, J. P. (2009b). New York: Past, present, future. In *When mayors take charge: School governance in the city,* edited by J. P. Viteritti (pp. 206–34). Washington, DC: Brookings Institution Press.

Wong, K. & Sunderman, G. (2007). Education accountability as a presidential priority: No Child Left Behind and the Bush presidency. *Publius: The Journal of Federalism, 37*(3), 333.

Wong, K., Shen, F. X., Anagnostopoulos, D., & Rutledge, S. (2007). *The education mayor: Improving America's schools.* Washington, DC: Georgetown University Press.

Yin, R. (1989). *Case study research.* Thousand Oaks, CA: Sage.

9

SCALING UP AND SUSTAINING CHARTER SCHOOL EFFECTS

Mark Berends and R. Joseph Waddington

With studies showing increasing inequality and the lack of social mobility in the United States, scholars, policymakers, and the general public are concerned about the short- and long-term effects of inequality on society and social cohesion (Duncan & Murnane, 2011; Picketty, 2014; Stiglitz, 2013).[1] Although support of families, living wages, health care, housing, tax reform and other key aspects of social life are targets for policymakers to improve opportunities for individuals, researchers and policymakers have renewed attention to how schools promote educational opportunity through their effects on student achievement, engagement, promotion, and attainment.

In part, this renewed interest in schools and educational opportunity has focused on school choice reforms. Many of these school choice initiatives have been in place for decades, and the landscape of school options has changed significantly, which has implications for how we analyze school effects (Berends, 2015, 2018). Today, although a vast majority of students continue to attend their neighborhood public schools, we have a greater variety of school choice options, including magnet schools, charters, and private schools. Roughly, 10 percent of the nation's youth attends some form of private schooling (e.g., Catholic, religious private, and non-religious private) and this proportion has been quite consistent over several decades (Kena et al., 2014). In the public sector, there has been a shift with the growth of charter public schools (Berends, 2018). Based on the data from the U.S. Department of Education (2016), 80 percent of students in the United States attend traditional public schools, 5.1 percent attend charter public schools, 4.7 percent attend magnet schools, 3.7 percent attend Catholic schools, 4.1 percent attend other religious private schools, and 2.5 percent attend nonsectarian private schools.

The increasing variety of school choice options available in the U.S. is striking (for an overview see Austin & Berends, 2018; Berends et al., 2009; Berends, 2018). Of course, there are bitter controversies surrounding school choice (see Henig, 2009; Berends et al., 2011), and proponents and opponents can point to the mixed findings (some positive, some negative, some no effects) to promote their positions, so additional research can help policy and research move forward by untangling some of these effects by looking at the impacts of various school types simultaneously. In this chapter, we focus on how various types of schools have an impact on student achievement and engagement outcomes with a particular focus on the charter school sector.

In Indiana, because students in traditional public, charter, magnet, and private schools all take the same state tests and report other annual data to the Indiana Department of Education, we are able to examine how the achievement and engagement effects vary across students and school types using longitudinally linked student records. Building on our previous research in Indianapolis (Berends & Waddington, 2018), we unpack the differences in longitudinal impacts on student achievement gains from baseline (math and English/language arts (ELA)) and engagement (attendance and discipline) for students transferring to charter, magnet, Catholic, and other private schools relative to their experiences in traditional public schools. We focus specifically on the following questions:

- What is the impact on student achievement, attendance, and discipline when students switch from a traditional public school to a charter, magnet, or private school in Indianapolis?
- How do the charter school impacts differ based on the charter school authorizer (Mayor's schools or other authorizer)?
- How do the charter school impacts differ for disadvantaged students (i.e., by race/ethnicity or socioeconomic status)?

In what follows, we highlight the growing phenomenon of cities using a variety of choice options. We then go on to describe the setting, motivation for this current work, the data and methods, and the results before we discuss the implications of our research.

Portfolio Management Models

In the past few years, there has been an emerging model of how to organize large urban school districts—relying on *portfolio management models*. That is, it is increasingly common that school districts' central offices oversee a portfolio of school options that offer diverse school missions and instructional designs, including traditional public schools, magnet schools, independent and franchised charter public schools, and private schools (see Bulkley et al., 2010; Hill et al., 2009, 2013).

As described by Bulkley et al. (2010), there are several core elements of a portfolio management model. First, a portfolio strategy involves the creation of new schools with increased autonomy, often through the expansion of charter schools, to help families find schools that suit their children's educational needs and interests without being constrained by neighborhood zoned schools. Second, portfolio management models have increased the accountability for schools based on clear and rigorous guidelines for student and school performance, primarily based on test score levels and gains. Third, and related, there is a system in place to close schools and end service provider partnerships when schools do not meet the accountability standards. Fourth, the entire strategy, according to Bulkley et al. (2010), is a district central office one to further school quality and improve student outcomes by having an array of options available to families.

Such portfolio management has become increasingly popular in urban areas such as Chicago, New Orleans, and Washington, DC, to name but a few places. One way in which the central offices in these locations can manage the portfolio of choice is that these locations often have mayoral control of the school system—providing the opportunity for greater coherence among the various educational programs and types of schools from which parents may choose.

Portfolio of Choice in Indianapolis

However, in some urban locales, the portfolio of choice is not coherent, but rather quite messy due to multiple actors having influence and to the politics of educational reform (Hill, 2010). For instance, some cities and urban locales may have a variety of parent choice options, but no mayoral control or control by a central office. This chapter examines the portfolio of choice available in the Indianapolis urban area, where the central school district office has not intentionally employed a portfolio management model. Yet, a portfolio model of choice exists in Indianapolis nonetheless, more *de facto* than *de jure*.

The Indianapolis urban area is almost exclusively contained within Marion County, Indiana. Approximately 56,584 students in grades 3–8 were enrolled in 146 traditional public schools in the urban area during the 2015–16 school year.[2] While the overall enrollment in traditional public schools in the Indianapolis urban area had increased over the decade prior due to population growth, the share of students in grades 3–8 enrolling in traditional public schools has fallen from 80.2 percent in the 2005–06 school year to 73.7 percent in the 2015–16 school year. The public schools in the Indianapolis urban area are organized into 11 independent districts, the largest of which is Indianapolis Public Schools. In our previous work (see Berends & Waddington, 2018), we extensively described the landscape of school choice in the Indianapolis urban area. As nearly one-in-four Indianapolis urban area students are enrolled in choice schools, we briefly review the types of schools and choice programs that are the focus of our analyses in this paper and display these findings in Table 9.1.

TABLE 9.1 Descriptive Statistics for All Indianapolis Students by School Type: 2015–16

	Public	Charter	Magnet	Catholic	Other Private
Students	56,584	8,628	3,586	5,645	2,823
Schools	146	34	15	27	31
Female	0.481	0.502	0.527	0.502	0.510
Black	0.343	0.437	0.521	0.084	0.173
Latino/a	0.199	0.124	0.237	0.154	0.083
Other Race/Ethnicity	0.093	0.063	0.059	0.069	0.089
Free/Red.-Price Lunch	0.706	0.700	0.677	0.282	0.369
Eng. Lang. Learner	0.222	0.101	0.220	0.136	0.126
Special Education	0.151	0.166	0.150	0.096	0.075
Math Score	−0.273	−0.497	−0.528	0.199	0.118
	[1.003]	[0.995]	[1.019]	[0.923]	[0.922]
ELA Score	−0.291	−0.392	−0.391	0.292	0.149
	[1.002]	[0.966]	[0.951]	[0.914]	[0.913]

Table displays all students within the Indianapolis urban area (Marion County) as of the 2015–16 school year. Proportions reported for demographic characteristics; means and standard deviations [in brackets] reported for test scores. Source: Authors calculations from Indiana Department of Education student-level administrative data.

In terms of public school choice, there is a growing set of charter schools throughout the Indianapolis urban area. As of 2015–16, there were 34 charter schools enrolling 8,628 students in grades 3–8 (11.2 percent). Most of these charter schools (23 of 34) were authorized through the Indianapolis Mayor's Office, the only mayor's office in the nation that has such a capacity. The Mayor's Office established the Office of Education Innovation to manage the charter schools and oversee their mission of providing high-quality schools to Indianapolis families. This Office of Education Innovation has been in existence across several mayoral administrations, starting with Bart Peterson in 2000 (Democrat), and continuing with Greg Ballard (2008–16, Republican) and Joseph Hogsett (2016–present, Democrat).

In addition to charter schools within the public school choice sphere, there are several magnet school options available to families. In 2015–16, 3,586 grade 3–8 students (4.6 percent) enrolled in 15 magnet schools. All but one of the magnet schools in Indianapolis are operated as thematic schools by Indianapolis Public Schools.

In the private sector, enrollments have increased since 2011 because of the state of Indiana implementing the Indiana Choice Scholarship Program (ICSP) (see Berends et al., 2018; Waddington & Berends, 2018). This program provides a voucher or "scholarship" to qualifying low- and modest-income families to help offset tuition at a private school of their choice. Over 3,700 students in grades 3–8 received and used a voucher to attend a private school in the Indianapolis urban area during the 2015–16 school year.

Within the private school sector, there are 27 Catholic schools overseen by the Archdiocese of Indianapolis that enrolled 5,645 students in grades 3–8 in

2015–16 (7.3 percent). All elementary and middle-grade Catholic schools participated in statewide testing and reporting. Another 2,823 grade 3–8 students (3.6
percent) were enrolled in 31 other religiously affiliated and non-religious private
schools that also participate in statewide testing and data collection.[3]

Looking across school types, public schools—whether traditional public, charter or magnet—enroll higher proportions of students from disadvantaged backgrounds, whether by race/ethnicity, socioeconomic status, or special education
status. English Language Learners (ELL) are over-represented in traditional public
and magnet schools. In terms of aggregate math and ELA achievement, traditional public school students in Indianapolis scored an average of roughly one-
fourth of a standard deviation below the statewide average. Meanwhile, students
in charter and magnet schools on average performed worse, with mean scores
one-half of a standard deviation below the statewide average in math and four-
tenths below in ELA. In the private sector, Catholic and other private school
students outperformed the statewide average, scoring an average of one- to two-
tenths of a standard deviation higher in math and 0.15 to 0.30 standard deviations
higher in ELA.

Together, the Indianapolis Mayor's Office has worked closely with the
state government (i.e., the Republican Governor and legislature), the Indiana
Department of Education, the superintendent of Indianapolis, the superintendents of the other districts, and key stakeholders that comprise the Indianapolis
school system. Although this may not be considered an intentional portfolio
management model, the concerted reform efforts among multiple actors make
Indianapolis an important focus of study for school choice (see Bulkley et al.,
2010). Parents of school-age children in Indianapolis do have several different
schooling options to choose for their children, and we can analyze the impact of
parental choice on comparable student outcomes (state test scores and engagement indicators) across all school types simultaneously. Despite the prevalence
of choice in the Indianapolis area, students sort into schools quite differently in
terms of demographic and academic background.

Questions Unresolved in Comparing School Sector Effects

When examining the school level, a challenging, yet critical task is to examine whether different school sectors produce more positive student outcomes,
whether that be state test scores, graduation rates, college enrollment, or
other academic and social outcomes (Hamilton & Stecher, 2010; Levin, 2010).
However, examining student outcomes across school sectors is often challenging because not all of the students in different schools within the same urban
locale take the same standardized tests or report other similar data. For the most
part, the bulk of the literature on the effects of choice schools has focused on
comparisons of one school type (e.g., charter schools) *vis-à-vis* traditional public
schools.

Overall Effectiveness

We provided an extensive review of the effects of different types of choice schools in our earlier work (see Berends & Waddington, 2018). Briefly speaking, the effects of choice schools on student achievement outcomes tend to be mixed (e.g., some positive, some negative, some neutral) and highly variable based on context. Recent studies of Catholic elementary and middle schools have found the achievement of students is similar or lower than traditional public school students (e.g., Carbonaro, 2006; Reardon et al., 2009; Elder & Jepsen, 2014). Studies of charter schools have also found mixed and variable effects on student achievement (for review see Austin & Berends, in press; Berends, 2015; Betts & Tang, 2019); however, studies using enrollment lotteries have found large, positive effects on student achievement for students enrolling in oversubscribed, non-profit charter schools. (e.g., Abdulkadiroglu et al., 2011; Angrist et al., 2011; Dobbie & Fryer, 2011; Hoxby & Murarka, 2008; Gleason et al., 2010). Studies of magnet schools have also found mixed and variable effects on student achievement outcomes (for review see Ballou, 2009; Bifulco, 2012).

Although researchers have examined the variation in school effects within and between sectors for decades, they have been unable to examine the variation across multiple school types simultaneously, which we are able to do with the unique Indiana data. In what follows, we are able to examine the impact of students switching from a traditional public school into different school types (charter, magnet, and private) on student achievement and engagement—something that has rarely been done in the school effects research (Waddington & Berends, 2018).

Charter School Authorizers

We are also able to dig deeper into the portfolio of choice in Indianapolis by examining whether the type of charter school authorizer moderates the impacts of charter schools. Examining whether charter school effects differ by authorizer has important implications for how policymakers frame charter laws and regulators and for parents who make choices based on better information about schools (Zimmer et al., 2014).

There has been little research on how charter school authorizers are related to the variation in charter school effects. In Minnesota, relying on 10 years of panel data at the school-level, Carlson et al. (2012) found little variation in charter school authorizers (local school boards, postsecondary education institutions, non-profit organizations, and Minnesota Department of Education). In Ohio, Zimmer et al. (2014) used state longitudinally linked student-level data to examine a similar variety of charter school authorizers (school district, higher education institutions, nonprofit organizations, Ohio State Board of Education). They found that schools authorized by nonprofit organizations have lower achievement gains in mathematics and reading than other charter schools.

Despite the limited amount of research, examining authorizers is important because they play some significant roles, including making decisions about which charter schools are permitted to open, monitoring charter school performance to target where additional support may be needed, and making decisions about which charter schools can be reauthorized (Vergari, 2001). Although not all authorizers aim to fulfill all these roles (Bulkley, 2001), in Indianapolis, the Mayor's Office has addressed all of these roles. It has held high standards about which charter schools to open and has closed charter schools over the past decade. In terms of monitoring performance, the Mayor's Office has focused on four core questions: (1) Is the educational program a success?; (2) Is the organization in sound health?; (3) Is the organization effective and well-run?; and (4) Is the school providing the appropriate conditions for success? (Office of Innovation, 2017). For each of these questions, the Mayor's Office collects data on between 30–40 indicators, each linked to performance standards ranging from not meeting the standard, approaching standard, meeting the standard, and exceeding the standard. The indicators and standards provide a level of specificity to better target improvement supports. Because of the Mayor's Office monitoring schools in specific ways and holding them accountable, our analyses that follow can help inform whether such monitoring and regulation moderates charter school impacts.

Data and Methods

Data Description and Measures

We used eight years (2008–09 school year through 2015–16) of longitudinal, student records from the Indiana Department of Education (IDOE) for this study. The records contain demographic, test score, and engagement information about students in grades 3–8 attending traditional public, charter, and private schools that participate in the annual English/language arts (ELA) and mathematics assessments of the Indiana Statewide Testing for Educational Progress Plus (ISTEP+) program.[4]

Indiana is unique because many private K–8 schools participate in the ISTEP+ program and other statewide reporting (52 percent statewide; 75 percent of Indianapolis urban area private schools).[5] Many private schools, including most Catholic schools, participated in ISTEP+ testing over the past decade as part of their accreditation process and to participate in statewide athletics competitions. Additional private schools began taking the ISTEP+ as a required part of their participation in the statewide school voucher program. All students in ISTEP+ participating schools take the test, regardless of whether they receive a voucher. With robust private school participation, we can make comparisons across school types in the public and private sectors.

Our academic outcomes of interest are students' annual ELA and math ISTEP+ test scores. We standardized each student's scores by the subject/grade/year mean and standard deviation of all test takers statewide.[6] The standardized measures allow us to draw comparisons, in standard deviation (SD) units, between individuals in different types of schools. We also investigated unexcused absences and suspensions as outcome measures of student engagement. Unexcused absences are recorded annually for students in all school types, while suspensions are recorded annually for all public-school types. We created dichotomous indicators for each year for each student for each measure; one for if a student had one or more unexcused absences (minimum of a full day), and one for if the student was suspended (either in- or out-of-school).

We use several student-level demographic and academic background characteristics reported in the annual IDOE data. These characteristics include each student's sex, race/ethnicity, grade level, free or reduced-price lunch recipient status, English proficiency status, and special education status. We recoded each of these variables into binary indicators.

The longitudinal records also contain information about the student's school of record, including the school name and National Center for Education Statistics (NCES) unique identification number. Using the NCES ID, we linked the schools to the Common Core of Data (CCD) and the Private School Universe Survey (PSS) to create binary indicators of the school type (e.g., traditional public, charter, magnet, Catholic, and other private) of each student's annual enrollment. We manually entered this information for schools with missing data.

From these indicators, we identified students who switch between school types, enabling us to parse the impacts of switching to a charter school amongst other school types. We also included additional hand-coded indicators for charter schools, honing in on differences between the authorizers of charter schools in the Indianapolis urban area. The primary authorizer of charter schools in the Indianapolis urban area is the Indianapolis Mayor's Office, for which we create a single indicator to distinguish these charter schools from those authorized by other entities such as Ball State University or the Indiana Charter School Board.

We also created two binary indicators to identify all students who switch schools between years, regardless of if they change school type. The first indicates whether a student made a structural move due to normal grade progression. The second indicates whether a student made a nonstructural move (switching schools for any other reason). Both variables indicate a switch only in the school year immediately after the switch took place (t), even though the switch takes place between years t and $t-1$. Although we do not observe the underlying reasons why students change schools, these two variables together help us to identify the charter school impacts beyond the negative association between mobility and student achievement (see Schwartz et al., 2017).

Sample Description

Our analytical sample comprises all Indianapolis urban area (Marion County) public and private schools participating in the ISTEP+ testing program.

The sizable, diverse population combined with the variety of public and private school types makes the Indianapolis urban area prime for investigating the impacts of different school types and narrowing in on the impacts of charter schools on student outcomes.[7]

When creating our analytical sample, we made several decisions along the way that excluded several students across all school types from our final analyses. We enforced several data restrictions prior to sample construction. These restrictions included requiring each student to have at least three years of test scores, including two years before changing school types (a pre-baseline and baseline year). As such, this excludes any choice school students whom we observed changing schools after their first observation in our data. We also only include choice and public students who transfer between schools within Marion County. Based on these decisions, we constrained our final analytical sample to meet the above criteria.

Our main research questions involve unpacking the academic achievement gains made by students who switch from public to charter schools (in comparison to gains made by students switching to other choice schools) and how the gains are moderated based on the authorizer of the charter school. Ideally, we would randomly assign students to attend a choice school (e.g., a charter school) or a traditional public school. Then, we could draw comparisons between the treatment and control groups from the assignment process. In the Indianapolis urban area, only a handful of charter schools implement enrollment lotteries, and no such mechanism exists for assigning students in a random manner across other school types.

Without random assignment of students to various school types or a natural experiment such as a lottery to determine enrollment, any assessment of the effects of school choice in the Indianapolis urban area is subject to selection bias due to many unobservable factors that influence a family's choice of school for their child. Thus, we cannot simply compare the achievement of choice and traditional public school students. However, we can use this set of robust, student-level longitudinal data in conjunction with our estimation approach and the creation of comparison groups to mitigate selection bias.

To aid in our estimation, particularly for the impacts of students switching to charter schools, we constructed comparison groups for each group of students switching from traditional public to charter, magnet, Catholic, and other private schools. One important takeaway from the within-study comparison literature within educational research and broader quasi-experimental literature (for examples, see Cook et al., 2008; Bifulco, 2012) is that treatment and comparison groups should be drawn from the same geographic location and time frame (i.e., the same school). Therefore, we construct comparison groups for each group of choice students that matches students based on a number of geographic, time, and demographic criteria.

To match choice and public students, we develop "matching cells" that exactly match students based on being of the same race and sex and in the same grade, year, and school as a choice student at baseline—that is, the year before a choice student switches schools and is still enrolled in a traditional public school. This approach has been used by researchers in some other recent evaluations of charter schools, particularly in instances where random assignment via lotteries does not exist (see Dobbie & Fryer, 2017) or in attempts to replicate experimental findings for subsets of students and schools (see Angrist et al., 2013). For all students transitioning from a public to a choice school, we constrain the comparison sample to the group of public school students who never attend a choice school and are in the same matching cell as the choice student's baseline year.[8] At baseline, choice and non-choice public students share the same race, sex, grade, year, and public school. Post-baseline, the estimated impact of attending a choice school is a comparison of choice students versus a counterfactual group of peers who remain in a public school.

The exact matching of students based on a number of criteria helps to mitigate selection bias in terms of who does and does not choose to leave a traditional public school and attend a choice school. By matching students by school, grade, and year, the choice and comparison students are compared, beginning at baseline, in the same schooling contexts. Also, matching exactly based on a student's race and sex further accounts for variation in the selection process. For example, if students of a certain race/ethnicity were more likely to opt for choice schools, we are now comparing them to their same-race peers who should share the same likelihood of selection into a choice school based on the observable characteristic of race/ethnicity.

This approach shares important characteristics with propensity score matching (Rosenbaum & Rubin, 1983). Both approaches rely on the matching of students based on a finite set of observable criteria that are associated with the selection process. The exact matching process is more precise than matching on propensity scores; however, the number of matching criteria is limited when using exact matching. We believe that race/ethnicity, sex, and sharing a baseline year, grade, and school are a reasonable set of criteria to mitigate selection bias. Yet, as with propensity score matching, we are adjusting for key observable differences between choice school and non-choice public school students. Our estimates of the impacts of switching to a choice school remain subject to bias based on any unobservable characteristics that may drive selection into a choice school. We further detail these concerns and our approach to estimating effects when describing our approach to estimation.

Estimation Strategy

Despite constructing comparable samples of choice and public students, a simple comparison of choice and public student achievement or engagement outcomes may still be biased if we have not accounted for unobserved factors that may drive a family's decision to select a choice school, nor regression-adjusted covariates.

Our basic empirical model relies on the inclusion of matched cell fixed effects as an approach to mitigate unobserved, between-group confounding influences.

We begin with an OLS regression model for estimating achievement outcomes, as shown in equation 1 below.

$$Y_{icgt} = a + \beta_1 Charter_{icgt} + \beta_2 Magnet_{icgt} + \beta_3 Catholic_{icgt} + \beta_4 OthPriv_{icgt}$$
$$+ \delta \mathbf{X}_{icgt} + \theta_{gt} + \tau_c + \upsilon_{icgt} \tag{1}$$

Here, the achievement level (Y) for each student (i) in matching cell (c) in grade (g) and year (t) is a function of choice school selection (charter, magnet, Catholic, or other private) versus remaining in a traditional public school. The matched cell fixed effect (τ_c) in the model accounts for unobserved differences between choice and non-choice students within each race-sex-grade-year-school cell at baseline. Thus, the choice school effects in this model ($\beta_1 - \beta_4$) represent the within-cell difference between choice and non-voucher student achievement in the years after baseline.

We also controlled for a vector of student and school characteristics ($\mathbf{X}_{icgt}$) that include a student's sex, race/ethnicity, free or reduced-price lunch status, ELL and special education status as well as structural and non-structural school changes in year (t) interacted with grade level (g). Grade-by-year effects (θ_{gt}) account for differences across exams and over time. The term υ_{icgt} represents school cluster-robust standard errors to account for serial correlation amongst students within the same school and is used in all models. We estimate separate models with math and ELA achievement as the outcome measures. We also estimate separate models for each year after baseline, yielding estimates for one, two, and three years after baseline.

Equation (1) estimates the impact of attending a choice school on a student's achievement levels in any one year after baseline. A student's prior achievement may also play a role in the selection process, and thus we need to account for prior achievement in our model. We deal with this issue by controlling for prior achievement only in the pre-treatment years, which includes the baseline (Y_{igt-1}) and pre-baseline (Y_{igt-2}) years, as shown in equation (2).

$$Y_{icgt} = a + \beta_1 Charter_{icgt} + \beta_2 Magnet_{icgt} + \beta_3 Catholic_{icgt} + \beta_4 OthPriv_{icgt}$$
$$+ \pi_1 Y_{icgt-1} + \pi_2 Y_{icgt-2} + \delta \mathbf{X}_{icgt} + \theta_{gt} + \tau_c + \upsilon_{icgt} \tag{2}$$

After accounting for pre-treatment prior achievement, we describe the estimates of the choice school effects as the value-added achievement gain in any one year from baseline. By controlling for prior achievement, we are netting out the differences between choice and non-choice student achievement within any one matching cell that may drive selection into attending a choice school. And, by accounting for baseline and pre-baseline achievement, we are accounting for pre-treatment *trends* in achievement.

If choice students experienced a substantial drop in student performance, this could be a signal to parents to switch to a different type of school. This phenomenon is known in the job-training literature as "Ashenfelter's Dip" (Ashenfelter 1978), and without adjusting for pre-treatment differences in achievement, our results may be biased. Thus, we control for two years of prior achievement to net out any differential trends in achievement between choice and non-choice students. As a result, most our estimates of choice school impacts are constrained to students in grades 5 to 8.

Student Engagement Models

We can use a similar estimation strategy as we used to estimate impacts on student achievement to estimate the effects of attending a choice school on student unexcused absences and suspensions. Our measures of absences and suspensions are dichotomous indicators by year, so we use a linear probability model, as shown in equation (3) below.[9]

$$Z_{icgt} = a + \beta_1 Charter_{icgt} + \beta_2 Magnet_{icgt} + \beta_3 Catholic_{icgt} + \beta_4 OthPriv_{icgt}$$
$$+ \pi_1 Z_{icgt-1} + \delta \mathbf{X}_{icgt} + \theta_{gt} + \tau_c + \upsilon_{icgt} \tag{3}$$

Here, the probability of a student (i) in having an unexcused absence or being suspended (Z) in each matching cell (c), grade (g), or year (t) is represented as a function of choice school attendance and a host of background characteristics, baseline year indicators of absences or suspensions, grade-by-year indicators, and matching cell fixed effects. The baseline indicators help to adjust for the absence of suspension issues that may lead to a student switching schools. Therefore, this model estimates the change from baseline in the probability of experiencing an unexcused absence or suspension, in percentage points, for students switching to charter (β_1), magnet (β_2), Catholic (β_3), and other private schools (β_4) in comparison to their traditional public-school peers within the same matching cell.[10] We estimated separate models for absences and suspensions, as well as separate models for each year after baseline.

For both the student achievement and engagement models, we parse the charter school impacts by subgroups. First, we estimated the different impacts by charter school authorizer, comparing charter schools authorized by the Indianapolis Mayor's Office to all other authorizers. We included a recoded set of two charter variables: one indicating charters authorized by the Indianapolis Mayor's Office and the second indicating all other charter schools. Second, we estimated differential impacts by race/ethnicity and socioeconomic status, focusing primarily on disadvantaged populations, which include Black students, Latino students, and free or reduced-price lunch recipients. For these estimates, we included the main effects of attending a charter along with race and free/reduced-price lunch (FRPL) status and then interaction between charter attendance and race or FRPL status in separate models.

Results

In Table 9.2, we describe the analytical sample of Indianapolis urban area students transitioning from traditional public to choice schools and their matched peers remaining within traditional public schools. Largely, the group of students making transitions to choice schools and the matched set of public school students is demographically and academically similar to the population of all students in the Indianapolis urban area as described in Table 9.1 in the introduction to this chapter. We primarily focus on the notable differences between students who transition to choice schools and the broader population of students in public and choice schools.

The proportion of Black students who transition from public to charter, Catholic, and other private schools is greater than the overall proportion of Black students in these three types of schools. Similarly, the proportion of Latino students and English Language Learners transitioning from public to Catholic schools is higher than the proportion of Latino and ELL students in the population of students enrolled in traditional public or Catholic schools. Students moving to magnet,

TABLE 9.2 Baseline Descriptive Statistics for Analytical Sample of Indianapolis Students

	Public	Charter	Magnet	Catholic	Other Private
Students	37,466	2,094	2,955	611	295
Schools	145	37	21	27	24
1 Yr. Obs. in Choice	–	981	1,116	162	119
2 Yrs. Obs. in Choice	–	622	1,468	215	85
3+ Yrs. Obs. in Choice	–	491	371	234	91
Female	0.503	0.506	0.555	0.514	0.536
Black	0.390	0.602	0.526	0.213	0.217
Latino/a	0.122	0.107	0.246	0.311	0.115
Other Race/Ethnicity	0.034	0.059	0.058	0.069	0.102
Free/Red.-Price Lunch	0.646	0.779	0.906	0.581	0.661
Eng. Lang. Learner	0.102	0.080	0.162	0.246	0.142
Special Education	0.112	0.139	0.140	0.090	0.115
Retained	0.005	0.022	0.015	0.008	0.003
Math Score	−0.104	−0.456	−0.351	−0.005	−0.185
	[1.007]	[0.924]	[0.864]	[0.818]	[0.956]
ELA Score	−0.176	−0.483	−0.410	−0.113	0.146
	[0.971]	[0.906]	[0.831]	[0.848]	[0.977]
Unexcused Absence	0.603	0.727	0.708	0.579	0.653
Any Suspension	0.124	0.164	0.170	0.074	0.085

Table displays descriptive information at baseline for our analytical sample of Indianapolis urban area (Marion County) students with at least three years of test scores. Proportions reported for demographic characteristics; means and standard deviations [in brackets] reported for test scores. For choice students, this includes students with at least two years of test scores prior to switching to a choice school. For public school comparison students, only students of the same sex and race/ethnicity in the same grade, school, and baseline year of choice students are included. Source: Authors calculations from Indiana Department of Education student-level administrative data.

Catholic, and other private schools are more socioeconomically disadvantaged than the overall population in these schools.[11] There are minimal differences in the proportions of special education students who transfer to choice schools relative to the proportion of special education students previously enrolled in all school types.

Students who transfer from a public school to a school of choice tend to be lower achieving at baseline. In Table 9.2, charter and magnet school students score between 0.35 and 0.48 SD below the state average. However, the average achievement of students making transitions to charter and magnet schools is roughly the same as the overall average achievement in charter and magnet schools in Indianapolis. Students transitioning to Catholic schools are nearly at the state average in mathematics and perform lower than the state average in ELA (-0.11 SD). In contrast, students transitioning to other private schools score below the state average in math (-0.19 SD) but above the state average in ELA (0.15 SD). On average, students making transitions from public to any private school are much lower achieving than the overall population of private school students in Indianapolis. Our matched comparison group of traditional public school students are below the state average in both subjects, but overall higher achieving than the traditional public school population in Indianapolis. Charter and magnet school students also have a greater percentage of unexcused absences and suspensions at baseline compared with traditional public school, Catholic, and private school students.

When looking at the overall effects of students switching from a traditional public school into another school choice type, we find that charter school students who attend a charter school for three years past baseline score 0.21 standard deviations higher in mathematics and ELA than their matched public school peers (see Table 9.3). The estimated achievement gains from baseline of charter students is nearly zero in both subjects in the first year after the transition, and slightly positive (albeit not statistically significant) in the second year. Charter students are also 14 to 16 percentage points more likely to be suspended in the first two years of attending a charter school as compared with their peers who remain in traditional public schools.

In contrast, students who transition into magnet and Catholic schools score lower on mathematics, and these effects decline even more the longer that the student is enrolled in a magnet or Catholic school since baseline compared with students who remain in traditional public schools. By year three, students in magnet and Catholic schools lose an average of 0.25 and 0.29 SD in math from baseline, respectively. Meanwhile, students who move into Catholic and other private schools experience lower rates of unexcused absences by 30 to 40 percentage points across all years compared to their public school peers.

In Table 9.4, we focus on two different types of effects for charter school students. First, the estimates show the effects on test scores and engagement indicators for students in charter schools authorized by the Indianapolis Mayor's Office and for students in different racial/ethnic and socioeconomic groups compared with their matched traditional public school peers. If the estimates are highlighted in **bold**, that means that mayor-authorized charter school students also significantly

TABLE 9.3 Achievement and Engagement Outcomes for Indianapolis Choice Students

	Math	ELA	Absences	Suspensions
Charter Schools				
Year 1	0.003	0.032	−0.063	0.139★★★
	(0.055)	(0.040)	(0.049)	(0.041)
Year 2	0.112	0.084	−0.075	0.156★★★
	(0.075)	(0.045)	(0.046)	(0.033)
Year 3	0.211★★	0.212★★★	−0.080	0.060
	(0.072)	(0.045)	(0.043)	(0.033)
Magnet Schools				
Year 1	−0.140★★★	−0.060	0.002	0.002
	(0.040)	(0.031)	(0.022)	(0.022)
Year 2	−0.183★★★	−0.072	−0.025	−0.056★
	(0.064)	(0.043)	(0.028)	(0.026)
Year 3	−0.240★	−0.036	0.034	−0.008
	(0.096)	(0.071)	(0.036)	(0.028)
Catholic Schools				
Year 1	−0.132★★★	−0.027	−0.303★★★	−
	(0.033)	(0.029)	(0.056)	
Year 2	−0.182★★★	0.017	−0.390★★★	−
	(0.046)	(0.045)	(0.061)	
Year 3	−0.287★★★	0.013	−0.352★★★	−
	(0.052)	(0.047)	(0.053)	
Other Private Schools				
Year 1	−0.168	−0.026	−0.358★★★	−
	(0.095)	(0.044)	(0.054)	
Year 2	−0.229★	−0.166★★	−0.373★★★	−
	(0.089)	(0.062)	(0.074)	
Year 3	−0.002	−0.040	−0.377★★★	−
	(0.123)	(0.077)	(0.073)	

★$p \leq 0.050$; ★★$p \leq 0.010$; ★★★$p \leq 0.001$. Results reported from preferred models (2) and (3) for test score and engagement outcomes, respectively. Results unavailable for suspension outcomes for private school students as private schools do not report disciplinary records to the Indiana Department of Education. We computed separate models by number of years after switching to a choice school. ISTEP+ Math and ELA scores measured in standard deviation units, relative to the Indiana mean and standard deviation within each grade and year (across all public and private school test takers statewide). Robust standard errors, adjusted for the clustering of students within schools, are in parentheses. Source: Authors calculations from Indiana Department of Education student-level administrative data.

differ from other charter school students; Black or Latino students differ from White students in charters; FRPL students from non-FRPL charter students.

Students who switch into charter schools authorized by the Mayor's Office score significantly higher in mathematics and ELA, and they also have higher rates of suspensions compared with their peers who remain in traditional public schools. Mayor-authorized charter school students score 0.10 SD higher in mathematics in year one since baseline and this increases to 0.29 SD in year three.

TABLE 9.4 Variation in Outcomes for Indianapolis Charter School Students

	Math	*ELA*	*Absences*	*Suspensions*
Mayor-Authorized Charters				
Year 1	**0.100***	**0.095****	−0.022	**0.192****
	(0.040)	**(0.032)**	(0.042)	**(0.039)**
Year 2	**0.244****	**0.142****	−0.072	0.182***
	(0.065)	**(0.040)**	(0.051)	(0.033)
Year 3	**0.287****	**0.247****	−0.064	**0.080***
	(0.067)	**(0.046)**	(0.047)	**(0.035)**
Black Students				
Year 1	**0.105***	**0.108****	**−0.024**	**0.209****
	(0.043)	**(0.034)**	**(0.045)**	**(0.042)**
Year 2	**0.213****	**0.135****	−0.034	**0.203****
	(0.075)	**(0.045)**	(0.040)	**(0.034)**
Year 3	**0.270****	**0.250****	−0.080	0.098*
	(0.077)	**(0.051)**	(0.045)	(0.041)
Latino Students				
Year 1	−0.072	−0.024	**−0.009**	0.073*
	(0.055)	(0.054)	**(0.051)**	(0.029)
Year 2	0.004	0.020	−0.076	**0.223****
	(0.099)	(0.056)	(0.099)	**(0.077)**
Year 3	0.159	0.226	−0.071	0.119
	(0.131)	(0.117)	(0.109)	(0.065)
FRPL Students				
Year 1	**0.039**	0.053	−0.053	0.150***
	(0.050)	(0.035)	(0.044)	(0.040)
Year 2	**0.161***	**0.118****	−0.057	**0.173****
	(0.065)	**(0.041)**	(0.048)	**(0.032)**
Year 3	**0.265****	**0.260****	−0.101*	0.071
	(0.072)	**(0.050)**	(0.047)	(0.038)

*$p \leq 0.050$; **$p \leq 0.010$; ***$p \leq 0.001$. **Bold** indicates statistically significant differences from reference group (non-mayor-authorized charters, White students in charters, and non-FRPL charter students) at the $p \leq 0.050$ level. Results reported from preferred models (2) and (3) for test score and engagement outcomes, respectively, with interactions by subgroups. To parse out subgroup effects, we include interactions between the subgroup indicators and choice school indicators. We then calculated the linear combination of the main effect plus interaction term to arrive at estimates for the subgroups displayed above. We computed separate models by number of years after switching to a choice school. ISTEP+ Math and ELA scores measured in standard deviation units, relative to the Indiana mean and standard deviation within each grade and year (across all public and private school test takers statewide). Robust standard errors, adjusted for the clustering of students within schools, are in parentheses. Source: Authors calculations from Indiana Department of Education student-level administrative data.

The impact on ELA test scores by year three is slightly more modest at 0.25 SD. These students also have higher rates of suspension in year one since baseline (0.19 percentage points), but more years in a mayor-authorized charter school reduces the effect on suspensions to only an eight-percentage point higher likelihood of being suspended as compared to their public school peers by year three.

All of these estimates also indicate the students who transition into charter schools authorized by the Mayor's Office significantly differ from students in charter schools authorized by a different entity. Although not shown in Table 9.4, students transitioning to Mayor's Office authorized charters scored 0.55 SD higher in math three years after baseline (indicating an overall loss from baseline of nearly 0.25 SD in math for non-Mayor's Office authorized charter students) and 0.25 SD higher in ELA three years after baseline (indicating null effects on ELA achievement in other charters). Students transitioning to Mayor's Office authorized charters are 15 to 20 percentage points more likely to be suspended than their non-Mayor's Office authorized charter peers.[12]

Looking across all charter schools in Indianapolis, Black students who move from traditional public to charter schools experience achievement gains in math and ELA compared with their peers remaining in traditional public schools. These effects increase the longer these students are enrolled in charters, to roughly one-fourth of a standard deviation from baseline. However, these Black students are also likely to experience higher rates of absences and suspensions compared with their traditional public school peers in the first two years since baseline, but in the third year the engagement indicators are either insignificant (absences) or slightly positive (10 percentage points more likely to be suspended). The achievement and disciplinary incident rate for Black students in charters is higher than that of White students.

Although there are few significant estimates for Latino students who transfer to charter schools in Indianapolis, students who receive FRPL and switch from public schools into charter schools have greater gains in mathematics compared with their public school peers. This math effect is null in the first year after switching to a charter and increased to 0.27 SD in year three. FRPL students also experience a significant gain in achievement from baseline of 0.25 SD in ELA compared with their public school peers. These three-year achievement effects for FRPL students in the charter schools are also significantly higher than the effects for non-FRPL students in charter schools.

Discussion

This study was one of the first to be able to analyze state administrative longitudinal records in an urban area to examine a wide range of school types and the differential effects on achievement and engagement in Indianapolis' portfolio of choice schools. Specifically, we investigated the effects for students who switch from a traditional public school to another school type, whether that be a charter, magnet, Catholic, or other private school.

Descriptively, African American students are more likely to switch from public to charter, Catholic, and other private schools, and Latino students and English Language Learners are more likely to transition to Catholic schools. Compared with their peers, socioeconomically disadvantaged students are more likely to move to magnet, Catholic, and other private schools. As a reflection of the voucher program, low- to modest-income families are those more likely to send their children to a private school after receiving a voucher.

All the students in Indianapolis schools tend to score below the state average in mathematics and reading. Students who transfer from a traditional public school into a choice school are lower achieving, especially those students who move into charters and magnet schools. These charter and magnet school movers also have a greater percentage of unexcused absences and suspensions compared with their peers in traditional public, Catholic, and private schools.

In general, we find that there is some variation in the effects on achievement and engagement for students who move from a traditional public school into a school of choice. Students who switch to a charter school experience higher achievement over time, but they also have higher suspensions in the first two years after the move compared with their peers who remain in traditional public schools. Students who move into Catholic schools experience losses in mathematics, but over time, these negative effects decline; students switching into Catholic schools also lower absenteeism compared with their peers who remain in public schools.

Charter schools authorized by the Indianapolis Mayor's Office are having some successes in terms of student achievement. Overall, students who move from a traditional public school in Indianapolis into one of the charter schools authorized by the Mayor's Office have significant improvement in their mathematics and ELA scores even though they also have higher rates of suspensions compared with their traditional public school peers.

Charter schools in Indianapolis, broadly speaking, are also helping to close achievement gaps between African American and White students. Compared with the traditional public school peers, Black students who transition from traditional public to charter schools experience about a quarter of a standard deviation improvement in their math and reading scores three years after attending the new school. These African American students, however, are also likely to experience greater rates of absences and suspensions, suggesting that there is a trade-off between achievement gains and engagement losses. Across grades 3–8 in Indianapolis, the Black-White achievement gap is a consistent 0.60 standard deviations. Based on our findings in this study, charter schools may cut this gap in half after three years of attendance.

Similar to other studies that rely on similar statistical models, an important limitation of our analyses to assess the causal impact of school type on student achievement gains and engagement indicators is that we are looking at students who switch from a traditional public school to a school of choice. These students and their families choose from within the choice options available to them in the Indianapolis urban area, whether that be a charter, magnet, Catholic, or another private school. Because of this, there may be something quite different about these students who switch rather than those who stay in public schools, which limits our generalizability of these findings.

Moreover, students transferring to these choice schools may be different at the outset than their peers already enrolled. We found this to be the case in our previous work (see Berends & Waddington, 2018), particularly that students transferring to Catholic and other private schools have academic achievement well behind their peers already enrolled in a private school. As we stated above, this and other differences about students who are switchers rather than those who enroll in a choice school from the outset limits the generalizability of the choice school effects we find to students who switch in the middle of their educational experience; they do not capture overall sector effects.

The finding that students who switch to mayor-authorized charter schools and Black students experience a significant increase in the likelihood of receiving a suspension needs further examination. This finding is somewhat troubling amidst claims that charter schools attempt to push out students who do not fit the school mission, particularly those who are low achieving (Ravitch 2010, 2013). Our results also run counter to those of Imberman (2011), who found sharp decreases in the rate of suspensions along with improvements in attendance. Could it be that the charter schools in our sample are pushing students out, even in a high-achieving, "no excuses"-type of schooling model? Because some researchers have shown that charter schools do not "push out" low-performing students (Zimmer & Guarino 2013; Zimmer et al., 2018), this is something to further examine within the Indianapolis urban area.

The variation in effects of students moving to different schools of choice also needs further investigation. The negative effects in mathematics for students moving to magnet and Catholic schools may be due to a number of factors. We hypothesize that the critical factors to explore have to do with the social context of the school—e.g., socioeconomic and racial/composition of the school and the schools' organizational and instructional conditions (Austin & Berends, in press; Berends, 2015; Waddington & Berends, 2018). We will be analyzing these factors in our future research.

In addition, the finding that the mayor-authorized charter schools are having positive effects on student achievement, particularly African Americans, is informative for our understanding of how charter schools may contribute to the closing of achievement gaps. Perhaps it is the support and monitoring of the Mayor's Office of Education Innovation that explains these positive effects. Perhaps it is also the organizational conditions of the schools, principal leadership, teacher quality, and rigorous instruction that explain these findings. Again, our future work aims to examine these factors to provide lessons not only for the portfolio of choice inIndianapolis but also for other locales implementing school choice reforms.

Notes

1 Author order was determined randomly; each contributed equally to this paper. This paper was supported by Notre Dame's Center for Research on Educational Opportunity (CREO), Institute of Educational Initiatives, the Spencer Foundation, and the Walton Family Foundation. We are grateful to the Indiana Department of Education for providing access to the state administrative records and for supporting independent analyses. All opinions expressed in this paper represent those of the

authors and not necessarily the institutions with which they are affiliated. All errors in this paper are solely the responsibility of the authors.

2 We report student enrollments in grades 3-8, as these are the grade levels of focus for our analyses.

3 We further describe the participation of private schools in statewide testing and data collection in the data and methods section of this paper.

4 The ISTEP+ is the NCLB-mandated state test for Indiana students in grades 3-8 and is aligned to the Indiana Academic Standards. The ISTEP+ tests students each spring in ELA and math. The ISTEP+ is vertically equated across grades and consists of multiple-choice, constructed-response, and extended-response items scored using item response theory methods. Reliability coefficients range from 0.88 to 0.94 in ELA and 0.88 to 0.95 in math (Indiana Department of Education, 2011). Some schools opt to have their students to take the multiple-choice section online.

5 There were 61 private schools serving students in grades 3-8 in the Indianapolis urban area (Marion County) between the 2008-09 and 2012-13 school years. This excludes all special education and small home schools. Of these 61 private schools, 46 participated in ISTEP+ testing (75 percent). All 28 Catholic schools, 17 of 28 other religious schools (61 percent) and 1 of 5 nonsectarian schools (20 percent) participated. Other private schools participating in ISTEP+ may be different than those not participating.

6 We standardized scores statewide as opposed to only within the sample to reflect the distribution used to scale the ISTEP+. The Indianapolis urban area distribution largely reflects the statewide distribution.

7 Marion is the most populous county in the state (i.e. also has the largest school age population) with just over 900,000 residents as of the 2010 Census. The vast majority of residents (91 percent) live within the city of Indianapolis, as the city boundaries are roughly co-terminus with the county boundaries. The county is also substantially more racially and ethnically diverse than the rest of the state. Approximately 59 percent of the population is non-Hispanic White, 27 percent African American, and 10 percent Hispanic/Latino (United States Census Bureau, 2014).

8 Some public-school students have peers who leave to attend a private school with a voucher across several grades and years. To avoid replicating individual students in our sample, we randomly choose which of a given public school student's years serves as the baseline year.

9 We opted to use a linear probability model instead of a logistic regression model as the inclusion of the matched-cell fixed effects in the logistic regression model results in the model failing to converge.

10 We previously mentioned that suspension data are only available for public students.

11 For the private schools, this is largely a function of low to modest income families sending their students to a private school after receiving a voucher in the state.

12 The results from all of these comparisons are available from the authors upon request.

References

Abdulkadiroglu, Atila, Joshua D. Angrist, Susan Dynarski, Thomas J. Kane, & Parag A. Pathak (2011). Accountability and flexibility in public schools: Evidence from Boston's charters and pilots. *Quarterly Journal of Economics, 126*(2), 699–748.

Angrist, Joshua D., Sarah R. Cohodes, Susan Dynarski, Jon B. Fullerton, Thomas J. Kane, Parag A. Pathak, & Christoper R. Walters (2011). *Student achievement in Massachusetts' charter schools*. Cambridge, MA: Center for Educational Policy Research, Harvard University.

Angrist, Joshua D., Parag A. Pathak, & Christopher R. Walters (2013). Explaining charter school effectiveness. *American Economic Journal: Applied Economics, 5*(4), 1–27.

Ashenfelter, Orley (1978). Estimating the effect of training programs on earnings. *The Review of Economics and Statistics, 60*(1), 47–57.

Austin, M. & Berends, M. (2018). School choice and learning opportunities. In *Handbook of the Sociology of Education in the 21st Century*, edited by B. Schneider (pp. 221–50). New York: Springer.

Ballou, Dale (2009). Magnet School Outcomes. In *Handbook of research on school choice*, edited by M. Berends, M. G. Springer, D. Ballou, and H. J. Walberg (pp. 409–26). New York, NY: Routledge.

Berends, Mark (2015). Sociology and school choice: What we know after two decades of charter schools. *Annual Review of Sociology, 41*(15), 159–80.

Berends, Mark (2018). The continuing evolution of school choice in America. In *Handbook of education policy*, edited by R. Papa & S. Armfield (pp. 97–118). Hoboken, NJ: Wiley-Blackwell.

Berends, Mark & Peñaloza, Roberto V. (2010). Increasing racial isolation and test score gaps in mathematics: A 30-year perspective. *Teachers College Record, 112*(4), 978–1007.

Berends, Mark & Waddington, R. Joseph (2018). School choice in Indianapolis: Effects of charter, magnet, private, and traditional public schools. *Education Finance and Policy, 13*(2), 227–55.

Berends, Mark, Cannata, Marisa, & Goldring, Ellen B. (2011). School choice debates, research, and context. In *School choice and school improvement*, edited by M. Berends, M. Cannata, and E. B. Goldring (pp. 3–14). Cambridge, MA: Harvard Education Press.

Berends, Mark, Matthew G. Springer, Dale Ballou, & Herbert J. Walberg (Eds.) (2009). *Handbook of research on school choice*. New York, NY: Routledge.

Berends, Mark, Waddington, R. Joseph, & Austin, Megan (2018). Lessons learned from Indiana. *Education Next, 18*(2), 50–1, 60–3.

Betts, Julian R. & Emily Tang (2019). Effects of charter schools on student achievement. In *Education at the crossroads: Research perspectives*, edited by M. Berends, R. J. Waddington, & J. Schoenig, J. New York: Routledge.

Bifulco, Robert (2012). Can nonexperimental estimates replicate estimates based on random assignment in evaluations of school choice? A within-study comparison. *Journal of Policy Analysis and Management, 31*(3), 729–51.

Bulkley, Katrina (2001). Educational performance and charter school authorizers: The accountability bind. *Education Policy Analysis Archives, 9*(37), 1–22.

Bulkley, Katrina E., Jeffrey R. Henig, & Henry M. Levin (Eds.) (2010). *Between public and private: Politics, governance, and the new portfolio models for urban school reform*. Cambridge, MA: Harvard Education Press.

Carbonaro, William (2006). Public-private differences in achievement among kindergarten students: Differences in learning opportunities and student outcomes. *American Journal of Education, 113*(1), 31–65.

Carlson, Deven, Lesley Lavery, John F. Witte (2012). Charter school authorizers and student achievement. *Economics of Education Review, 31*(2), 254–67.

Cook, Thomas, William R. Shadish, & Vivian C. Wong (2008). Three conditions under which experiments and observational studies produce comparable causal estimates: New findings from within-study comparisons. *Journal of Policy Analysis and Management, 27*(4), 724–50.

Dobbie, Will & Roland G. Fryer (2011). Are high quality schools enough to close the achievement gap? Evidence from a social experiment in Harlem. *American Economic Journal: Applied Economics, 3*, 158–87.

Dobbie Will & Roland G. Fryer. (2017). Charter schools and labor market outcomes. NBER Working Paper No. 22502. Cambridge, MA: National Bureau of Economic Research. Retrieved from https://sites.google.com/site/willdobbie/

Duncan, Greg J. & Richard J. Murnane (2011). (Eds.). *Whither opportunity? Rising inequality, schools, and children's life chances.* New York: Russell Sage Foundation.

Elder, Todd & Christopher Jepsen (2014). Are Catholic primary schools more effective than public primary schools? *Journal of Urban Economics 80*(1), 28–38.

Elmore, Richard (2007). *School reform from the inside out: Policy, practice, and performance.* Boston, MA: Harvard Education Press.

Finnegan, Kara S. (2007). Charter school autonomy: The mismatch between theory and practice. *Educational Policy, 21*(3), 503–26.

Gleason, Philip, Melissa Clark, Christina Clark Tuttle, & Emily Dwoyer (2010). *The evaluation of charter school impacts: Final report.* NCEE 2010-4029. Washington, DC: National Center for Education Evaluation and Regional Assistance, Institute of Education Sciences, U.S. Department of Education. Retrieved from http://ies.ed.gov/ncee/pubs/20104029/pdf/20104029.pdf.

Hamilton, Laura & Brian M. Stecher (2010). Expanding what counts when evaluating charter school effectiveness. In *Taking measure of charter schools: Better assessment, better policymaking, better schools,* edited by J. R. Betts & P. T. Lanham, (pp. 33–54). MD: Rowman and Littlefield.

Henig, Jeffrey R. (2009). *Spin cycle: How research is used in policy debates: The case of charter schools.* New York: Russell Sage Foundation.

Hill, Paul T. (2010). *Learning as we go: Why school choice is worth the wait.* Stanford, CA: Hoover Institution Press.

Hill, Paul T., Christine Campbell, David Menefee-Libey, Brianna Dusseault, Michael DeArmond, & Betheny Gross (2009). *Portfolio school districts for big cities: An interim report.* Seattle, WA: Center on Reinventing Public Education, University of Washington.

Hoffer, Thomas B. (2009). Perspectives on private schools. In *Handbook of school choice,* edited by M. Berends, M. G. Springer, D. Ballou, & H. J. Walberg (pp. 429–46). New York: Routledge.

Hoxby, Caroline M. & Sonali Murarka (2008). Methods of assessing achievement of students in charter schools. In *Charter school outcomes,* edited by M. Berends, M. G. Springer, & H. J. Walberg (pp. 7–37). Mahweh, NJ: Taylor and Francis Group.

Imberman, Scott A. (2011). Achievement and behavior in charter school: Drawing a more complete picture. *The Review of Economics and Statistics, 93*(2), 416–35.

Kena, Grace, Susan Aud, Frank Johnson, Xiaolei Wang, Jijun Zhang, Amy Rathbun, Sidney Wilkinson-Flicker, & Paul Kristapovich (2014). *The condition of education 2014* (NCES 2014-083). U.S. Department of Education, National Center for Education Statistics. Washington, DC. Retrieved from http://nces.ed.gov/pubsearch.

Levin, Henry M. (2010). A framework for designing governance in choice and portfolio districts: Three economic criteria. In *Between public and private: Politics, governance, and the new portfolio models for urban school reform,* edited by K. E. Bulkley, J. R. Henig, & H. M. Levin, H. M. (pp. 217–40). Cambridge, MA: Harvard Education Press.

Office of Education Innovation (2017). Performance framework for mayor-sponsored charter schools, 2016–2017. Indianapolis, IN: Office of the Mayor.

Picketty, Thomas (2014). *Capital in the twenty-first century.* Cambridge, MA: Belknap Press.

Ravitch, Diane (2010). *The death and life of the great american school system: How testing and choice are undermining education.* New York: Basic Books.

Ravitch, Diane (2013). *Reign of error: The hoax of the privatization movement and the danger to America's public schools*. New York: Alfred A. Knopf.

Reardon, Sean, Jacob Cheadle, & Joseph Robinson (2009). The effect of Catholic schooling on math and reading development in kindergarten through fifth grade. *Journal of Research on Educational Effectiveness*, 2(1), 45–87.

Rosenbaum, Paul R. & Donald B. Rubin (1983). The central role of the propensity score in observational studies for causal effects. *Biometrika, 70*(1), 41–55.

Schwartz, Amy Ellen, Leanna Stiefel, and Sarah A. Cordes (2017). Moving matters: The causal effect of moving schools on student performance. *Education Finance and Policy, 12*(4), 419–46.

Stiglitz, Joseph E. (2013). *The price of inequality: How today's divided society endangers our future.* New York: W. W. Norton and Company.

Tienda, Marta & David B. Grusky (1990). Foreward. In *Equality and achievement in education*, edited by James. S. Coleman (pp. ix–x). Boulder, CO: Westview Press.

U.S. Census Bureau (2014). *State and county quickfacts for Marion County, Indiana*. Retrieved from http://quickfacts.census.gov/qfd/states/18/18097.html.

Vergari, Sandra (2001). Charter school authorizers, public agents for holding charter schools accountable. *Education and Urban Society, 33*(2), 129–140.

Waddington, R. Joseph & Mark Berends (2018). Impact of the Indiana Choice Scholarship Program: Achievement effects for students in upper elementary and middle school. *Journal of Policy Analysis and Management* (Early View).

Zimmer, Ron, Brian Gill, Jonathon Attridge, & Kaitlin Obenauf (2014). Charter school authorizers and student achievement. *Education, Finance, and Policy, 9*(1), 59–85.

Zimmer, Ron W. & Cassandra M. Guarino (2013). Is there empirical evidence that charter schools 'push out" low-performing students? *Educational Evaluation and Policy Analysis, 35*(4), 461–80.

Understanding the Context of School Choice

10

ACHIEVEMENT VERSUS ATTAINMENT

Are School Choice Evaluators Looking for Impacts in the Wrong Places?

Collin Hitt, Patrick J. Wolf, and Michael Q. McShane

Almost every major education reform of the last 20 years at both the state and national level has rested on a common assumption: standardized test scores are an accurate and appropriate measure of success and failure. It has followed that programs or policies that increase student scores on standardized tests are "good" and programs that fail to do so are "bad." School choice research followed this route.

A growing number of studies, however, are finding that school choice programs can improve high school graduation rates, college attendance, and earnings without producing gains in test scores. Conversely, studies of other school choice programs have found large short-term test score gains, but no lasting benefits in terms of graduation rates or college attainment. Improving test scores appears to be neither a necessary nor a sufficient condition for improving the later life outcomes that truly matter.

This chapter is a meta-analysis, the most thorough yet conducted, on the effect that school choice has on educational attainment. We have attempted to collect every experimental and quasi-experimental study of school choice in the U.S. that examines attainment impacts. Most of these studies also examine impacts on test scores. We use an expansive definition of school choice, including private school voucher programs, charter schools, early college high schools, magnet schools, vocational schools, and other forms of public school choice. We compare impacts on test scores to impacts on later attainment outcomes. Our question is whether, across studies, program impacts on test scores predict impacts on later outcomes.

We review every known study that contains participant-effect estimates for *both* student achievement and attainment. We exclude studies that look only at achievement scores or only at attainment outcomes. We use a simple "vote counting" analytical approach. We collapse findings into four categories: significantly positive, insignificantly positive, insignificantly negative, and significantly negative. We then map achievement findings against attainment findings.

We find that school choice program impacts on achievement are inconsistent, perhaps on balance weakly positive, thus replicating the findings of more sophisticated meta-analyses of the test score effects specifically of vouchers (Shakeel et al., 2016; Egalite & Wolf, Chapter 4) and charters (Betts & Tang, Chapter 5). However, impacts on attainment are much more consistently positive (Foreman, 2017). This pattern itself implies that some programs have produced clearer attainment impacts than achievement impacts; but, the pattern of findings is actually more complicated.

A school choice program's impact on test scores is a positive but very weak predictor of its impacts on longer-term outcomes. Our findings are based on 39 unique impact estimates across studies of more than 20 programs. In the coming months and years, more studies of school choice will be released. Perhaps over time a stronger connection between achievement and attainment impacts will emerge. We suspect not.

Our findings beg serious questions about the use of standardized tests as the exclusive or primary metric upon which to evaluate school choice programs. If test score gains are neither a necessary nor a sufficient condition for producing long-term gains in crucial student outcomes, then current approaches to accountability for school choice programs are questionable at best. Our findings suggest that focusing on test score gains may lead regulators to favor schools whose benefits could easily fade over time and punish schools that are producing long-lasting gains.

Methods

The goal of our systematic literature search was to identify studies that examined the effect of school choice on the following outcomes: reading and math scores, high school graduation, college attendance and completion of a four-year college degree. We limited our search to studies set in the United States.

We searched the following terms on Google Scholar:

- "school choice" + "attainment"
- "school choice" + "graduation"
- "charter school" + "attainment"
- "charter school" + "graduation"
- "school voucher" + "attainment"
- "school voucher" + "graduation"

We then screened the titles of the first 200 studies returned for each search term. If the title appeared in any way relevant, the study was logged for a review of its abstract. The abstract review process essentially screened for a sufficiently rigorous study design and relevant outcomes.

Students attend schools of choice, *by choice*. Researchers can easily observe test scores and educational-degree attainment after students enroll in schools of choice. The fundamental question of program evaluation is, what would those outcomes have looked like if students had not attended that school?

This causal question is difficult to answer, because students who select to attend schools of choice are obviously different—by virtue of their choice of school—than students who elect to or who have no choice but to attend school elsewhere. This reality creates a problem called selection bias—a problem that impacts everything from educational to pharmaceutical research. Students who select into schools of choice may naturally score differently on tests and graduate at different rates than students who do not exercise school choice, in ways that researchers cannot observe.

Various methods exist for addressing selection bias, some more rigorous than others. In order for a study to be included in our meta-analysis, it must have used random assignment, regression discontinuity, instrumental variables, statistical matching, or statistical modeling to control for differences between choice students and the students with whom they were compared.

Any study not eliminated during the abstract review was given a full reading, whereupon we determined the research methods used and the outcomes of interest. Only quantitative studies were included in our analysis. Studies with data flaws—such as major problems with attrition from the study—were eliminated, as were studies that failed to report point estimates of effect sizes on test scores and attainment outcomes. Studies that passed these standards were included in our main analysis.

Studies in our main analysis then formed the basis for a secondary network search. We searched the citations *in* each study, beginning with a title search as outlined above, as well as the citations *of* each study, as indicated by Google Scholar. We also searched the entire publication history of the author of every included study. Finally, we searched the entire databases of research centers that supported or published the studies selected, including the American Institutes of Research, the Brookings Institution, the Everyone Graduates Center at Johns Hopkins University, Mathematica Policy Research, Manpower Demonstration Research Corporation, the National Bureau of Economic Research, the RAND Corporation, the School Choice Demonstration Project at the University of Arkansas, and SRI International. In each instance that a title was identified through the network search, the entire process described above was repeated.

This meta-analysis focuses on the relative effect that individual school choice programs have had on achievement and attainment. During our search, we identified several rigorous studies that examined attainment impacts but not achievement (e.g. Cullen et al., 2005). We identified many more studies that examined only achievement impacts. Ultimately, a study (or a series of studies) was included only if it provided both achievement and attainment impacts.

In total, we included studies of more than 20 programs, which provided 39 unique estimates of the impact that school choice programs have had on both achievement and attainment.

We then coded each finding in one of four ways: positive and statistically significant, positive and statistically insignificant, negative and statistically insignificant, negative and statistically significant. The data, coded as such, could be treated as nominal or ordinal variables. This distinction makes little difference to our findings.

Our coding scheme may seem rigid. One can criticize the exactitude that we are imposing on the data, as achievement and attainment results must match regarding both direction and statistical significance. We believe this exactitude is justified by the fact that the conclusions one draws about whether or not school choice "works" depends on the direction and significance of the effect parameter. We are testing whether the results of the hypothesis tests are similar whether achievement or attainment is the chosen outcome, in a given study. If they are not, as we generally show, then the selection of outcome is critical to the assessment of school choice.

There are several policy options for offering school choice. The studies we collect cover a number of these mechanisms.

One mechanism is private school vouchers, where students are awarded vouchers to cover tuition at any one of a number of private schools of their choosing. Another mechanism is public school open-enrollment programs, where students can choose to attend whichever local public school they want. These initiatives might be labeled macro choice programs.

Another mechanism is the creation of specific schools of choice. Such micro choice programs, which may overlap with each other, include charter schools, selective enrollment high schools, career and technical schools, early college high schools, inclusive STEM schools, and new small schools of choice.

We examine a very specific question: whether the relative impacts of school choice on achievement are correlated with the relative impacts on attainment, for the population of empirical studies that examine both outcomes. We present results only from studies that examine impacts on *both* achievement and attainment, either within the same report or within a clearly linked series of reports from a common research project. We exclude several school choice studies that examine only attainment impacts, and we exclude the very large number of choice studies that examine only test score impacts. Our results should not be interpreted as the overall effect that school choice has had on achievement test scores. Likewise, our findings do not represent the totality of evidence that school choice has had on attainment.

Summary of Results

Overall, we identify 36 unique estimates of school choice impacts on reading and math tests from studies that also examine impacts on attainment. Among those studies, 34 contain unique estimates of the impact on high school graduation, 19 contain unique estimates of the impact on college enrollment, and 11 contain unique estimates of the impact on completion of a four-year college degree. Tables 10.1, 10.2, and 10.3 summarize the results by outcome, with English Language Academy (ELA) as the test score domain. The results with math as the test score measure show an even weaker association with attainment than the ELA results and are available from the authors by request. The impacts on achievement tests together lean slightly positive, though most findings are statistically insignificant. The impacts on attainment altogether lean more heavily positive.

Among ELA impact estimates, 11 (32 percent) are positive and significant, 13 (38 percent) are positive and insignificant, seven (21 percent) are negative and insignificant, and three (nine percent) are negative and significant.[1]

Among attainment high school graduation impact estimates, 16 (47 percent) are positive and significant, 13 (38 percent) are positive and insignificant, three (9 percent) are negative and insignificant, and two (6 percent) are negative and

TABLE 10.1 High School Graduation Impacts versus ELA Impacts

Number of Estimates by Sign and Statistical Significance

	High School Graduation Impacts				
	Negative Significant	Negative Insignificant	Positive Insignificant	Positive Significant	Total
ELA Impacts					
Negative Significant	1	0	1	1	3
Negative Insignificant	0	1	3	3	7
Positive Insignificant	1	1	5	6	13
Positive Significant	0	1	4	6	11
Total	2	3	13	16	34

Pearson chi2(9) = 5.8434 Pr = 0.755
gamma = 0.2047 ASE = 0.223

TABLE 10.2 College Attendance Impacts versus ELA Impacts

Number of Estimates by Sign and Statistical Significance

	College Attendance Impacts				
	Negative Significant	Negative Insignificant	Positive Insignificant	Positive Significant	Total
ELA Impacts					
Negative Significant	0	0	0	0	0
Negative Insignificant	0	2	3	1	6
Positive Insignificant	0	1	3	4	8
Positive Significant	0	0	1	4	5
Total	0	3	7	9	19

Pearson chi2(4) = 5.0114 Pr = 0.286
gamma = 0.6883 ASE = 0.191

TABLE 10.3 Four-Year College Degree Impacts versus ELA Impacts

Number of Estimates by Sign and Statistical Significance

	Four-Year College Degree Impacts				
	Negative Significant	Negative Insignificant	Positive Insignificant	Positive Significant	Total
ELA Impacts					
Negative Significant	0	0	0	0	0
Negative Insignificant	0	2	3	0	5
Positive Insignificant	0	1	2	0	3
Positive Significant	0	0	0	3	3
Total	0	3	5	3	11

Pearson chi2(4) = 11.0489 Pr = 0.026

gamma = 0.8065 ASE = 0.201

significant (Table 10.1). For estimates of impact in enrolling in college, nine (47 percent) are positive and significant, seven (37 percent) are positive and insignificant, three (16 percent) are negative and insignificant, and none is negative and significant (Table 10.2). Only 11 studies in our analysis examine the effects on college completion, three (27 percent) find significant positive effects, five (46 percent) find positive and insignificant effects, and three (27 percent) find negative and insignificant effects (Table 10.3).

If achievement results perfectly predicted attainment results, all of the counts of studies in the tables would appear in the "primary diagonal" of the results matrix, from the upper left corner to the lower right corner. That would mean that each finding of a positive significant effect of school choice on ELA test scores was accompanied by a similar finding of a positive significant effect on attainment, while positive insignificant ELA results always matched up with positive insignificant attainment results, etc. We see in Table 10.1 that only 13 of the 34 study results (38 percent) regarding ELA impacts and high school graduation impacts lie on the primary diagonal. The remaining 21 of 34 results (62 percent) are aberrant in that either the direction or the statistical significance (or both) of the ELA result and high school graduation result are different. The results in Table 10.1 are so dispersed that our diagnostic measures indicate that ELA results, on average, are not statistically significant predictors of high school graduation results in this set of school choice studies.

The results in Table 10.2 are hardly better. Only nine of the 19 sets of results (47 percent) regarding school choice impacts on ELA scores and college attendance match up on the primary diagonal. The ELA results are not statistically significant predictors of the college enrollment results either.

Table 10.3 is the only one to reveal a statistically significant correlation, in this case between ELA impacts and four-year college degree impacts of school choice. Seven of the 11 studies of that question (64 percent) report ELA findings that perfectly align with their college degree attainment results. However, due to the very small number of studies examined, any statistical test of association is extremely sensitive to the inclusion of even one additional study. This is an instance where, literally, every additional study has the ability to affect how we understand this issue.

Our primary finding is that evaluating school choice interventions based on achievement measures tends to yield different results than evaluating those same programs based on attainment metrics.

Multiple factors could lead to a significant finding for attainment to follow an insignificant finding on achievement. One possible explanation is measurement error: test scores are a noisy, imperfect measure of reading and math ability, while graduation and college attainment statistics are measured far more accurately, if done so honestly. Random noise in measurement causes impact estimates to attenuate. The greater noise with which an outcome is measured, the more likely that estimated impacts on that outcome will be insignificantly different from zero.

However, measurement error cannot entirely explain the differences in findings across outcomes. There are multiple instances in which school choice programs produced significant test score gains but no significant gains in high school graduation, for example. Testing error can perhaps explain why estimated impacts would be clearer for attainment than for achievement—but statistical noise can in no way explain why impacts would ever be clearer for achievement than attainment.

Overall, we have asked a simple question: Do test-score impacts of school choice programs serve as a reliable predictor of attainment impacts? Across the existing literature, the answer generally is no. This pattern of findings may change as more studies are published on school choice. Should the pattern remain consistent, however, the implications for school choice policy are massive.

Conclusions and Policy Recommendations

Under current K–12 regulatory regimes, the growth of school choice is actively managed. Take the example of charter schools, where caps are commonly placed on the number of charters that can open. Because only a limited number of charter schools can operate at a given time, the authorities who grant approval to charter schools to open tend to focus on replicating schools with a demonstrated record of success. If that record of success is judged on test scores, authorities will privilege schools that produce test score gains.

With respect to school choice, a "portfolio model" of regulation has grown substantially in popularity. The concept borrows its name from investment banking: managers should begin with a diverse array of investments, and thereafter transfer resources towards the assets producing the best results, while dumping assets with poor returns. This method, or philosophy, of governance also draws heavily on the principles of program evaluation—the use of social scientific methods to determine whether a program is producing benefits.

Program evaluation follows a simple logic model. Define the outcomes that a program is supposed to impact. Assess the extent to which the program has impacted those outcomes. If the program produces positive impacts at an acceptable cost, recommend it for expansion or replication. If a program fails to do so, recommend it for reformation or elimination.

The portfolio model of school choice governance goes like this. First, allow new schools to open. Second, evaluate their effectiveness, identifying schools that produce gains. Third, select those schools for replication and expansion. Fourth, close the schools that fail to produce gains. The process is intended, over time, to increase the overall quality of schools within a portfolio.

The portfolio model of education governance is highly attractive, but its success depends on one key factor: the appropriateness of the metric used to judge the success of the assets within the portfolio. This consideration takes us back to the basics of program evaluation—the outcomes that researchers choose to focus upon.

The outcome measure that is chosen by researchers and policymakers is a fundamental part of the evaluation process (Hatry, 2006). Ambitious programs such as school choice have ambitious goals: to leave children better off in the long-run. But long-run outcomes naturally take a long time to observe. Program evaluators often choose to focus on short-term outcomes, at least in the early years of a program. If there is a disconnect between effects on test scores and later life outcomes, particularly when it comes to evaluating schools of choice, the regulatory regime might need to be rethought.

Test scores and measures of educational attainment likely capture different constructs that are only weakly related to each other. Test scores might measure changes in knowledge or intelligence (or merely test-taking skills). High school graduation, college attendance, or earnings later in life could capture something more—habits like perseverance and conscientiousness. Some schools might be better at promoting such non-cognitive skills than others.

Now, perhaps these attainment measures do not matter as much as we might think. Perhaps schools of choice have watered down graduation requirements so that students who should not be receiving diplomas are graduating.[2] Perhaps schools of choice are sending unprepared students into college only to fail. We do not believe this explains our results. The impacts that choice programs have on high school graduation are a strong predictor of impacts on college attendance and graduation—more so than test score impacts.

There is a robust literature on the impact of high school graduation on later life outcomes (summarized in Wolf & McShane, 2013). Recent policy changes, however, might be weakening that relationship. After many of the studies were conducted, new incentives for increased graduation rates and college attendance were put in place. These incentives might have led to the watering down of graduation and admissions standards, consistent with "Campbell's Law," which holds that an outcome measure inevitably becomes corrupted once it is used for accountability purposes.

Even with these caveats in mind, the policy implications from this analysis are clear. The most obvious implication is that policymakers need to be much more humble in what they believe that test scores tell them about the performance of schools of choice. Measures of achievement are not giving us the whole education picture. Insofar as test scores are used to close (or expand) schools, policymakers might be making errors. Test scores should be put in context and should not automatically occupy a privileged place over parental demand and satisfaction as short term measures of school choice success or failure.

Policymakers should not give up trying to evaluate how well school choice programs or the students or schools that participate in them are performing. What we are simply saying is that if test scores are their only barometer, policymakers are using highly imperfect evaluative information. As it becomes easier to track later life outcomes by linking student information to census or tax records, those looking to evaluate school choice policies have the opportunity to make a more holistic evaluation of the meaningful effects of these programs.

We are still a long way from fully understanding how schooling affects children. Our analysis points us in a direction of diversifying the data sources that we use to evaluate schools and school programs and investigating new metrics that might be better correlated with the types of life outcomes that we, ultimately, value.

The unprecedented growth in school choice begs two related questions. Are school choice programs improving student outcomes? What is the best way for policymakers to manage the growth of school choice in order to maximize the benefits to students? For both of these questions, researchers and policymakers have looked mainly at standardized tests to provide the answers. Our findings tell us to start looking elsewhere.

Notes

1 Among math impact estimates not presented here, 11 (33 percent) are positive and significant, 15 (46 percent) are positive and insignificant, six (18 percent) are negative and insignificant, and one (three percent) is negative and significant.
2 A particularly outrageous example of such diploma fraud took place recently in Washington, DC (McGee, 2018).

References

Studies included in the meta-analysis indicated with *

*Abdulkadiroğlu, A., Angrist, J. D., & Pathak, P. A. (2014). The elite illusion: Achievement effects at Boston and New York exam schools. *Econometrica*, *82*(1), 137–96. doi:10.3982/ECTA10266

*Abdulkadiroğlu, A., Hu, W., & Pathak, P. A. (2013). *Small high schools and student achievement: Lottery-based evidence from New York City*. (National Bureau of Economic Research No. 19576). Cambridge, MA: National Bureau of Economic Research. Retrieved from http://www.nber.org/papers/w19576.pdf.

Angrist, J. D., Cohodes, S. R., Dynarski, S. M., Pathak, P. A., & Walters, C. R. (2016). Stand and deliver: Effects of Boston's charter high schools on college preparation, entry, and choice. *Journal of Labor Economics, 34*(2), 275–318. doi:10.3386/w19275

Barrow, L., Classens, A., & Schanzenbach, D. W. (2015). The impact of Chicago's small high school initiative. *Journal of Urban Economics, 87*, 100–13. doi:10.3386/w18889

Barrow, L., Sartain, L., & de la Torre, M. (2017). *The role of selective high schools in equalizing educational outcomes: Heterogeneous effects by neighborhood socioeconomic status.* (Federal Reserve Bank of Chicago No. 2016–17, 2016) Chicago: University of Chicago Consortium on School Research. Retrieved from https://www.chicagofed.org/publications/working-papers/2016/wp2016-17.

★Berger, A., Turk-Bicakci, L., Garet, M., Song, M., Knudson, J., Haxton, C., … & Cassidy, L. (2013). Early college, early success: Early college high school initiative impact study. Washington, DC: American Institutes for Research. Retrieved from https://www.air.org/sites/default/files/downloads/report/ECHSI_Impact_Study_Report_Final1_0.pdf.

★Bitler, M. P., Thurston, D., Penner, E. K., & Hoynes, H. W. (2015). Distributional effects of a school voucher program: Evidence from New York City. *Journal of Research on Education Effectiveness, 8*(3), 419–50. doi:10.3386/w19271

★Bloom, H. S. & Unterman, R. (2012). *Sustained positive effects on graduation rates produced by New York City's small public high schools of choice* (MDRC Policy brief 34). Retrieved from https://www.mdrc.org/sites/default/files/policybrief_34.pdf.

★Bloom, H. S. & Unterman, R. (2013) Sustained progress: *New findings about the effectiveness and operation of small public high schools of choice in New York City.* (ERIC No. ED545475). New York, NY: Manpower Demonstration Research Corp. Retrieved from https://files.eric.ed.gov/fulltext/ED545475.pdf.

★Chingos, M. M. & Peterson, P. E. (2015). Experimentally estimated impacts of school vouchers on college enrollment and degree attainment. *Journal of Public Economics, 122*, 1–12. doi:10.1016/j.jpubeco.2014.11.013

★Cowen, J. M., Fleming, D. J., Witte, J. F., Wolf, P. J., & Kisida, B. (2012). Student attainment and the Milwaukee Parental Choice Program: Final follow-up analysis. (School Choice Demonstration Project Report No. 30). Fayetteville, AR: University of Arkansas. Retrieved from http://www.uaedreform.org/downloads/2012/02/report-30-student-attainment-and-the-milwaukee-parental-choice-program-final-follow-up-analysis.pdf.

Cullen, J. B., Jacob, B. A., & Levitt, S. D. (2005). The impact of school choice on student outcomes: an analysis of the Chicago Public Schools. *Journal of Public Economics, 89*(5–6), 729–60.

★Cullen, J. B., Jacob, B. A., & Levitt, S. (2006). The effect of school choice on participants: Evidence from randomized lotteries. *Econometrica, 74*(5), 1191–230. doi:10.1111/j.1468-0262.2006.00702.x

★Deming, D. J., Hastings, J. S., Kane, T. J., & Staiger, D. O. (2014). School choice, school quality, and postsecondary attainment. *The American economic review, 104*(3), 991–1013. doi:10.1257/aer.104.3.991

★Dobbie, W. S. & Fryer Jr., R. G. (2011). *Exam high schools and academic achievement: Evidence from New York City.* (NBER Working Paper No. 17286). Massachusetts: National Bureau of Economic Research. Retrieved from http://www.nber.org/papers/w17286.pdf.

★Dobbie, W. S. & Fryer Jr., R.G. (2014). The impact of attending a school with high-achieving peers: Evidence from the New York City exam schools. *American Economic Journal: Applied Economics, 6*(3), 58–75. Retrieved from https://scholar.harvard.edu/files/fryer/files/dobbie_fryer_shs_07_2013.pdf.

★Dobbie, W. S. & Fryer Jr., R. G. (2015). The medium-term impacts of high-achieving charter schools. *Journal of Political Economy, 123*(5), 985–1037. Retrieved from https://scholar.harvard.edu/files/fryer/files/dobbie_fryer_hcz_01062015_1.pdf.

★Dobbie, W. S. & Fryer Jr., R. G. (2016). *Charter schools and labor market outcomes.* (NBER Working Paper No. 22502). Massachusetts: National Bureau of Economic Research. Retrieved from http://www.nber.org/papers/w22502.pdf.

★Dougherty, S. M. (2016). The effect of career and technical education on human capital accumulation: Causal evidence from Massachusetts. *Education Finance and Policy*, 1–30. doi:10.1162/edfp_a_00224

★Edmunds, J. A., Unlu, F., Glennie, E., Bernstein, L., Fesler, L., Furey, J., & Arshavsky, N. (2017). Smoothing the transition to postsecondary education: The impact of the early college model. *Journal of Research on Educational Effectiveness, 10*(2), 297–325. doi:10.1080/19345747.2016.1191574

★Edmunds, J.A.; Unlu, F., Glennie, E., Furey, J., & Arshavsky, N. (2016). Impact of the early college model on postsecondary outcomes. Poster presented at the Institute of Education Sciences Principal Investigator's meeting, Washington, DC. (Conference poster, shared by author).

Foreman, L. M. (2017). Educational attainment effects of public and private school choice. *Journal of School Choice, 11*(4), 642–54. doi:10.2139/ssrn.3045987

★Furgeson, J., Gill, B., Haimson, J., Killewald, A., McCullough, M., Nichols-Barrer, I., … Lake, R. (2012). *Charter-school management organizations: Diverse strategies and diverse student impacts.* Mathematica Policy Research, Inc. Retrieved from https://files.eric.ed.gov/fulltext/ED528536.pdf.

★Garet, M., Knudson, J. & Hoshen, G. (2014). *Early college, continued success: Early college high school initiative impact study.* Washington DC: American Institutes for Research. Retrieved from https://www.air.org/sites/default/files/downloads/report/AIR%20ECHSI%20Impact%20Study%20Report-%20NSC%20Update%2001-14-14.pdf.

Hatry, H. P. (2006). *Performance measurement: Getting results (2nd Edition).* Washington, DC: Urban Institute Press.

★Hemelt, S. W., Lenard, M. A., & Paeplow, C. G. (2017). *Building better bridges to life after high school: Experimental evidence on contemporary career academies.* (CALDER Working Paper 176). Washington DC: American Institutes for Research. Retrieved from https://caldercenter.org/sites/default/files/WP%20176_0.pdf.

★Howell, W.G., Wolf, P. J., Campbell, D. E., & Peterson, P. E. (2002). School vouchers and academic performance: Results from three randomized field trials. *Journal of Policy Analysis and Management, 21*(2), 191–217. doi:10.1002/pam.10023

★Hoxby, C. M., Murarka, S., & Kang, J. (2009). *Technical How New York City's charter schools affect achievement.* Cambridge, MA: New York City Charter Schools Evaluation Project National Bureau of Economic Research. Retrieved from http://users.nber.org/~schools/charterschoolseval/how_nyc_charter_schools_affect_achievement_technical_report_2009.pdf.

★Kemple, J. J. (2001). *Career academies: Impacts on students' initial transitions to post-secondary education and employment.* Manpower Demonstration Research Corp. Retrieved from https://www.mdrc.org/sites/default/files/full_47.pdf.

★Kemple, J. J. & Snipes, J. C. (2000). *Career academies: Impacts on students' engagement and performance in high school.* Manpower Demonstration Research Corp. Retrieved from https://www.mdrc.org/sites/default/files/Career_Academies_Impacts_on_Students.pdf.

*Kemple, J. J. & Willner, C. J. (2008). *Career academies: Long-term impacts on labor market outcomes, educational attainment, and transitions to adulthood.* Manpower Demonstration Research Corp. Retrieved from https://www.mdrc.org/sites/default/files/full_50.pdf.

*Krueger, A. B. & Zhu, P. (2004). Another look at the New York City school voucher experiment. *American Behavioral Scientist, 47*(5), 658–98. doi:10.1177/0002764203260152

*Lauen, D. L., Fuller, S., Barrett, N., & Janda, L. (2017). Early colleges at scale: Impacts on secondary and postsecondary outcomes. *American Journal of Education, 123*(4), 523–51. doi:10.1086/692664

McGee, K. (2018, January 29). In *D.C., 34 percent of graduates received a diploma against district policy.* nprEd, All Things Considered. Retrieved from https://www.npr.org/sections/ed/2018/01/29/581036306/in-d-c-thirty-four-percent-of-graduates-received-a-diploma-against-district-poli.

*Mayer, D. P., Peterson, P.E., Myers, D. E., Tuttle, C. C., & Howell, W. G. (2002). *School choice in New York City after three years: An evaluation of the school choice scholarships program. Final report.* (MPR Ref No. 8404-045) Retrieved from Mathematica Policy Research, Inc. and Harvard University, Program on Education Policy and Governance website: https://sites.hks.harvard.edu/pepg/PDF/Papers/nyc%20yr3%20MPR-PEPG%20exec.summ%202.19.02.pdf.

Mills, J. N. & Wolf, P. J. (2017). Vouchers in the bayou: The effects of the Louisiana scholarship program on student achievement after two years. *Education Evaluation and Policy Analysis, 39*(3), 464–84. doi:10.3102/0162373717693108

Mosteller, F. & Boruch, R. F. (Eds.). (2002). *Evidence matters: Randomized trials in education research.* Washington DC: Brookings Institution Press.

Murray, M. P. (2006). Avoiding invalid instruments and coping with weak instruments. *Journal of Economic Perspectives, 20*(4), 111–32. doi:10.1257/jep.20.4.111

*Neild, R. C. & Byrnes, V. (2014). *Impacts of career and technical schools on postsecondary outcomes.* Retrieved from John Hopkins University, Center for Social Organization of Schools, Everyone Graduates Center website http://new.every1graduates.org/wp-content/uploads/2014/10/Impacts-of-Career-and-Technical-Schools-on-Postsecondary-Outcomes.pdf.

*Neild, R. C., Boccanfuso, C., & Byrnes, V. (2013). *The academic impacts of career and technical schools: A case study of a large urban school district.* Retrieved from John Hopkins University, Center for Social Organization of Schools, Everyone Graduates Center website http://new.every1graduates.org/wp-content/uploads/2013/02/The-Academic-Impacts-of-Career-and-Technical-Schools.pdf.

*Sass, T. R., Zimmer, R. W., Gill, B. P., & Booker, T. K. (2016). Charter high schools' effects on long-term attainment and earnings. *Journal of Policy Analysis and Management, 35*(3), 683–706. doi:10.1002/pam.21913

Shakeel, M. D., Anderson, K. P., & Wolf, P. J. (2016). *The participant effects of private school vouchers across the globe: A meta-analytic and systematic review* (Working Paper 2016–07). Retrieved from University of Arkansas, Economics Research Network, Department of Education Reform, College of Education and Health Professions website http://www.uaedreform.org/downloads/2016/05/the-participant-effects-of-private-school-vouchers-across-the-globe-a-meta-analytic-and-systematic-review-2.pdf.

*Tuttle, C. C., Gill, B., Gleason, P., Knechtel, V., Nichols-Barrer, I., & Resch, A. (2013). *KIPP middle schools: Impacts on achievement and other outcomes. Final report.* Retrieved from ERIC database. (ED540912) Princeton, NJ: Mathematica Policy Research, Inc. website: https://files.eric.ed.gov/fulltext/ED540912.pdf.

★Tuttle, C. C., Gleason, P., Knechtel, V., Nichols-Barrer, I., Booker, K., Chojnacki, G., … & Goble, L. (2015). *Understanding the effect of KIPP as it scales: Volume I, impacts on achievement and other outcomes. Final report of KIPP's investing in innovation grant evaluation.* Washington DC: Mathematica Policy Research, Inc. Retrieved from http://www.kipp. org/wp-content/uploads/2016/09/kipp_scale-up_vol1-1.pdf.

★Unterman, R., Bloom, D., Byndloss, D. C., & Terwelp, E. (2016). *Going away to school: An evaluation of SEED DC.* New York: Manpower Demonstration Research Corp.

★Witte, J. F., Wolf, P. J., Cowen, J. M., Fleming, D. J., & Lucas-McLean, J. (2009). *The MPCP longitudinal educational growth study second year report.* (SCDP Milwaukee Evaluation Report# 10). Retrieved from University of Arkansas, Department of Education Reform, College of Education and Health Professions, School Choice Demonstration Project website http://www.uaedreform.org/downloads/2009/03/report-10-the-mpcp-longitudinal-educational-growth-study-second-year-report.pdf.

★Wolf, P. J., Kisida, B., Gutmann, B., Puma, M., Eissa, N., & Rizzo, L. (2013). School vouchers and student outcomes: Experimental evidence from Washington, DC. *Journal of Policy Analysis and Management, 32*(2), 246–70. doi:10.1002/pam.21691

★Wolf, P. J. & McShane, M. Q. (2013). Is the juice worth the squeeze? A benefit/cost analysis of the District of Columbia opportunity scholarship program. *Education Finance and Policy, 8*(1), 74–99. doi:10.1162/EDFP_a_00083

★Wong, M. D., Coller, K. M., Dudovitz, R. N., Kennedy, D. P., Buddin, R., Shapiro, M. F., … & Chung, P. J. (2014). Successful schools and risky behaviors among low-income adolescents. *Pediatrics, 134*(2), e389-e396. Retrieved from http://pediatrics. aappublications.org/content/pediatrics/134/2/e389.full.pdf.

★Young, V., Adelman, N., Cassidy, L., House, A., Keating, K., Park, C.J., … & Yee, K. (2011). *Evaluation of the Texas high school project: Third comprehensive annual report.* (SRI Project P18092). Menlo Park, CA: SRI International.

★Zimmer, R., Gill, B., Booker, K., Lavertu, S., Sass, T. R., & Witte, J. (2009). *Charter schools in eight states: Effects on achievement, attainment, integration, and competition.* Santa Monica, CA: RAND Corporation. Retrieved from https://www.rand.org/pubs/monographs/ MG869.html.

11

SEARCHING FOR POLICIES AND PRACTICES THAT MAKE CHARTER SCHOOLS SUCCESSFUL

What Can Research Tell Us?

Philip M. Gleason

Charter schools are a central component of current efforts to reform the public education system in the United States. These schools are publicly financed, but free of many regulations that govern traditional public schools, such as those involving staffing, curriculum, and budget decisions. The first charter schools opened in Minnesota in 1992, and the sector has grown to nearly 7,000 charter schools serving 3 million students since then.

An original hope for charter schools was that they would serve as an educational laboratory. Without the oversight and regulations of traditional public schools, charter schools would be free to innovate and test new ideas. Some would fail, but the hope was that others would succeed and the new ideas and approaches they had successfully tested out could be used in other schools. In a May 2014 proclamation for National Charter Schools Week, President Obama highlighted this point, saying that charter schools "that are successful can provide effective approaches for the broader public education system."

Research on charter schools suggests that on average they perform about as well as but not better than traditional public schools in terms of boosting student achievement. Among studies that examined relatively broad groups of charter schools, for example, most have found that these schools either did not significantly affect student achievement or had effects that were very small in magnitude (Gleason et al., 2010; Furgeson et al., 2012; Zimmer et al., 2012; CREDO, 2013a). However, another key finding from the literature is that the effects of charter schools vary greatly. Some charter schools are successful in boosting student achievement and others are not. CREDO (2013a) found that many charter schools (25 to 29 percent) had positive effects and many (19 to 31 percent) had negative effects on students' math and reading achievement. Furgeson et al. (2012) found that among the 22 charter management organizations (CMOs) they studied, 11 had significant positive effects and seven had significant negative effects in math. Gleason et al. (2010) also found substantial variation in the impacts of 36 oversubscribed charter schools around the country.[1]

This variation in charter school effects raises the question of what characteristics distinguish good charter schools from bad ones. Can we identify the policies and practices that make a charter school successful? And can these policies and practices be replicated in other charter or traditional public schools equally successfully? This chapter addresses these questions by summarizing the research on factors associated with successful charter schools.

Framework for Studying Factors Related to Charter School Success

Analyzing what school policies and practices may lead to charter school success requires three steps: (1) defining and measuring school success; (2) measuring factors—school characteristics, policies, and practices—that may be related to success; and (3) estimating the relationship between those factors and measures of school success. A growing set of research studies have used reasonably similar approaches to these steps in investigating factors related to charter school success.

Defining School Success

While a successful charter school should lead to a wide variety of positive student outcomes, most prior research studies have focused on the outcome of student achievement as measured by performance on standardized assessments in reading and math. In addition, studies have measured charter school success in relative terms, based on a comparison of charter schools with an alternative set of schools (usually nearby traditional public schools) that their students might otherwise have attended. Thus, a successful charter school is one in which student test scores are better than they would have been in this alternative, or counterfactual, set of schools. The specific set of students and schools used as a comparison or control group depends on the study's design and methodology. Lottery-based studies follow lottery losers to whatever schools they ended up attending in the years following the lottery. Many non-experimental studies select students with similar characteristics and baseline achievement levels as the charter school students but who attend traditional public school students in the same district as the charter school.

School Characteristics, Policies, and Practices

One way of thinking about why some charter schools are more successful than other involves considering the three Cs: treatment contrast, clients, and context (Weiss et al. 2014). *Treatment contrast* refers to the difference in services/resources received by treatment group members who attend charter schools, with control group members who do not. It is this difference rather than simply the quantity and quality of services/resources provided by the program that mediates a school's impacts. The services/resources received by students are captured using measures of school characteristics, policies, and practices. Just a few examples include:

- Amount of instruction received (e.g., length of the school day).
- Curriculum/instructional approach.
- Approach to regulating student behavior.
- Quality of teachers and school leaders.
- Characteristics of student peers in the school.

Ideally, studies examining factors related to charter school impacts would measure the treatment contrast using difference in these characteristics between the charter schools being evaluated and the traditional public schools that control or comparison group students attend. In practice, most studies only have detailed information on the charter schools' characteristics, policies, and practices, and not on those of the nearby traditional public schools.[2] Rather than measuring the treatment contrast these studies employ variables measuring the characteristics and practices of the charter schools alone.

A school's *clients* are the charter school students who make up the treatment group. Student characteristics may influence, or moderate, the school's impacts, as some types of students may be helped more by the school than others. For example, students who are low achieving at the time they enter charter schools may benefit particularly from the typical charter school. If so, one would expect to see larger impacts for charter schools serving larger proportions of low-achieving students.

The *context* in which a charter school operates is another possible moderator. The school's neighborhood may influence its impacts, perhaps because the neighborhood affects the school's ability to attract good teachers or students' ability to focus on their schoolwork during non-school hours. More generally, charter schools in urban settings may have different impacts than those in non-urban settings because of the characteristics of traditional public school districts in these areas.

Methods for Identifying Factors Related to Charter School Success

To really understand how particular policies or practices influence a charter school's success, one would ideally randomly assign these policies and practices to a group of charter schools and then measure their influence on the schools' impacts. This is not an easy design to implement, however, and has not been used within the charter school sector. This type of experimental approach has been conducted within the traditional public schools sector, with a set of schools randomly assigned to implement a particular practice or set of practices (e.g., Garet et al., 2011; West et al., 2016; Agodini et al., 2013; Fryer, 2014).

Studies that have addressed the question of what factors may be responsible for the success of certain charter schools have used a non-experimental or observational approach. This approach involves observing how policies and practices actually implemented by charter schools are correlated with measures of their success. As discussed above, most studies of the factors related to charter school success use either a lottery-based or strong non-experimental design to rigorously estimate charter school impacts. To measure schools' characteristics, policies, and practices in some detail, the studies typically use surveys of school leaders or staff.

These studies then estimate the correlation between factors thought to influence charter school success and the schools' impacts on student achievement. In some cases, this correlational analysis is bivariate, where the basic question being addressed is whether a set of charter schools that have a particular feature (Feature A) have more positive (or negative) impacts than charter schools without Feature A. In other cases the analysis is multivariate, with statistical controls added to the analysis for other relevant features of the school (e.g., Wolf & Lasserre-Cortez, 2017).

This methodology for determining what factors may explain charter school success has several limitations. Most importantly, correlation is not the same as causation. Policies and practices correlated with positive charter school impacts may also be correlated with other characteristics, policies, and practices actually driving the school's success. Without random assignment, one cannot be certain that the factors included in the analysis are causally related to charter school impacts.

Another limitation of this research is that these studies have relied on small samples of charter schools. The typical study has analyzed factors related to impacts using a sample of about 30 charter schools. Thus, the statistical power of these analyses is low, a problem made worse by the fact that the number of factors that could potentially influence a charter school's success is large. So while the typical study has a sample of about 30 to 40 charter schools to analyze, the number of different characteristics, policies, or practices that could conceivably influence the schools' impacts on student achievement likely exceeds 30 to 40.[3]

Finally, many factors one might expect to be the most important contributors to a charter school's ability to boost student achievement are difficult to measure and are not included in these analyses. As previously mentioned, a charter school's impacts depend in part on the characteristics and quality of the traditional public schools to which they are compared, which are difficult to measure and often excluded. Similarly, some key charter school characteristics are difficult to measure, such as the effectiveness of the school's principal and teachers.

Factors Associated With Charter School Success

The findings presented here are from studies that set out explicitly to examine a wide range of factors that might explain charter school success. Other studies have presented evidence on how one or two individual factors are related to charter school impacts, but they did not aim to systematically explain factors related to charter school success. Those studies are not reviewed here. Collectively, the studies cover a range of locations, time periods, and methodologies and include over 400 schools in their analyses (although a few schools are included in more than one study). Table 11.1 lists the studies and shows key features of them.

Conclusions about the studies' findings were based on the following rules of thumb. Findings were based on strong evidence if at least four studies found a consistent significant relationship between a factor and charter school impacts with no strong counterevidence.[4] Findings were based on moderate evidence if at least two studies found a consistent significant relationship with minimal evidence to the contrary. A conclusion of no relationship between a factor and charter school impacts was made if at least two studies examined the relationship and found no significant relationship with minimal evidence to the contrary.

Charter School Characteristics, Policies, and Practices Consistently Associated with Positive Impacts

Several factors were positively related to charter school impacts on student achievement.

- *The most successful charter schools are located in urban areas.*

Just three of these studies directly examined the association between a charter school's urban location and its achievement impacts, but each study found a strong positive relationship (Gleason et al., 2010; Angrist et al., 2013; Chabrier et al., 2016) In addition, the pattern of results in studies that focus only on urban schools versus those that include both urban and non-urban schools is consistent with this finding. Studies with entirely urban samples have generally found positive impacts, including charter school studies in Boston (Abdulkadiroglu et al., 2011), Chicago (Hoxby & Rockoff, 2005), Los Angeles (CREDO, 2014), and New York City (Hoxby et al., 2009; Dobbie & Fryer, 2013; CREDO, 2013b). In contrast, broader studies that include urban and non-urban charter schools have found impacts that are close to zero and not statistically significant (Bifulco & Ladd, 2006; Sass, 2006; Gleason et al., 2010; Furgeson et al., 2012; Zimmer et al., 2012; CREDO, 2013a).

A caveat about this evidence is that these studies did not examine random samples of urban or non-urban schools. Most importantly, the lottery-based studies examined only oversubscribed schools that hold admissions lotteries. If the nature of selection of schools into the studies differed in urban and non-urban areas,

TABLE 11.1 Summary of Studies Systematically Examining Factors Related to Charter School Impacts

Study	Location	Years	Number of charter schools	Number of factors examined	Design for estimating impacts	Data source for measuring school characteristics and other factors related to charter school impacts	Design for estimating relationship between factors and charter school impacts
Hoxby et al. (2009)	New York City	2000–1 through 2007–8	33	28	Lottery-based	Charter schools administrators, NYC Dept. of Education (measured for charter schools only)	School-level bivariate and multivariate analysis[a]
Berends et al. 2010	National	2002–3 through 2005–6	76	12	Non-experimental	Teacher and principal surveys (charter schools and traditional public schools)	Student-level regression model[b]
Gleason et al. (2010)	15 states	2004–5 through 2007–8	36	18	Lottery-based	Principal survey (charter schools and traditional public schools)	School-level bivariate and multivariate analysis[a]
Furgeson et al. (2012)	8 states	2002–3 through 2009–10	22 CMOs, 68 schools	6 (43)[c]	Non-experimental / lottery-based[d]	Principal survey (charter schools and traditional public schools) and teacher survey (charter schools only)	School-level bivariate and multivariate analysis[a]
Angrist et al. (2013)	Massa-chusetts	2001–2 through 2010–11	33	11 (42)[e]	Non-experimental / lottery-based[d]	School administrator survey (charter schools only)	School-level bivariate and multivariate analysis[a]
Dobbie and Fryer (2013)	New York City	2003–4 through 2010–11	39	9 (40)[f]	Non-experimental / lottery-based[d]	Principal, teacher, and student surveys and video observations (charter schools only)	School-level bivariate and multivariate analysis[a]

(continued)

TABLE 11.1 Continued

Study	Location	Years	Number of charter schools	Number of factors examined	Design for estimating impacts	Data source for measuring school characteristics and other factors related to charter school impacts	Design for estimating relationship between factors and charter school impacts
Tuttle et al. (2013)	13 states	2003–4 through 2010–11	36	17	Non–experimental / lottery-based[d]	Principal survey (charter schools only)	School-level bivariate and multivariate analysis[a]
Knechtel et al. (2015)	9 states	2013–14	34	13	Non–experimental / lottery-based[d]	Principal survey (charter schools only)	School-level bivariate and multivariate analysis[a]
Chabrier et al. (2016)	Multiple districts and states[g]	2001–2 through 2010–11	87	11	Lottery-based	Principal survey (charter schools only)	School-level bivariate and multivariate analysis[a]

[a]The bivariate analysis involved regressing a measure of charter school impacts on a single characteristic of charter schools or examining this relationship between school characteristics and impacts in some similar way. The multivariate analysis involved regressing impacts on several school characteristics simultaneously.

[b]Berends et al. (2010) estimated a regression model in which student achievement was regressed on the student's prior achievement level, demographic characteristics, and characteristics of the student's school (regardless of whether or not the school was a charter school). One of the school characteristics included in the regression was charter school status. Thus, this study used variation in school characteristics across schools in the charter and traditional public school sectors to capture the relationship between school characteristics and student achievement.

[c]Furgeson et al. (2012) conducted the primary, confirmatory analysis using 6 factors, but conducted exploratory analysis with a total of 43 factors.

[d]Non-experimental estimates were the primary estimates used in estimating the relationship between charter school characteristics and impacts, though as part of the larger study impacts were estimated using lottery-based methods as well.

[e]Angrist et al. (2013) conducted the primary, confirmatory analysis using 11 factors but conducted exploratory analysis with a total of 42 factors.

[f]Dobbie and Fryer (2013) conducted the primary, confirmatory analysis using 9 factors but conducted exploratory analysis with a total of 40 factors.

[g]Chabrier et al. (2016) conduct their analysis using an aggregated data set based on data from three prior studies (Gleason et al. 2010; Angrist et al. 2013; Dobbie & Fryer 2013), with lottery-based impact estimates from those studies only.

CMO = charter management organization.

that differential selection could lead to an artificial difference in impacts between urban and non-urban charter schools.

- *The most successful charter schools consistently enforce a comprehensive behavior policy with rewards for positive behavior and sanctions for negative behavior.*

Although different studies used different measures of schools' behavior policies, several found that charter schools with high expectations for student behavior and that strictly enforced their rules governing behavior had more positive impacts on student achievement. For example:

- Furgeson et al. (2012) found more positive impacts among schools with that used "consistent behavior standards and disciplinary policies," zero-tolerance policies for potentially dangerous behaviors, rewards and sanctions, and parent or student responsibility agreements.
- Hoxby et al. (2009) found more positive impacts among schools with disciplinary policies "based on the idea that expecting small courtesies and punishing small infractions ... is important."
- Dobbie & Fryer (2013) found more positive impacts among schools with higher values of a 10-item index capturing the extent to which schools had a "strict disciplinary policy."
- Angrist et al. (2013) found that the extent to which the school emphasized "discipline and comportment" was positively correlated with impacts. They argued that this policy is an important part of schools' "No Excuses" identity, which they also found to be strongly correlated with achievement impacts.

Finally, several studies examined charter school networks known for an emphasis on high expectations for student behavior, and found positive impacts among these charter schools. Teh, McCullough, and Gill (2010) found positive impacts among schools in the Achievement First and Uncommon Schools CMOs. KIPP schools have also been found to have strong positive impacts on student achievement (Gleason et al., 2014; Angrist et al., 2012; Tuttle et al., 2015). While all KIPP schools use an approach that includes high expectations for student behavior, Tuttle et al. (2013) showed that even within the KIPP network, the schools with the most positive impacts were those that had more positive values of an index capturing the extent to which behavior standards and discipline policies with rewards and sanctions were established and enforced consistently across the entire school.

- *Charter schools that prioritize the objective of boosting students' academic achievement above other possible educational objectives have more positive impacts on student test scores.*

Several studies examined schools' focus on improving their students' academic achievement. While all schools presumably want their students to do well, these studies attempted to measure which schools placed more emphasis on this goal than on others. Berends et al. (2010) measured "focus on achievement" using teachers' ratings on items such as the extent to which they expected students to complete assignments and the extent to which they set high expectations for students' academic work. Hoxby et al. (2009) measured the extent to which the school's mission statement emphasized academic performance. Furgeson et al. (2012) used school principals' reports on whether the school places high importance on students "exceeding state academic standards." Dobbie and Fryer (2013) used principals' reports on whether the school places a "relentless focus on academic goals and having students meet them," noting that other potential priorities not selected by these schools involved "the social and emotional needs of the whole child" and "building a student's self-esteem through positive reinforcement." In all of these studies, the authors found a positive correlation between charter schools' focus on academic achievement on their impacts on students' math and/or English/language arts scores.

- *Charter schools with longer school days and/or school years have more positive impacts on student achievement.*

Nearly all studies reviewed here found a positive association between a charter school's instructional time (length of the school day/year) and impacts on student achievement (Hoxby et al., 2009; Gleason et al., 2010; Furgeson et al., 2012; Dobbie & Fryer, 2013; Angrist et al., 2013; Chabrier et al., 2016). However, several found that while this relationship was statistically significant in bivariate models, it was not significant in multivariate models (Gleason et al., 2010; Furgeson et al., 2012; Angrist et al., 2013). This pattern of results suggests that it may not be the additional time in school that leads to more positive impacts, but rather some other policies or practices associated with time in school.[5]

An interesting relationship between time in school and impacts was evident in KIPP schools (Tuttle et al. 2013). On average, KIPP schools have long school days (nine hours), so the positive impacts across the KIPP network (Gleason et al., 2014) support the notion that long school days could contribute to positive impacts. Within the network, KIPP school days range from about eight to 10 hours, and Tuttle et al. (2013) found more positive impacts among KIPP schools with shorter days. Upon further exploration, however, they found that schools that spent more time on core instruction had more positive impacts, while those that spent more time on activities other than core instruction had less positive impacts. In other words, a long school day was still associated with more positive impacts so long as the time was spent on core instruction.

Research on extended time in traditional public schools also suggests that extra time may have beneficial effects only if devoted to core subject instruction.

An evaluation of an expanded learning time (ELT) initiative in Massachusetts, which added at least 300 hours to the school year but did not restrict the additional time to instructional activities, found that the additional time did not significantly affect student achievement (Checkoway et al., 2012). By contrast, Cortes, Goodman, and Nomi (2015) found that a "double dose" of algebra instruction had positive impacts on student achievement and educational attainment.

Characteristics, Policies, and Practices with Moderate Evidence of Positive Associations with Charter School Impacts

Based on somewhat more limited evidence, the research has identified several additional factors potentially related to charter school impacts.

- *Charter schools providing frequent feedback and coaching to teachers may have more positive impacts on student achievement.*

Furgeson (2012), Dobbie & Fryer (2013), and Chabrier et al. (2016) each found that the most successful charter schools provided teachers with the most coaching and feedback, based on both the bivariate and multivariate analysis. Among KIPP schools, on the other hand, Tuttle et al. (2013) found no significant relationship between a measure of teacher professional development and mentoring and achievement impacts. Among traditional public schools, Glazerman et al. (2010) studied a teacher induction intervention that provided teachers with various forms of coaching and support. They found positive impacts of this intervention, but only after three years.

- *Charter schools that encourage the use of student data to guide teachers' instructional practices may be more successful in boosting student achievement.*

One approach for improving teachers' instructional practices involves using data from interim student assessments to provide real-time information to teachers on students' mastery of particular concepts (Hamilton et al., 2009). Several studies offer support for the promise of this "data-driven instruction" approach in charter schools. Hoxby et al. (2009) found that charter schools administering more interim assessments had more positive impacts, though this relationship was not significant in multivariate analysis. Angrist et al. (2013) found that using informal tests to gauge understanding was positively correlated with impacts. Chabrier et al. (2016) also found data-driven instruction to be significantly related to impacts.

Other studies present a more nuanced picture. Dobbie and Fryer (2013) found that an index of data-driven instruction was positively associated with impacts, although not significantly. Furgeson et al. (2012) found that while measures of a school's efforts to get student data to teachers were not significantly associated with impacts on student achievement, a measure of how much teachers actually used data to help with their instruction was positively associated with impacts. By contrast, Knechtel et al. (2015) found a negative and significant relationship between KIPP schools' use of data-driven instruction and impacts. Evidence from traditional public schools has not shown a strong positive relationship between data-driven instruction and student achievement. Carlson, Borman, & Robinson (2011), Slavin et al. (2013), Konstantopoulos, Miller, and van der Ploeg (2013), and West et al. (2016) all found either no significant effects of data-driven instruction on student achievement, or small positive effects.

- *Limited evidence suggests that high-dosage tutoring helps charter schools improve student achievement.*

Dobbie and Fryer (2013) measured the extent to which charter schools offered high-dosage tutoring to students, or frequent instruction in very small groups—groups of six or fewer students four or more times a week. They found a positive association between tutoring and charter school impacts, particularly in English/language arts. Angrist et al. (2013) also found a positive relationship between a measure of tutoring for all students and charter school impacts, in this case in math. Other studies did not directly examine the relationship between the availability of tutoring in charter schools and their impacts. Research in traditional public schools is mixed, but a recent study of the provision of Supplemental Educational Services under the *No Child Left Behind* (NCLB) *Act* such as tutoring and other academic services showed no evidence of positive impacts on student test scores (Deke et al., 2014).

Characteristics, Policies, and Practices Not Associated with Charter School Impacts

Studies have also identified factors that do not appear to be related to impacts. This does not necessarily mean that these factors are not relevant or important, given the limitations of the studies' research designs. Just as we cannot necessarily conclude that factors correlated with charter school impacts are responsible for these schools' success, we cannot rule out the possibility that factors not correlated with impacts do contribute to their success. However, the evidence to date shows no significant relationships between the following factors and charter school impacts:

- *Class Size.* Several studies found no relationship between class size or student-teacher ratio and charter school impacts (Hoxby et al., 2009; Furgeson, 2012; Dobbie & Fryer, 2013; Tuttle et al., 2013). Gleason et al., (2010) found a significant relationship, but in a counterintuitive direction with impacts more positive in charter schools with a larger student-teacher ratio. Knechtel et al. (2015) found significantly more positive impacts in schools with smaller classes, but this relationship was not significant in multivariate models. The major piece of experimental evidence on the effects of class size in traditional public schools comes from the evaluation of Project STAR, which showed evidence of positive effects of very small classes, especially in the early grades (Finn & Achilles, 1990).

- *Teacher Qualifications.* Dobbie and Fryer (2013) and Chabrier et al. (2016) found no bivariate association with charter school impacts of teacher certification or having a master's degree. Gleason et al. (2010) and Tuttle et al. (2013) found no association between the proportion of experienced teachers in a charter school and the school's impacts. Similarly, research in traditional public schools has found no consistent link between student learning and teacher qualifications, with the exception of teacher experience (Rivkin, Hanushek, & Kain, 2005; Aaronson, Barrow, & Sander, 2007).

- *Charter Management Organization Affiliation.* While some individual CMOs have been found to have strong positive impacts on student achievement (Teh et al., 2010; Gleason et al., 2014), studies have found that overall, there is no significant relationship between whether a charter school is affiliated with a CMO and its impacts (Hoxby et al., 2009; Gleason et al., 2010). [6] In addition, studies that directly estimated impacts of CMO schools across multiple CMOs found that average impacts were not significantly different from zero (Furgeson, 2012; CREDO, 2013c).

- *Policies Promoting Parent Involvement.* Some charter schools make a special effort to involve parents in their children's education. Dobbie and Fryer (2013) developed an index of parent engagement capturing feedback provided to parents on students' behavior, academic performance, and other issues. Hoxby et al. (2009) and Angrist et al. (2013) measured whether charter schools used parent contracts. Tuttle et al. (2013) developed an index of parent involvement. In each case, the researchers found no significant relationship between these parent engagement measures and charter school impacts.

- *Charter School Age.* Hoxby et al. (2009) and Gleason et al. (2010) found no significant relationship between a charter school's age and student achievement impacts. A caveat is that both were lottery-based studies focused on oversubscribed charter schools. Very young charter schools, which presumably are less likely to be oversubscribed, may have been underrepresented.

- *Enrollment.* Furgeson et al. (2012) found that total school enrollment was not significantly related to charter school impacts. Similarly, Berends et al. (2010) found no significant relationship between enrollment and student achievement. Gleason et al. (2010) found a significant negative relationship between total school enrollment and charter school impacts—impacts were more positive in schools with lower enrollment. However, the relationship between enrollment per grade and impacts was not statistically significant, suggesting that the enrollment effect may have been related to the number of grades served.

What Do We Know and How Can We Learn More?

Research on the relationship between charter schools' policies and practices and their impacts on student achievement is motivated by a desire to understand what explains the success of certain charter schools. By understanding factors linked to charter school success, these policies and practices might be used successfully in other schools. Charter school networks that employ these policies and practices might be expanded. New charter schools might be encouraged to use the same policies and practices. Traditional public schools might adopt them. Ultimately, the hope is that the education system as a whole might be improved.

Summary of Research Findings

The research provides consistent evidence that some policies and practices are correlated with more positive charter school impacts on student achievement. The most successful charter schools tend to be those that consistently enforce a comprehensive behavior system, put their highest priority on helping students meet high expectations for academic achievement, and have long school days and/or years. More limited evidence suggests that successful charter schools give teachers frequent feedback and coaching, encourage and facilitate the use of student data to help teachers improve their practices, and provide high dosage tutoring to students.[7] However, a number of charter school characteristics, policies, and practices have been found to be uncorrelated with their impacts, including the school's age, CMO affiliation, funding, average class size, teacher qualifications, and efforts to encourage parent involvement.

The wisdom of encouraging the use of policies and practices that have been found to be correlated with charter school impacts depends in part on two characteristics of the underlying research. First, does the research have good internal validity? In other words, are these policies and practices actually responsible for the success of the schools included in these studies, or is the observed correlation spurious? Second, does the research have good external validity? Even if we conclude that certain policies and practices are responsible for the success of the charter schools in these studies, would these relationships also hold in other samples of charter schools or in traditional public schools?

The research in this area provides little guidance on questions of internal and external validity. As discussed previously, the limitations of the studies' research designs—small samples and limited ability to control for confounding factors—give us reasons to be skeptical of their internal validity. The policies and practices found in successful charter schools may simply be correlated with other factors that are actually responsible for the schools' positive impacts. For example, charter school impacts may truly be driven by a principal's ability to identify and hire effective teachers, and principals with this ability may also happen to work in schools with long school days. Because we cannot observe a principal's ability to hire good teachers, we simply observe a positive correlation between the length of the school day and charter school impacts. However, if we were to open a new charter school and require that it use a long school day, that school would not necessarily be successful because it would not necessarily have a principal with the ability to identify and hire good teachers.

The external validity of existing studies is questionable because these studies have focused on a limited set of charter schools with particular characteristics and operating in a particular context. The studies have relied heavily on urban charter schools and oversubscribed charter schools. What is true for these schools may not be true for suburban or rural charter schools that are not oversubscribed. In addition, the studies have focused on charter schools operating at a time in which charter schools make up a relatively small proportion of all public schools in the U.S. Would the policies and practices associated with charter school success in this context work equally well in a context in which charter schools served a larger proportion of students? In a situation like that, charter schools might have to adapt their practices to attract students or might struggle to find enough teachers who could work effectively in their schools.

Believing that the policies and practices correlated with charter school impacts would work equally well in traditional public schools requires an even greater leap. Charter schools are schools of choice. Students do not have to attend charter schools and the schools may have attributes that make them less attractive to certain types of students. Students who are especially unmotivated are unlikely to choose to attend a school with nine-hour school days, for example. Traditional public schools, by contrast, are less likely to be schools of choice and typically must serve all students living in a particular geographic area (unless these students choose to go elsewhere). It is difficult to know whether the policies and practices that are effective in boosting student achievement in a school of choice would be equally effective in a traditional public school serving all students who live in a given neighborhood. For example, if charter schools attract and/or retain only the most motivated or best behaved students in a neighborhood, then students attending these schools may benefit from positive peer effects.

Scaling up successful charter school networks brings additional challenges. For successful networks to remain successful as they grow larger, they must be able to maintain the policies and practices that made them successful. As they open new schools, can they continue to attract enough students and the right kind of students to fill their seats? Can they attract enough teachers and school leaders to be able to effectively implement these policies and practices? At KIPP, for example, the average principal reported working 74 hours per week (Tuttle et al., 2013). If the number of KIPP schools in a district doubles or triples, will they continue to be able to attract principals willing to work that hard and who remain effective school leaders? Finally, as CMOs grow, they face increasing administrative burden and their internal bureaucracy presumably must grow to meet this burden. Will this growing internal bureaucracy lead to unanticipated problems?

Next Steps

Research examining factors related to charter school impacts should best be thought of as hypothesis-generating research. Although not providing conclusive evidence about what policies and practices will bring school success, the research provides suggestive evidence about policies and practices that are worth further investigation. The best strategy for learning more about the effectiveness of these promising policies and practices involves testing them elsewhere and carefully measuring their effects. For example, policies and practices that have been found to be correlated with charter school impacts can be purposefully implemented in new schools, allowing researchers to study their effects on student achievement in these schools.

In practice, such research studies could take two approaches. First, a package of policies and practices associated with successful charter schools might be randomly assigned to a group of schools that would agree to participate in a research study. After these policies and practices had been carefully implemented in the randomly selected schools, subsequent student achievement and other student outcomes in these schools could be compared with those in other schools in the study that were not randomly selected to implement the intervention. Alternatively, charter school networks already implementing the policies and practices associated with success could expand, opening new schools using the same policies and practices. As the network grew, the impacts of the newly opened schools could be compared with estimates of the impacts of schools that opened when the network was smaller. If the newly opened schools were equally successful, this would be evidence that the network's policies and practices remained successful in this new context.

Fryer (2014) provides an excellent example of the first approach. The author identified a bundle of five policies and practices found by Dobbie and Fryer (2013) to be consistently present in successful New York City charter schools, and implemented these practices in traditional public schools in Houston, Texas. These practices included increased instructional time, strategies to increase human capital of teachers and administrators, high-dosage tutoring, frequent use of data to inform instruction, and a culture of high expectations. Fryer (2014) found that the implementation of these policies and practices in Houston led to an increase in student achievement of 0.206 standard deviations in math and 0.043 standard deviations in reading, per year. The study also reported that a similar set of policies and practices implemented in traditional public schools in Denver, Colorado had similar positive effects (based on a non-experimental design).

We know less about the extent to which successful charter school networks maintain positive impacts as they grow and reach a scale at which they could struggle to replicate their practices effectively. Most charter school networks are relatively small, especially in terms of their presence in a single city or district. KIPP is currently the largest network with about 200 schools, and only a few individual districts have a large number of these schools, with 26 KIPP schools operating in the network's largest region. Tuttle et al. (2015) examined trends in impacts among 37 KIPP schools during a period of rapid network growth from 2001–2 through 2013–14, finding that impacts were positive throughout but largest during the earliest years of that period.

Overall, learning more about the policies and practices likely to lead to success among charter schools, and potentially traditional public schools, requires continuing research in three areas. First, researchers should continue conducting research in which rigorous methods are used to estimate charter school impacts and these impacts are correlated with school policies, practices, and other relevant factors. This research will generate hypotheses about what factors actually lead to school success. Second, to the extent possible, researchers should work with policymakers to purposefully implement these factors in other schools and investigate their effects. Third, to the extent that charter school networks that have been found to have positive effects expand, researchers should examine whether schools in the network remain as effective as the size of the network increases, especially within individual districts.

Notes

1 One might question whether there is similar variation in the impacts of individual traditional public schools. Zimmer et al. (2012) examined this issue and found significantly greater variation in school-level impacts in the charter school sector than in the traditional public school sector in most of the states they examined.

2 There are three exceptions: Gleason et al. (2010) and Furgeson et al. (2012) measured a treatment contrast for selected school characteristics using the charter school-traditional public school difference based on data from a principal survey. Berends et al. (2010) used a different methodology and did not directly measure a treatment contrast, but did account for the characteristics of both charter schools and traditional public schools based on both principal and teacher surveys.

3 The studies reviewed here have explicitly tried to limit the number of factors they have examined given the limited degrees of freedom in analysis based on a sample of 30 to 40, but still have examined correlations with charter school impacts of between 11 and 43 different factors.

4 Evidence was also considered strong if three studies found a significant relationship and there was compelling supporting evidence.

5 An alternative possibility is that time is schools is so strongly correlated with these other policies and practices that it is not possible to disentangle their effects.

6 One study did find some evidence of a relationship between CMO status and charter school impacts. Dobbie and Fryer (2013) found that New York City charter schools affiliated with a CMO had significantly more positive impacts at the elementary school level, though differences at the middle school level were not significant.

7 Some evidence suggests that successful charter schools tend to have most or all of these policies and practices in clusters, rather than just one or two of them (Furgeson et al., 2012; Angrist et al., 2013; Dobbie & Fryer, 2013).

References

Aaronson, D., Barrow, L., & Sander, W. (2007). Teachers and student achievement in the Chicago public high schools. *Journal of Labor Economics, 25*(1), 95–135.

Abdulkadiroglu, A., Angrist, J. D., Dynarski, S. M., Kane, T. J., & Pathak, P. A. (2011). Accountability and flexibility in public schools: Evidence from Boston's charters and pilots. *Quarterly Journal of Economics, 126*(2), 699–748.

Agodini, R., Harris, B., Seftor, N., Remillard, J., & Thomas, M. (2013). *After two years, three elementary math curricula outperform a fourth.* Washington, DC: Institute of Education Sciences, U.S. Department of Education.

Angrist, J. D., Dynarski, S. M., Kane, T. J., Pathak, P. A., & Walters, C. R. (2012). Who benefits from KIPP? *Journal of Policy Analysis and Management, 31*(4), 837–60.

Angrist, J. D., Pathak, P. A., & Walters, C. R. (2013). Explaining charter school effectiveness. *American Economic Journal: Applied Economics, 5*(4), 1–27.

Berends, M., Goldring, E., Stein, M., & Cravens, X. (2010). Instructional conditions in charter schools and students' mathematics achievement gains. *American Journal of Education, 116*(3), 303–35.

Bifulco, R. & Ladd, H. F. (2006). The impact of charter schools on student achievement: Evidence from North Carolina. *Education Finance and Policy, 1*(1), 50–90.

Carlson, D., Borman, G. D., & Robinson, M. (2011). A multistate district-level cluster randomized trial of the impact of data-driven reform on reading and mathematics achievement. *Educational Evaluation and Policy Analysis, 33*(3), 378–98.

Chabrier, J., Cohodes, S., & Oreopoulos, P. (2016). What can we learn from charter school lotteries? *Journal of Economic Perspectives, 30*(3), 57–84.

Checkoway, A., Gamse, B., Velez, M., Caven, M., de la Cruz, R., Donoghue, N., Kliorys, K., Linkow, T., Luck, R., Sahni, S., & Woodford, M. (2012). *Evaluation of the Massachusetts Extended Learning Time (ELT) initiative.* Cambridge, MA: Massachusetts Department of Elementary and Secondary Education.

Cortes, K. E., Goodman, J. S., & Nomi, T. (2015). Intensive math instruction and educational attainment: Long-run impacts of double-dose algebra. *Journal of Human Resources, 50*(1), 108–58.

CREDO (2013a). *National charter school study: 2013.* Stanford, CA: Stanford University Center for Research on Educational Outcomes.

CREDO (2013b). *Charter school performance in New York City.* Stanford, CA: Stanford University Center for Research on Educational Outcomes.

CREDO (2013c). *Charter school growth and replication.* Stanford, CA: Stanford University Center for Research on Educational Outcomes.

CREDO (2014). *Charter school performance in Los Angeles.* Stanford, CA: Stanford University Center for Research on Educational Outcomes.

Deke, J., Gill, B., Dragoset, L., & Bogen, K. (2014). Effectiveness of supplemental educational services. *Journal of Research on Educational Effectiveness, 7*(2), 137–65.

Dobbie, W. & Fryer, Jr, R. G. (2013). Getting beneath the veil of effective schools: Evidence from New York City. *American Economic Journal: Applied Economics, 5*(4), 28–60.

Finn, J. D. & Achilles, C. M. (1990). Answers and questions about class size: A statewide experiment. *American Educational Research Journal, 27*(3), 557–77.

Fryer, R. G. (2014). Injecting charter school best practices into traditional public schools: Evidence from field experiments. *Quarterly Journal of Economics*, *129*(3), 1355–407.

Furgeson, J., Gill, B., Haimson, J., Killewald, A., McCullough, M., Nichols-Barrer, I., Teh, B., Verbitsky-Savitz, N., Bowen, M., Demeritt, A., Hill, P., & Lake, R. (2012). *Charter-school management organizations: Diverse strategies and diverse student impacts.* Cambridge, MA: Mathematica Policy Research.

Garet, M. S., Wayne, A. J., Stancavage, F., Taylor, J., Eaton, M., Walters, K., Song, M., Brown, S., Hurlburt, S., Zhu, P., Sepanik, S., & Doolittle, F. (2011). *Middle school mathematics professional development impact study* (NCEE 2011–4024). Washington, DC: Institute of Education Sciences, U.S. Department of Education.

Glazerman, S., Isenberg, E., Dolfin, S., Bleeker, M., Johnson, A., Grider, M., & Jacobus, M. (2010). *Impacts of comprehensive teacher induction: Final results from a randomized controlled study.* Washington, DC: Institute of Education Sciences, U.S. Department of Education.

Gleason, P., Clark, M., Tuttle, C. C., & Dwoyer, E. (2010). *The evaluation of charter school impacts: Final report* (NCEE 2010–4029). Washington, DC: Institute of Education Sciences, U.S. Department of Education.

Gleason, P. M., Tuttle, C. C., Gill, B., Nichols-Barrer, I., & Teh, B. (2014). Do KIPP schools boost student achievement? *Education Finance and Policy*, *9*(1), 36–58.

Hamilton, L., Halverson, R., Jackson, S. S., Mandinach, E., Supovitz, J. A., & Wayman, J. C. (2009). *Using student achievement data to support instructional decision making.* Institute of Education Sciences Practice Guide (NCEE 2009–4067). Washington, DC: Institute of Education Sciences, U.S. Department of Education.

Hoxby, C. M. & Rockoff, J. E. (2005). Findings from the city of big shoulders. *Education Next*, *5*(4), 52–8.

Hoxby, C. M., Murarka, S., & Kang, J. (2009). *How New York City's charter schools affect student achievement.* Cambridge, MA: New York City Charter Schools Evaluation Project.

Knechtel, V., Anderson, M. A., Burnett, A., Coen, T., Sullivan, M., Tuttle, C. C., & Gleason, P. (2015). *Understanding the effect of KIPP as it scales: Volume II, leadership practices at KIPP.* Washington, DC: Mathematica Policy Research.

Konstantopoulos, S., Miller, S. R., & van der Ploeg, A. (2013). The impact of Indiana's system of interim assessments on mathematics and reading achievement. *Educational Evaluation and Policy Analysis*, *35*(4), 481–99.

Rivkin, S. G., Hanushek, E. A., & Kain, J. F. (2005). Teachers, schools, and academic achievement. *Econometrica*, *73*(2), 417–58.

Sass, T. R. (2006). Charter schools and student achievement in Florida. *Education Finance and Policy*, *1*(1), 91–122.

Slavin, R. E., Cheung, A., Holmes, G. C., Madden, N. A., & Chamberlain, A. (2013). Effects of a data-driven district reform model on state assessment outcomes. *American Educational Research Journal*, *50*(2), 371–96.

Teh, B., McCullough, M., & Gill, B. P. (2010). *Student achievement in New York City middle schools affiliated with achievement first and uncommon schools.* Cambridge, MA: Mathematica Policy Research.

Tuttle, C. C., Gill, B., Gleason, P., Knechtel, V., Nichols-Barrer, I., & Resch, A. (2013). *KIPP middle schools: Impacts on achievement and other outcomes.* Washington, DC: Mathematica Policy Research.

Tuttle, C. C., Gleason, P., Knechtel, V., Nichols-Barrer, I., Booker, K., Chojnacki, G., Coen, T., & Goble, L. (2015). *Understanding the effect of KIPP as it scales: Volume I, impacts on achievement and other outcomes.* Washington, DC: Mathematica Policy Research.

Weiss, M. J., Bloom, H. S., & Brock, T. (2014). A conceptual framework for studying the sources of variation in program impacts. *Journal of Policy Analysis and Management, 33*(3), 778–808.

West, M. R., Morton, B. A., & Herlihy, C. M. (2016). *Achievement network's investing in innovation expansion: Impacts on educator practice and student achievement*. Cambridge, MA: Harvard University, Center for Education Policy Research.

Wolf, P. J. & Lasserre-Cortez, S. (2017). *Features of New Orleans charter schools associated with student achievement growth based on an exploratory analysis*. Washington, DC: U.S. Department of Education, Institute of Education Sciences, National Center for Education Evaluation and Regional Assistance, Regional Educational Laboratory Southwest. Retrieved from http://ies.ed.gov/ncee/edlabs.

Zimmer, R., Gill, B., Booker, K., Lavertu, S., & Witte, J. (2012). Examining charter school achievement effects across seven states. *Economics of Education Review, 31*(2), 213–24.

12

THE POLITICS OF CHARTER SCHOOL EVIDENCE IN LOCAL CONTEXT

The Case of Los Angeles

Janelle Scott, Elizabeth DeBray, Christopher Lubienski, Johanna Hanley, Elise Castillo, and Samantha L. Hedges

Introduction and Policy Context

Incentivist educational policies advance from the logic that public school systems cannot improve because they are not structured to be externally accountable, and that actors within the system (including teachers, administrators, and students) are not positioned in ways that would allow them to sense and respond to competition (Chubb & Moe, 1990; Coleman, 1997; Walberg & Bast, 2003). Charter schools are an example of incentivist policies because a key aspect of the theory in action is that increased freedom will produce not only greater academic outcomes, but also redress inequality. The role of charter schools in making public education more equitable has advocates and detractors, many of whom are active in funding incentivist reforms, and producing or promoting evidence to policymakers on their promise or pitfalls.

Since 2000, we have conducted a comprehensive review of the research on charter schools in conjunction with our research on the politics of research utilization. We find little consensus among researchers about charter school efficacy—even when efficacy is construed in the broadest sense to include equity, academic outcomes, teacher quality, parental satisfaction, or democratic participation. Moreover, the kinds of incentivist measures policymakers and intermediary organizations (IOs) are advancing beyond charter schools shift with the political preferences of those actors in public office, and foundations' and other IOs' policy preferences.

For example, when we initially began our research, the adoption of school voucher policies had stalled to a handful of states and cities, but has now gained political footing at the state level in Indiana and Louisiana, for example. And "Parent Trigger" laws, which allow parents in low-performing schools to vote for their schools to undergo radical transformation by a number of policy mechanisms, including becoming charter schools, or be operated by a non-profit charter management organization (CMO), are gaining in popularity in state legislatures (Rogers et al., 2015). In California, where the legislation originated, parents have "pulled" the so-called trigger to convert their children's schools several times, primarily in the Los Angeles Unified School District and surrounding suburbs.

Although the specifics vary by state, charter schools are essentially publicly funded schools that are managed by non- or even for-profit groups, usually independent of local districts and free from many regulations. They are intended to induce schools to compete for students by adopting more effective organizational behaviors. In fact, despite the enthusiastic, bipartisan endorsement these schools have enjoyed in Washington, DC, and strong support they have received from philanthropic organizations such as the Gates Foundation, the Broad Foundation, the Walton Family Foundation and the Fisher Fund/Pisces Foundation, the research record on charter school achievement is actually quite modest, showing great variability within and across states (CREDO, 2009; 2013; Betts & Tang, Chapter 5). There are currently approximately 6,000 charter schools in operation, serving some 2.5 million children.

Non-governmental organizations have grown in number and influence in educational policymaking in the United States and internationally (Gunter & Mills, 2016; Ball & Junemann, 2012; Henig, 2013; McDonnell & Weatherford, 2013; McGuinn, 2012; Reckhow, 2013). These intermediary organizations (IOs) are active in promoting, participating in, or opposing "incentivist" educational policies like charter schools, vouchers, "parent trigger" laws, and merit-pay systems for teachers that seek to encourage individuals and institutions to be more effective. These reforms operate under a theory that incentivized individuals and organizations will improve educational practice and outcomes, especially for some of the nation's most impoverished and disadvantaged K–12 students. The evidence on these reforms, and the extent to which policymakers attend to such evidence, stands to affect the educations of millions of U.S. children, making the political contexts under which effective research utilization takes place a key area for empirical investigation.

The adoption and implementation of incentivist policies depends in part on the understanding or acceptance of their track record or potential by policymakers and other stakeholders such as parents, community organizations, and journalists or bloggers. And this acceptance is in turn informed by the promotion and translation of various forms of evidence through a number of IO knowledge mobilization strategies (Qi & Levin, 2013). In addition, the nature of policymaking is highly complex—made even more so by the entry of new policy entrepreneurs and IOs which act as *de facto* policymakers even when they have limited official public authority to do so. These "heterarchical" conditions (Ball & Junemann, 2012) make research on the political context of evidence used by IOs to promote their effectiveness especially timely and important.

This chapter presents evidence from research in Los Angeles Unified School District (LAUSD) to investigate the multiple forms of evidence IOs are producing and promoting and across social media, and how political contexts might inform policymakers' and IOs' use of it. Charter schools have proliferated in LAUSD, as in other urban school districts, making LAUSD an important case to examine how evidence on charter school equity operates in local contexts, and how national and state-level politics inform evidence use.

Los Angeles Unified School District

Demographics and Budget

The second-largest school district in the nation, LAUSD enrolled 664,774 K–12 students across over 700 schools during the 2016–17 school year. In addition, LAUSD hosts 338 charter schools, serving 107,142 students. LAUSD encompasses most of the city of Los Angeles, as well as part or all of 31 adjacent cities and unincorporated areas. Demographic data for 2016–17 illustrate that Latinx students comprise the majority of the district, at 74.4 percent, followed by White students, at 9.8 percent. African American and Asian students comprise 8 percent and 6 percent of the district's overall population, respectively. About a quarter of LAUSD students are English language learners; 93 languages other than English are spoken among the district's student population. Additionally, about 80 percent of all students qualify for free or reduced-price lunch. In 2016–17, LAUSD's General Fund was $7.59 billion, and covered personnel salaries and benefits, books and supplies, capital outlay, and other operating expenses. Over 85 percent of the General Fund comes from the state.

Governance/Leadership

LAUSD is governed by an elected Board of Education, consisting of seven members, which approves the superintendent. Like many urban districts, LAUSD has experienced churn in system-level leadership. In 2014, the board appointed Ramon C. Cortines as superintendent of the district after the resignation of former Superintendent John Deasy; Cortines had led the district twice before. At the time of our research Michelle King served as superintendent, and an announcement about her successor was pending in 2018.

Intermediary Sector

Active intermediary organizations in Los Angeles include local chapters of high-profile national organizations, such as Educators 4 Excellence. The advocacy organization Children Now works on state-level education reform issues, and has offices in Sacramento, Oakland, and Los Angeles. Charter advocacy organizations, such as the California Charter Schools Association, are also active on the district-level, perhaps most notably by endorsing candidates for school board. Finally, Los Angeles is the birthplace of Parent Revolution, which mobilizes California parents to leverage the state's Parent Trigger Law and organize to transform their children's schools.

Blogs

As is the case in New York City, LAUSD parents and educators also engage in the online discourse on local education policy and reform, specifically to voice opposition to corporate reform. Examples include the blogs 4LAKids (http://4lakidsnews.blogspot.com), authored by LAUSD parent and PTA leader Scott Folsom, and the blog of Chris Thinnes, a parent and veteran teacher (http://chris.thinnes.me). The websites for local reform organizations, including Educators 4 Excellence and Parent Revolution, also maintain regular blogs. Finally, the online news site LA School Report, while not a blog, also provides regular media coverage of local education issues.

Foundations

Foundations supporting Los Angeles education reform efforts include the Wasserman and Stuart Foundations. LA is also supported by foundations with a statewide reach, such as the California Community Foundation and the California Education Policy Fund. In addition, foundations with national reach are heavy investors, including the Walton Family Foundation, the Gates Foundation, and the Broad Foundation. Among this heavy philanthropic investment, the Broad Foundation has been highly influential in Los Angeles, providing significant funding for charter schools, reform organizations, and school board candidates who ascribe to the Broad Foundation's preferences for market-oriented educational policies. Another way in which the Broad Foundation has been influential has been its investment in urban school leadership preparation through its Broad Fellows program.

State Governance/Political Context

The California State Board of Education (SBE) is responsible for creating all K–12 education policy for the state, including those pertaining to academic standards, curriculum, assessments, and accountability. The SBE consists of 11 members, who each serve a four-year term and are appointed by the governor; a student member serves a one-year term. The current president of the SBE is Dr. Michael Kirst, professor Emeritus of education at Stanford University, who was first appointed to the board in 2011 and reappointed in 2014. The state superintendent of public instruction presides over the California Department of Education (CDE), and is responsible for executing policies enacted by the SBE. Currently, the state superintendent is Tom Torlakson, who was re-elected in November 2014 to serve a second four-year term.

California's Parent Trigger law has inspired much debate among district leaders, community members, and reform advocates since its enactment in 2010. For example, in August 2014, then-Superintendent of LAUSD, John Deasy, argued that districts such as LAUSD, having received a federal waiver from the U.S. Department of Education, are exempt from the state's Parent Trigger law. In response, the parent advocacy organization Parent Revolution threatened to sue LAUSD if the district blocked parents from utilizing the law to turn around their schools (Reid, 2014b). Following Deasy's resignation in October 2014, interim (and now officially appointed) Superintendent Ramon C. Cortines expressed his support of the law, thus clearing the way for parents to use the Parent Trigger law to petition for school reform (Reid, 2014a).

In 2014, former Senator Gloria Romero, who helped write the law in 2010, founded the non-profit California Center for Parent Empowerment, which works to educate parents and help them to make use of the law (California Center for Parent Empowerment, 2015; Reid, 2015a). However, California's Parent Trigger law has inspired another camp of education reform advocates who believe that the law creates too much political antagonism. Notably, Jesus Sanchez, a former Parent Revolution organizer, criticizes the "divisive" impact of Parent Trigger, and, with other Parent Revolution veterans, founded Excellent Educational Solutions, a private consulting firm, to help foster more collaborative discourse and negotiations among district and school leaders, educators, and families to create school reform. For example, during 2014 negotiations over proposed reforms to Lexington Elementary in the Pomona Unified School District, "the threat of using options under the Parent Trigger was ever-present throughout the discussions," such that the law functioned to "leverage" school change, without actually being used by parents. Excellent Educational Solutions was instrumental to the successful negotiations over Lexington Elementary (Reid, 2015b).

Literature Review and Conceptual Framework

Our literature review and conceptual framework draw from political, economic, and sociological research on the changing nature of the central state in an era of neoliberal governance, where tasks formerly performed by public policy officials are increasingly contracted out to private sector actors, and where the ability of the state to provide social services like public education is hindered by shrinking tax bases, a general antipathy toward government, and racial, ethnic, and socioeconomic segregation (Schneider & Ingram, 1997; Skocpol et al., 1985; Hacker & Pierson, 2010; Reardon et al., 2012; Orfield, Kuscera, & Siegel-Hawley, 2012). This political context influences the use of research evidence as system leaders shape and implement governance, instructional, and personnel policies (Wohlstetter & Houston, 2015). We are also informed by more recent studies, such as Cucchiara's (2013) work on urban regimes, urban renewal, and the role of market-based reforms like charter schools in marketing living in the city to young, affluent residents. Central to urban regime theory is the notion that school politics are embedded in city politics. The regime concept also focuses on the particular ways public and private actors relate to one another, or the political arrangements among various actors. In addition, scholars working on the study of philanthropy, and its role in helping with policy transfer, continue to inform and shape our understanding of the political ecology of urban school district regimes (Reckhow, 2013; Quinn et al., 2014, Reckhow & Tompkins-Stange, 2015; AU & Ferrare, 2014, 2015).

Since 2011, we have studied IOs and their efforts to produce and share research evidence on these reforms in three urban school districts of varying sizes and with different governance structures, and in national IO policy coalitions. We have learned about the importance of local relationships for translating and lending legitimacy to research findings, the centrality of foundations in nurturing research evidence utilization through advocacy networks, the emergence of local and national bloggers as important producers and distributors of research evidence, and the ways in which IOs are using the blogs and social media to promote and disseminate their findings within their particular advocacy networks (Castillo et al., 2015).

Overall, our findings, and our review of the extant literature, point to the need for research utilization scholars to acquire a deeper understanding of political contexts, and how IOs are informing and being informed of those contexts. Yet there is need for explication regarding what elements constitute a political context. We draw from Weaver-Hightower's framework of policy ecologies to examine the politics of research utilization. Weaver-Hightower (2008) critiques the linear policy stages model of educational policymaking that he argues largely emerged out of the spate of 1960s government studies scholarship in the wake of federal and state expansion of civil rights and social welfare programs.

Political Ecology and Research Utilization

The ecology metaphor helps us to conceptualize policy processes as complex, interdependent, and intensely political. It models policy processes on concepts from the natural sciences, bringing new understandings and attention to often overlooked aspects of policy creation and implementation. The metaphor of an ecosystem is more appropriate than one of stages or circuits because the interactions of environments, groups, and events capture better the fluidity of the policy processes (Weaver-Hightower, 2008, p. 154).

Weaver-Hightower argues that a given policy ecology might consist of actors, relationships, environments, structures, and processes where individuals are members of multiple groups simultaneously. "Mapping these relationships reminds us that policy is not simply creating a text or artifact but is rather a struggle among human beings for validation or funding of their own interests, meanings, and forms of knowledge" (2008, p. 158). We theorize that the policy ecology shaping charter schools will include federal and state education policies and agencies, local ideologies, and histories, foundations, local district policy traditions and community characteristics, and IO functions. Figure 12.1 displays our application of the policy ecology framework to incentivist educational reforms.

Policy ecologies also involve flows of discourses between these areas. Attention to the flows of discourse and information can enable researchers to consider policies that were not enacted but were otherwise advanced. Weaver-Hightower (2008, p. 158) explains, "The ecological metaphor also demands that analysts account for the multiple levels at which policies interact, exert or receive influence, are created, and are implemented. Such thinking in terms of interconnections is a particular strength of the metaphor."

In our cross-case analysis of our research sites from the first phase of our work (2011–15), we discovered similarities and differences with respect to configurations of local IO networks and how they are related to local political history and governance. In general, we found that the movement of evidence through IO networks is related to the influence of sponsoring brokers. We found across sites that in each, there were "alpha" intermediary organizations, which tended to have well-funded research and policy staffs, and a dominant presence in policy discussions. Quite often, these were IOs funded by philanthropy, or a consortium of local and national philanthropies, which then served the function of coordinating much of the IO network. For instance, these "alpha" IOs tended

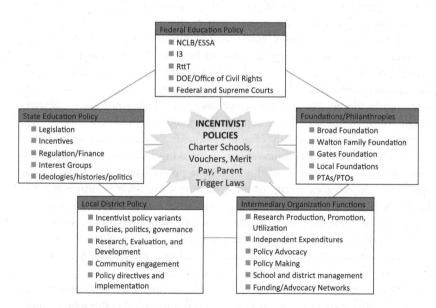

FIGURE 12.1 Policy Ecology of Research Utilization.

to play a leadership and convening function within their respective IO sectors (Scott et al., 2016). These exceptions notwithstanding, the actual research capacity within most local IOs to date has been fairly low, meaning that policymakers operate in a climate with few independent, empirical sources for research evidence (DeBray et al., 2014). Some IOs have staff with expertise in research production and/or staffers able to understand and translate research, while others lack anyone with basic understandings of methodology, or research design—a difference that, based on our data, does not appear to predict their degree of impact with policymakers. We have seen that much of what counts as research evidence in our case school districts is descriptive analyses.

Emerging from this research, however, is an awareness that the role of the broader political ecologies of school districts and their impact on the use of research evidence is, as yet, an under-examined, yet potentially critical, component in the research utilization field's collective and more comprehensive understanding of research evidence production, promotion, and utilization. To date, however, there has not been sufficient study of the political contexts in which research evidence is produced, promoted, and utilized, and the notion of "political context," when engaged conceptually or empirically, remains largely undertheorized, especially in light of the emergence of IOs and their impact on public policymaking (Weaver-Hightower, 2008). According to Weaver-Hightower, the ecological metaphor for political contexts "demands that analysts account for the multiple levels at which policies interact, exert or receive influence, are created, and are implemented" (p. 158). In this chapter, we apply the policy ecology model to the political context in Los Angeles, with particular attention to how it shapes research use and interpretation around charter school reform.

The framework we employ pushes against the strand of policy analysis that embraces a "policy stages" approach utilized by Kingdon (1995) and others (see Smrekar & Mavrogordata, Chapter 8). While this strand adds important insights into research utilization in the adoption of a historically contested issue, it supposes neatly identifiable and distinct phases of the policy process. As Weaver-Hightower (2008) notes, "These and other contemporary policy theories ... fail to capture the true complexity of policy contexts, or cannot account for all of the various components that influence policymaking and implementation across time" (p. 153). This critique of the traditional policy stages approaches can be applied to the complex terrain of the Common Core State Standards (CCSS). Hodge & Benko (2014) discuss the growing opposition to the CCSS, and contends that many analyses of the CCSS' policy formation tend to focus on elite actors, overlook the importance of funding (private and public) to US policy processes, and underestimate the tensions around race, ideology, and governance that characterize US public education policy contexts.

As McDonnell & Weatherford (2013) note, groups were supported by the Gates Foundation to write op-eds, offer expert testimony, and otherwise promote the standards to their state departments of education. Despite a comprehensive process of vetting the standards before state departments of education (SDEs) formally adopted them, by neglecting the broader policy ecology that Weaver-Hightower (2008) and other policy scholars encourage the architects and supporters of the CCSS (and many scholars who provided early analysis of their adoption) misread the near certainty that there would be intense resistance from a number of political and ideological sources that effectively derailed the standards after they were formally adopted in SDEs in a number of states. Yet, this opposition has not manifested itself in a coordinated opposition movement. Rather, it is fractured along ideological lines, and according to local and state political cultures (McGuinn, 2012).

We have mapped intermediary organizational networks in the context of educational politics and research utilization across several urban regimes. Our conceptualization of intermediary organizations includes entities that have an advocacy bent and their intermediary organizations networks also extends the way more sociologically oriented scholars have typically theorized IOs. In similar veins, we note scholars like Julie Marsh's study of the micropolitics of implementing teacher compensation in New York City (2014), and Maia Cucchiara's (2013) updated work on urban regimes, which encompasses market-based reforms like charters. In addition, scholars working on the study of philanthropy, and its role in helping with policy transfer continue to inform and shape our understanding of the political ecology of urban school district regimes (Reckhow, 2013; Quinn et al., 2014; Reckhow & Tompkins-Stange, 2015). As yet, political scientists working on educational policies have not comprehensively connected theories on politics and governance to research utilization studies.

We are informed by political, economic, and sociological research that has wrestled with the changing nature of the central state in an era of neoliberal governance, where tasks formerly performed by public policy officials are increasingly contracted out to private sector actors, and where the ability of the state to provide social services like public education is hindered by shrinking tax bases and a general antipathy toward government, and hyper racial, ethnic, and socioeconomic segregation (Schneider & Ingram, 1997; Skocpol, 1985; Hacker & Pierson, 2010; Reardon et al., 2012; Orfield et al., 2012).

Our framework understands policymaking to be informed by policy networks involving myriad actors, including interest groups, formal public policymakers, private foundations and donors, teachers, teachers unions, school and system leaders, taxpayers, and universities operating in urban political ecologies that share similarities, but also differ on key characteristics and democratic processes. We are also centrally interested in understanding how research is produced (and by whom), and how it is (or is not) utilized in policymaking processes in different urban regimes, and how networks, ideas, evidence, and policies might get mobilized through policy networks to other urban educational policy contexts.

Evidence Use and Policy Mobility

Charter management organizations (CMOs) and their networks are successfully moving the debate on charter school equity and effectiveness from school districts, City Hall, and state capitols to Congress, often through social and traditional news media, by finding new political support and strengthening existing political ties to powerful state and national allies. Much of the advocacy activity within these networks includes sharing evidence of the reforms' effectiveness in school districts with policymakers, the public, and other IOs (e.g., Hassel et al., 2012). Similarly, recently proposed federal legislation (2015) would have allowed states to seek federal money to replicate "successful" charter school models (Camera, 2015). In addition, researchers are at the early stages of examining the central role foundations are playing in IO advocacy networks, and exploring foundations' influence on education reform for theories on the policymaking process and for research production and utilization (Scott, 2009; Reckhow, 2013; Scott & Jabbar, 2013; 2014).

IO advocacy networks are interested in transfer of these reforms to other districts within and across states through the enactment of state and national legislation and regulations, based on the evidence promoted through foundation-funded venues and dissemination events (Hess et al., 2010). International and domestic research is also helping to vivify the field of educational policy analysis, bringing fresh theoretical perspectives, utilizing mixed-methods to investigate and map the new emerging policy and IO networks, investigating the changing nature of public policy and governance, and theorizing the implications of these alterations for democracy.

Thus, in this chapter, we are also informed by McCann and Ward's (2013) discussion of *policy mobilities* across particular contexts through policy networks. We are interested in understanding how research is produced (and by whom), and how it is (or is not) utilized in policymaking processes in different urban regimes, and how ideas, evidence, and policies are mobilized through policy networks to other urban school districts.

As McCann and Ward (2013) explain, the geospatial mobility of policy models has been narrowly conceptualized in political science. According to these authors:

> *policy transfer*, narrowly defined, has indeed lost intellectual currency outside of political science, precisely because it tends to have been *narrowly defined*. The emergence of multi-disciplinary perspectives on how, why, where, and with what effects policies are mobilized, circulated, learned, reformulated, and reassembled highlights, on the other hand, the benefits of understanding policy-making as both a local and, simultaneously, a global socio-spatial and political process.
>
> *(p. 4)*

McCann and Ward build on the policy transfer literature and move beyond it to conceptualize policy assemblages, mobilities, and mutations. Assemblage is a mechanism for understanding policies within a social process where the policy has an identity of its own and fits with a place. The mobilization of a policy is a "complex, power-laden process" (p. 9). For a policy to be mobile, it becomes fluid and free of a specific territory, and the term "mobilities" describes the varying contexts and social processes in which a policy can be imported.

As policies are mobilized and pass through places, institutions, and communities, they undergo mutations. Through mutation, policies are interpreted and reinterpreted as certain elements are abstracted and molded into a story that fits the place and the people within that place. Furthermore, policies move through, and are adapted by, networks of social relations, involving diverse participants with overlapping ideological understandings, interests, commitments, aspirations, purposes, and influence, and at least partly congruent political ventures. Through these network relations, favored policy fixes are co-produced and legitimated, and are held together by subscription to a particular discourse (Ball, 2012; Peck & Theodore, 2010).

The Case of Los Angeles

Our mixed-methods study (2016–18) in New York and Los Angeles investigates how political contexts inform research utilization, and how IOs are working within and across urban district contexts around charter schools. In this chapter, we examine how these dynamics constitute the policy ecology and regime politics in LAUSD. We selected LAUSD because of the complexity of its policy ecology, which includes the following characteristics that Weaver-Hightower (2008) includes in his framework: diverse *actors*, including local, state, and national-level IOs; contested *relationships* among actors; *environments and structures* shaping the relationships and interactions among actors; and *processes* that contribute to the ongoing evolution of the ecology. In particular, we investigate the policy ecology surrounding charter schools in LAUSD, a topic of much political controversy. Moreover, we examine the transfer of policy ideas *vis-à-vis* charter schools within LAUSD's policy ecology and how political and ideological divides across actors on the issue of charter schools constrains the development of a stable and durable urban regime. Consistent with urban regime theory, in Los Angeles, we see evidence of an unstable or contested regime as private actors seek to gain influence, yet there is strong pushback from district and the teachers' union folks.

The infusion of large-scale philanthropic activity on charters in LAUSD began in the early 2000s. Reckhow describes this growth, noting that "both the Gates Foundation and the Broad Foundation were significant grant makers by 2005" (2013, p. 65) to LAUSD, and that CMOs such as Green Dot and Aspire Charter schools were among the early beneficiaries (Walton funded individual schools only). The largest grantee from each of these foundations, writes Reckhow, was Pacific Charter School Development, Inc. (2013, p. 65). Political tensions around charters in LA began to grow as the economic recession was at its height and the school district rolled out a "Public School Choice Initiative" (PSCI). As Marsh (2016, p. iii) writes: "Adopted in 2009, the PSCI allowed teams of internal and external stakeholders to develop plans for and compete to turn around the district's lowest performing schools and to operate newly constructed schools designated to ease overcrowding." One of the tensions that arose during this competitive process was that "charter school proponents found themselves on the losing team with very few plans selected. The board was significantly more likely to select plans from internal teams than from external charter school organizations and network partners" (Marsh, 2016, p. 22). The UTLA "infused strong messages of PSCI as 'giving away' public schools to private operators in a PR campaign" (Marsh, 2016, p. 24). Drawing on the lessons from the dynamics during that period in LA, Marsh predicted (2016, p. 39):

> Without safeguards to ensure the dissemination of objective information, policies that expand charter schools will have a difficult time simultaneously empowering greater voice for parents and community members in decision-making. The high stakes of charter expansion create incentives for co-option and manipulation among actors seeking to preserve the status quo (which may include labor unions, current district employees, and elected officials), which greatly complicates efforts to educate stakeholders and engage them in meaningful participation

More recent developments regarding charter schools in LAUSD illustrate a complex policy ecology. During the initial phase of our study, these events included the school board's resistance in fall 2015 to the leaked Broad Foundation plan to give an additional $500 million to expand charter schools and a teachers' union-commissioned report alleging that charter school expansion has exacerbated declining LAUSD enrollment and further drained the district of funds (Whitmire, 2016). In addition, out-of-state donors have spent heavily to support the campaigns of charter-friendly candidates competing against candidates supported by the teachers' union, United Teachers of Los Angeles (UTLA) (Reckhow et al., 2016). Indeed, for the March 2017 school board primary race, which involved only three seats, charter school advocates together spent about $5.4 million to support their favored candidates. UTLA, in contrast, spent $1.6 million, around $1 million of which supported the candidacy of current board president Steve Zimmer (Favot, 2017b). Meanwhile, Superintendent Michelle King, who was appointed in January 2016, has indicated her support for charter schools, as well as a commitment to the district's traditional public schools. She stepped down due to health reasons in January 2018 (Blume & Resmovits, 2018), leaving the political landscape in greater uncertainty as acting Superintendent Vivian Ekchian took over.

The IO sector is also continuing to become more diverse, and characterized by strong national influences on its networks. While there are still established groups like Parent Revolution promoting the California "Parent Trigger" law, and many longstanding foundations such as the California Community Foundation, there are new philanthropically supported organizations Great Public Schools Now (founded in the aftermath of the failed attempt by Broad to fund district charters directly in 2015). Many of the groups work in tandem with the California State Charter Schools Association, as well as with national groups. There are also numerous CMOs, such as Green Dot and KIPP, which increasingly attempt to influence local, state, and federal policies. Many out-of-state donors supporting charter-friendly school board candidates in Los Angeles have ties to these and other education reform organizations (Reckhow et al., 2016).

In light of the complexity Carol Weiss (1980) describes regarding the application of research in policymaking, our data collection is grounded in varied policy and organizational settings. We agree with Heck (2004) that "because actors construct meanings within a social context, understanding the context in which a policy is developed and implemented is essential to understanding its particular implementation—that is, how the policy may be interpreted and acted on by the people in that setting" (p. 216). This contextual awareness of local policy ecology not only requires a flexible understanding of policymaking processes; it also requires a broad interpretation about the multiple forms of research utilization. For the purpose of our study, these include: 1) The *adoption or enactment of specific policies;* 2) *Confirmatory application of research;* 3) *Tactical use or misuse;* 4) *Hortatory application of research;* 5) *Knowledge creep and decision accretion;* and, 6) The generation of *common-sense understandings* of educational policy and alternatives (Davis & Nutley, 2008; Weiss, 1980; Shaker & Heilman, 2004).

Research Questions

1. What factors constituted the political ecology for research evidence production, promotion, and utilization in LAUSD in 2016–17?
2. How can policy mobility and ecology frameworks contribute to an understanding of the politics of research use in the intermediary organization sector for charters in LAUSD?

Methods, Data, and Analysis

Interviews

Between 2016 and 2018, we conducted semi-structured interviews with policymakers, journalists, IO representatives, and university-based researchers in Los Angeles, and with researchers, bloggers, and journalists around the United States. All interviews have been recorded and transcribed. This chapter draws from a subset (N=30) of our overall study's interviews. We embed our questions about research use within the overall questions about the organization's policy goals, ideology, and mission. We ask them for information to talk about partner organizations and individuals that work with them around specific efforts, but also for indications of groups or individuals who hold differing positions or interpretations of research.

Documents

In our larger study, which includes New York City, Denver, New Orleans, and Washington, DC, we are collecting academic and IO-generated policy reports, working papers, and peer-reviewed academic articles on charter schools and Parent Trigger laws. We are examining financial data on foundation spending. We are also conducting systematic searches of the literature on the reforms of interest, using Google Scholar, Web of Knowledge, and Publish or Perish. In addition, we are collecting official policy documents from LAUSD. We have drawn from media reports as important sources, and consider them part of the IO network—particularly since many foundations sponsor media networks in education such as *Education Week*, NPR, and The 74. The media reports in this analysis point to the contentious policy ecology and political context in Los Angeles regarding charter schools, and help to provide the necessary context and detail to help understand the perspectives and insights our respondents shared. In conjunction with interviews, at this phase of our research, media reports provide helpful triangulation and further insights into the city and school district political dynamics.

Observations

We have observed key research promotion and dissemination events, both virtually and in person. These events include board meetings and community-based events, such as rallies or hearings. Our team takes detailed field notes, focusing in particular on references to research, evidence, or anecdotes in support of statements about incentivist reforms. In October 2016, we attended and observed a monthly LAUSD board meeting that primarily concerned debate over several charter school renewals.

Findings

We integrate these multiple data forms into a comprehensive case study that we discuss across four findings (Yin, 2009). Because we theorize that IOs within and across advocacy networks are assuming different roles within policymaking, and that policymaking takes place at multiple political tiers and across different regulatory, legislative, and fiscal interventions, our analysis considers different ways we see such application. We are coding and analyzing our qualitative data using Dedoose software, beginning with a provisional "start list" of deductive codes that we derive from the constructs in our theoretical framework, and findings from the literature on research utilization and policymaking (Miles & Huberman, 1994).

As we code each transcript, document, and field note, we also create inductive codes in order to capture recurring themes that emerge from the data.

Our first research question is about the factors that constitute the political ecology for research evidence production, promotion, and utilization. Our preliminary findings reveal the range of factors that shaped the political context of intermediary organizations and how they brokered research during this period. These include a contested policy about charter schools, and varied interpretations about research evidence about charter school performance; the powerful involvement of outside interests and financial resources in school politics, as well as community pushback on these external influences; as well as continued patterns of traditional interest group and union politics. While there are multiple university-based researchers who have studied LA's incentivist policies, a strong and cohesive research-practice partnership structure—similar to what is evident in Chicago, New York, and New Orleans—involving multiple stakeholders is not yet in place.

Finding 1: Contested Policy on Charter Schools

As enrollments declined during this period, both charter school expansion, and philanthropists' promotion of them was contested. Employing Weaver-Hightower's typology of a policy ecology, the factors in play may be termed *pressures, inputs*, and *consumption* (2008, p. 166). That is, charter school expansion is under financial pressure that is forcing closer examination, via public political discourse, of how resources are employed. Inputs are the money and time expended in the charter sector, and it is being alleged by the union and some board members that there is excessive depletion of resources, particularly in the form of declining enrollments.

School Board Politics

As described earlier, Weaver-Hightower (2008) argues that a policy ecology experiences *entropy* "when an ecology breaks down and becomes disordered" (p. 156). Entropy can lead to *fragmentation*, "wherein ecologies are split or dissected, as when a governmental body … is divided in two" (p. 157). Further, actors in relationship to one another characterize policy ecologies; the relationship can be one of *competition, cooperation, predation*, or *symbiosis* (p. 156). The deep divisions within the LAUSD school board and the contested nature of the school board elections, particularly around the issue of charter schools, highlight fragmented policy ecology and competitive relationships.

The March 2017 school board primaries, which involved only three seats, centered heavily on candidates' positions on charter schools, and, while school board elections across the nation have typically been low-profile affairs, spending on these campaigns has reached unprecedented levels. Candidates opposed to charter schools have drawn financial support primarily from UTLA, which spent about $1.6 million to support its favored candidates. Yet in the open policy ecology that is LAUSD, candidates in favor of charter schools have drawn over $6 million in financial support from non-local groups, including the state-level California Charter Schools Association and an array of state- and national-level donors (Berkshire, 2017; Favot, 2017b; Reckhow et al., 2016). The current board members themselves have split on endorsements—Zimmer, McKenna, and Schmerelson have endorsed Imelda Padilla, while Rodriguez and Ratliff supported Kelly Gonez. Ratliff's endorsement of Gonez came most recently in mid-April, after initially encouraging Padilla to run early on in the race. Ratliff, who did not receive enough votes to make the run-off election for a city council seat, believes that both candidates for her board seat are qualified, but stated that "Gonez seeks to be an independent voice on the school board" and "recognizes the need to be conscientious of potential saturation of charters" (as quoted in Szymanski, 2017b). Non-local actors have also endorsed these candidates. Former Secretary of Education Arne Duncan, in fact, endorsed two charter-friendly candidates, Kelly Gonez and Nick Melvoin, whose opponents, LAUSD graduate and community organizer Imelda Padilla and then-current school board president Steve Zimmer, were supported by UTLA and other local labor groups (Szymanski, 2017a). Gonez and Melvoin were both elected in November of 2017.

Weaver-Hightower (2008) contends that an ecological metaphor allows us to see policy ecologies, like the natural world, as ever changing. Indeed, school board politics are continuously unfolding, especially in light of the upcoming school board elections in May 2017. Yet the contested and fragmented nature of the policy ecology to date signals the existence of what Stone (2001) and other urban politics scholars describe as an unstable regime, wherein diverse stakeholders have been unable to unify around a common policy agenda or goals. As described above, scholars have demonstrated that such fragmented civic coalitions can constrain meaningful and sustained school reform efforts (Ansell et al., 2009; Gold et al., 2007). Although the politics around LAUSD's school board elections continue to evolve, events to date appear to signal ongoing fragmentation.

To understand the political interplay of these factors, it is helpful to first summarize the various competing recent research reports and their claims about charter effects in LAUSD.

Overview of Studies on Charters

There has been a series of research studies and reports recently released on the effects of charter schools in LA. The purpose of sharing these research results is not to determine the rigorousness of research methodology or reliability and validity of results, but rather to contribute to a better understanding of the political context. UTLA, Stanford, UC Berkeley, UCLA, and the ACLU of Southern California conducted the studies described.

The UTLA study was conducted by a national consulting company, MGT of America (MGT), and was released in May 2016. It examined the fiscal impact of independent charter schools on LAUSD and found that independent charter schools are costing LAUSD about $500 million each year (Favot, 2016b). The study had 12 findings (both LA-specific and statewide)—major findings included charter schools not paying a required fee for using LAUSD facilities or co-location with traditional public schools (TPS), and the fiscal impact on students with special needs (MGT, 2016).

As Grace Regullano, research director of the UTLA, explained during our July 2016 interview:

> This is not an anti-charter analysis, this is simply saying, what are the impacts, is this sustainable, and what can we do about it … The sustainable system is extremely important, our research has shown that we were looking at the system as it currently is, is set up to increase costs at the same time decreasing revenues, which is fundamentally not a sustainable model.
>
> *(personal communication, July 15, 2016)*

Alex Caputo-Pearl, head of the UTLA, went further to say, "having unregulated charter growth that ultimately does, as our fiscal impact report shows, it does undermine the broader system, that's not a pathway to sustainability" (personal communication, July 15, 2016).

Shortly after the report was released, an LAUSD internal document was leaked showing that "district staff and others" criticized the study as inaccurate and a diversion from drains on LAUSD's finances that are much larger (Favot, 2016b). The California Charter Schools Association (CCSA) also issued a detailed response calling it "riddled with inaccuracies" (Favot, 2016b).

The Stanford study examined whether charter school students in LAUSD outperformed their counterparts in TPS. Their findings included that a student in an LA charter school typically gains more learning per year than their peer in a TPS—approximately 50 additional days in reading and 79 days in math (CREDO, 2014). Additionally, 13 percent of LA charter schools have reading results "significantly worse than TPS" and 22 percent are underperforming in math (CREDO, 2014, p. 40). The report concluded that there is a balance between the share of underperforming and high-performing charter schools.

Shin, Fuller, and Dauter (2015) also examined variations in student achievement. These researchers differentiated between "conversion," "start-up," and a third model run in LAUSD charter schools and found that compared with start-up charter schools, conversion schools (where TPS campuses were converted to charter status) consistently drew more experienced and credentialed teachers and enrolled students from comparatively advantaged families (p. 1). They also found that overall, charter school students had relatively higher academic performances compared with their peers in TPS, and that students attending a charter school for elementary or middle school outperformed their TPS peers; however, they found no effects for high school students attending a charter school versus a TPS (Shin et al., 2015).

The UCLA study was conducted by Wong et al. (2014) and examined high-performing charter high schools located in low-income neighborhoods in LA in order to determine whether a student's attendance at a high-performing school reduces risky health behaviors and if so, what the primary mechanism is. They found that attendance at a high-performing high school reduced risky health behaviors and was primarily due to improved retention of students and improved academic performance (Wong et al., 2014). Finally, the ACLU of Southern California studied California's charter school enrollment policies to determine the level of equity and found that approximately 253 out of 1,200 California charter schools (over 20 percent) have clearly exclusionary enrollment and retention policies (Leung & Alejandre, 2016). They found this was for a number of reasons including: 1) grades, 2) test scores, 3) denial of students not meeting a minimum English proficiency level, 4) burdensome application/pre-enrollment requirements (such as essays or interviews), 5) discouraging or burdensome requirements for parents/guardians of immigrant students, and 6) parent/guardian volunteer or donation requirements (Leung & Alejandre, 2016, p. 2). The ACLU contends these findings are "likely only the tip of the iceberg" (p. 2).

These reports are being researched, released, and disseminated in a context of diminished research capacity within the system. The research staff has been radically cut in recent years (personal communication, July 15, 2016). A research consortium, the Los Angeles Education Research Initiative (LAERI), has been established with the goal of involving multiple policy and practice stakeholders, but it has not yet focused on choice and charter schools (personal communication, July 15, 2016). Thus, external reports are promulgated without substantial district influence.

Finding 2: Outside Influence

LAUSD's policy ecology is constituted not only by local policy and advocacy actors, but also by external IOs that are working to expand charter schools, and that are using the LAUSD example to promote policy mobility in other settings. Outside influence is evident in the politics of IO's in several ways, from philanthropic efforts to expand charter schools, to connections to national interest groups, to unprecedented spending in the spring 2017 board election cycle.

During the summer of 2015, a proposal written by the Broad Foundation was leaked; it included a $490 million plan to rapidly expand charter schools to serve half of LAUSD students (Blume, 2015a; Blume 2015b; Favot, 2016c, Janofsky, 2015). The reaction was mostly scathing, prompting even the LAUSD board to unanimously vote to oppose it (Favot, 2016c). Out of the aftermath emerged a new organization called Great Public Schools Now (GPSN), which has donors including Broad and the Walton Family Foundation and board members from the same foundations. GPSN's agenda has appeared to backtrack since the original proposal, releasing a plan in 2016 for, "A new, community-centric plan for improving schools across the region—regardless of governance model, curricular orientation or operational platform. This plan is designed to give parents in low-income areas a real choice, real access for their kids, while preserving and augmenting things that are working today" (GPSN, 2016; Tully, 2016).

In June, GPSN announced that it had awarded $4.5 million to its first grant recipients, including a charter school (Equitas Academy), Teach for America, and an after-school program (Heart of LA) (Favot, 2016a). In November 2016, GPSN announced it would award two $20,000 planning grants to replicate successful and quality educational practices used at the Diego Rivera Learning Complex Public Service and King-Drew Senior High Medicine & Science Magnet schools (Blume, 2016). Superintendent King described these grants as an opportunity for LAUSD to "increase the number of high-quality choices for … families within the existing framework of successful district schools," whereas UTLA President Alex Caputo-Pearl declared the grants a "cheap-as-you-can-get publicity stunt" (as quoted in Blume, 2016). In February 2017, GPSN announced approximately $900,000 in grants would be given to six schools and organizations toward teacher retention efforts (Blume, 2017; Favot, 2017a; Hollyday, 2017).

Spending on the LA 2017 Board Races: Blurring of National and Local Interests

Spending and outside influence on the 2017 LAUSD board elections has been unprecedented; $6.7 million was spent for three seats prior to the March 7 primary, with about $5.4 million of that spent by outside labor groups and charter school supporters (Favot, 2017b). This follows similar trends found by Reckhow et al. (2016) that school board elections have evolved from low-profile, low-interest affairs into political contests increasingly influenced by outside donor involvement. Reckhow et al. (2016) study's findings raise important implications for democracy: "If local attention, engagement, and voting are enhanced by national-ized campaigns, the rise of large outside donors in school board elections could support 'new localism,' making local elections more vibrant and relevant, in spite of growing state and national policy leadership" (p. 22–3). On the other hand, "outside donors' policy preferences for education may differ from the preferences of voters in school districts that attract outside donor interest" (p. 23). In all cities, unions were the primary outside contributor early on, but outside donors played a substantially larger role by 2013. Large national donors tended to support pro-reform candidates in all case sites (Denver, Bridgeport, Los Angeles, and New Orleans). These findings bolster the empirical research demonstrating that reform groups aim to counter the political efforts of teachers' unions. These trends were fully apparent in 2017 as well. In addition to unprecedented spending, two Fair Political Practices Complaints (FPPCs) have been filed regarding potential viola-tions by the UTLA of the *Political Reform Act* in their supportive advertisements for Steve Zimmer and Imelda Padilla (Favot, 2017b).

This elections' results led to a runoff on May 16 between Board President Steve Zimmer and Nick Melvoin for District 4, and between Kelly Gonez and Imelda Padilla for District 6. Voter turnout was approximately 21 percent (Favot, 2017c).

Finding 3: Community Pushback and City Politics

Weaver-Hightower (2008, p. 166) introduces two descriptors of policy processes relevant to the current political situation in Los Angeles. Those are "emergence" and "entropy." The former refers to "the appearance of new ecologies when the resources and actors are available for their sustenance," whereas entropy is "the breakdown or disordering of an ecology" (p. 166). We find evidence of both types of processes, with uncertainty and flux about which political interests and/or investments will prevail. For this new dynamic to be understood, it is important to posit how crucial community interests have historically been in education reform efforts in Los Angeles from the 1990s on (Kerchner et al., 2008). For example, beginning in 2001, members from the mostly working-class Latino community of Pico Union, where the public schools long struggled with poor performance and overcrowding, effectively advocated for the development of new small schools. As Martinez and Quartz (2012) note, in Pico Union, strategic alliances "of unprecedented proportions" among community groups, LAUSD, university partners, and their local and national allies were key to sustaining the reform effort (p. 26). As one of our interviewees representing a local education foundation explained:

> You probably want to follow … the thing about Los Angeles, which is a little different than other communities, is the homegrown-ness of community organizing, and community mobilization efforts that have been successful on the education front. So, you know, a few years ago there was a big building campaign, and there was community organizing that really helped on getting schools built in communities where there had not been a school, and there was a need to build a school, and these community organizers really got youth involved, parents involved, the community involved.
>
> *(Personal communication, July 15, 2016)*

Yet as new actors, including education reform, advocacy, and philanthropic organizations, entered the terrain beginning in the early 2000s, LAUSD's policy ecology experienced the emergence process Weaver-Hightower (2008) describes. As these reformers gained influence, stakeholders with longstanding influence in LAUSD, including many community organizations, were sidelined and, in turn, largely uninformed of these emerging actors' reform agendas. As the community foundation leader added:

> Everything we've heard from the Great Public Schools Now people … has been that they fully intend to have dollars allocated for the replication of

successful district schools, public district schools. How that is gonna happen and play out and what it's gonna look like, I don't think anybody has seen details, or heard any details around what that's gonna look like.

(Personal communication, July 15, 2016)

Steve Barr, the founder of Green Dot Public Schools and, for a while, a Los Angeles mayoral candidate in 2016, corroborated this context of LA reforms in a media interview:

L.A.'s a little bit different than almost all of the other cities. All of the reform here has come from the bottom up. I think the problem now is that there are not a lot of activists doing it, it's becoming very donor-driven. So Eli Broad puts out a plan instead of somebody in the field and everyone's got to fit into that plan—it's OK, it's nice that there's support out there, but I think if you go to the troops, they're a little beaten down.

(Quoted in Bermudez, 2016)

These and other events around charter school policy point to the fragility of LAUSD's *civic capacity*, or the broad participation of diverse constituents in the pursuit of a shared education reform agenda (Stone, 2001). Scholars studying urban politics and education note that strong levels of civic capacity are key to mobilizing broad support for a particular reform, in turn maximizing the durability and longevity of the reform (Ansell et al., 2009; Gold et al., 2007; Henig et al., 1999; Reckhow, 2013; Shipps, 2003). Yet civic capacity is difficult to build and maintain. Indeed, studying Philadelphia, Gold et al. (2007) argue that district leaders' privatization agenda constrained civic capacity. Specifically, the private organizations with which the district contracted operated with minimal transparency and opportunity for public input, thus excluding key constituents; these events led to the erosion of public trust in the school district. We see similar dynamics currently unfolding in LAUSD around charter school policy. Indeed, as new entrants to the policy ecology, such as Great Public Schools Now, appear to be making decisions behind closed doors, the public remains relatively uninformed, as the foundation official quoted above describes.

This has led to instances of community pushback, such as during the October 2016 monthly meeting that we observed. During this meeting, the authorization of charter schools and addition of grade levels was considered; throughout the day, the LAUSD board and Superintendent King heard emotional testimonies from students, administrators, and parents from these and other charter schools. Most schools had relatively large groups there in supportive roles, wearing school colors and t-shirts. Cassie Horton, the acting managing director of the CCSA, also appealed to the board for consistency and transparency in charter renewals and denials—that there be no "blindsiding," and citing concern that this may happen during the afternoon meeting. By the afternoon and into the evening, hundreds of supporters stood in line outside LAUSD headquarters for the Magnolia, Celerity, and Citizens of the World charter school networks up for renewals. Supporters chanted and carried posters, reporters interviewed students, parents, and administrators, and police officers ensured the safety of the massive crowd (Fieldnotes, 2016).

This marginalization of community concerns has inspired some to run for vacant seats on the LAUSD School Board. For example, in an interview, a candidate running for the LAUSD board spoke about the necessity of change and leadership coming directly from the community—what she feels would be her biggest asset as a board member. A product of LAUSD schools herself, the candidate described her decision to run as dependent upon two conditions: "Somebody completely unqualified has to be running, and I have to feel like the community is asking me to do it" (Interview, October 19, 2017). Both conditions had been met for her, and she believes her roots and connection to the community has and will continue to enable her to give voice to community concerns that someone from outside the district is unable to do. Additionally, she explained, "there's a big disconnect, in my opinion, with what board members are being told, versus what they see," and accessibility between the community and the board (Interview, October 19, 2016). Yet with certain candidates, it is unclear whether they're giving voice to community concerns, or the concerns of their fundraisers.

In ecology terms, then, there are certainly new resources entering the system, but many members of the policy and community-based groups are unclear whether they are only going to be deployed for charters, or for the district's public schools as a whole. Thus, both research and policy are contested, and often work through traditional institutional politics; it is difficult to say whether there will be a tendency toward entropy, or a breakdown of traditional interests. So far, however, we see evidence of their reassertion, as described below.

The Los Angeles Area Chamber of Commerce held a 2016 meeting at which it flagged the expansion of charters as an economic concern to the system at large. UTLA has spearheaded a new initiative to involve community groups in challenging charters.

Finding 4: Complex Intermediary Sector

Our initial interviews preliminarily findings reveal that intermediary organizations supportive of charter school expansion in LAUSD are frequently working in concert with each other to affect both local and state policy, as well as drawing on the capacity of national-level organizations. These findings are consistent with research demonstrating that out-of-state donors and national philanthropic organizations provide robust financial support to charter school expansion efforts in LAUSD, and that these groups share ties to national organizations supportive of charter schools, including Teach For America, the New Schools Venture Fund, and Democrats for Education Reform (Reckhow, 2013; Reckhow et al., 2016; Scott, 2009) (Figure 12.2).

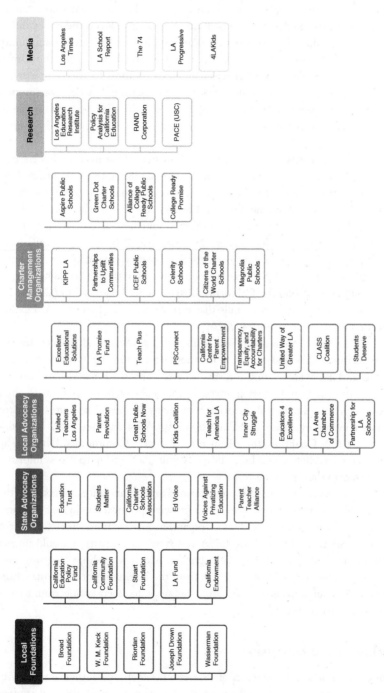

FIGURE 12.2 Intermediary Organization Sector in Los Angeles.

Parent Revolution, for instance, increasingly collaborates with community groups in its efforts to educate parents about choice. Gabe Rose, the policy director, informed us that the organization works with 40 to 50 such community groups, and in their efforts to affect local policy, collaborate with the Urban League, ACLU, and faith-based groups. Parent Revolution has become increasingly active in its attempts to influence various state-level policy decisions around accountability via the federal *Every Student Succeeds Act* (ESSA), with an eye to summative ratings that parents can easily understand (G. Rose, personal communication, July 14, 2016).

During an interview with Green Dot, Annabelle Eliashiv noted their collaboration with Parent Revolution and other similar groups mentioned by Parent Revolution, such as the ACLU. They also mentioned consulting with the Education Trust-West, Students First, and Students Matter at the state level and the Center for American Progress, Third Way, Democrats for Education Reform, the National Charter School Alliance (NCSA), and KIPP at the national level, displaying the wide range of their network ties. Furthermore, they noted relying on the Partnership for LA Schools "to figure out how they're handling things" at the school level and on the California Charter School Association (CCSA) for updates on "any policy, laws or bills that directly impact charters" (A. Eliashiv, personal communication, July 14, 2016).

The CCSA functions as a state and local policy advocate and provides leadership on accountability and resources for member schools. The CCSA also provides data and information on California's charter schools for parents, authorizers, legislators, the press, and other interested groups. As such, in addition to their work with Green Dot, they also partner with many organizations across the state, including Parent Revolution and Education Trust-West. Furthermore, they work with the CLASS Coalition, the Alliance for a Better Community, United Way, Educators for Excellence, and Educational Results Partnership to access information and inform their policy advocacy.

The inter-woven nature of these intermediary organizations allows for the spread of policy ideas and illuminates their growing political savviness. For example, the groups we interviewed used organizational partners like the NCSA and the CCSA to understand the ESSA and how the legislation would impact their work. The NCSA and the CCSA both provided workshops to groups like Green Dot to inform them of the ESSA from the beginning of its construction. Additionally, associations like CCSA are relied upon for their connections to legislators and other policymakers.

Conclusion and Discussion

Although advocates and detractors of charter schools approach their stances with apparent certainty about the effects of charter schools on equity and student achievement, they draw from different sources of evidence to substantiate their positions. Research on the effects of charter schools in Los Angeles was deeply contested during this time period, and the IO sector in Los Angeles and nationally was actively pushing evidence into the political ecology shaping policymaking in the city. UTLA drew on its commissioned study from MGT to substantiate its contention that charters were a massive financial drain on the public school system. The initial period of the study also revealed an evolution of the LAUSD board as a charter oversight body, exemplified by the uncommon denial of charter renewals for three Magnolia Public Schools and two Celerity charter network schools. While far from a large withdrawal of support, this served as an indication that the board was responsive to criticism of the unchecked expansion of charters.

The Los Angeles Area Chamber of Commerce also convened stakeholder meetings in 2016 to discuss concerns about the aggregate fiscal effects of charters on the district system. Our observations and interviews have shown how charter schools are a politically polarizing topic across Los Angeles, and how organizations are using, commissioning, or rejecting research in ways that 1) reinforce their position and 2) reinforce the politically charged nature of charter policy in the district. So, within this policy ecology, research serves to deepen political polarization. Or, to use Weaver-Hightower's terms, research is deployed in ways that facilitate entropy and fragmentation of the policy ecology, as well as competitive, rather than cooperative, relationships among actors.

In May 2018, the LAUSD Board named Austin Beutner as the superintendent in a 5-2 vote. Board members who voted against Beutner's appointment cited reasons such as his lack of education experience and the absence of transparency in a rushed selection process. Beutner, a former investment banker, CEO, editor of the Los Angeles Times, and philanthropist, helped lead the LAUSD Advisory Task Force under Michelle King's leadership of the district.

LAUSD Board member Ref Rodriguez's tenure came to a dramatic end in July 2018, when he plead guilty and resigned from the Board. He was charged with campaign money-laundering the previous fall, stepped down from his newly elected position as Board President, but chose to remain on the Board until his guilty plea. The Board has until the end of September to decide how to fill the now-vacant District 5 seat—Board members can choose to appoint someone to fill the seat for the remainder of Rodriguez's term (until June 2019), call for a special election and leave the seat empty until the election (which would likely be held in March 2019), or appoint someone to fill the seat until a special election is held. The implications of the Board's decision are weighty, as it will determine whether the pro-reform side maintains its majority held prior to Rodriguez's resignation or it swings back. The transparency of the Board's decision, its relationship to its students and families, and how it will affect votes between now and the next election cycle are key considerations.

Drawing on Weaver-Hightower's policy ecology framework, we find that the political debate in LA centers on *pressures*, *inputs*, and *consumption* (2008, p. 166). That is, charter school expansion is financial pressure that is forcing the change of closer examination, via public political discourse, of how resources are deployed. Inputs are the money and time expended in the charter sector, and it is being alleged by the union and some board members that there is excessive depletion of resources, particularly in the form of declining enrollments.

Further, the influx of an unprecedented amount of external financial involvement in the 2017 board elections was a dramatic illustration of how much LA remains important to charter supporters as a national symbol. LAUSD's policy ecology is not a closed system; instead, IOs are intent on promoting evidence on LAUSD charter schools to other settings. Simultaneous with the activities of these new IO's like GPSN, however, we also see the persistence of many of the traditional political patterns of education reform in LA: notably, the concern of community groups and foundations that their voices be heard and their needs consulted.

The nature of philanthropic involvement in charter schools nationally can best be characterized as being in a state of flux. The Broad Foundation, for instance, issued a letter criticizing the proposed Trump education budget for the harm its cuts to programs would inflict on the public school system; however, it was quickly noted that the budget would allocate less to charter schools. It remains to be seen whether and how philanthropies will align themselves with the same charter school policy agenda they have in the past, in light of the overall negative public perceptions of DeVos's privatization goals (Siders, 2017).

Respondents in Los Angeles have also noted that there exists a diminished capacity for research and evaluation at the school district level. Further, while there is one consortium, LAERI, whose goal it is to develop a coordinated research agenda on district initiatives among university-based researchers, the district, and stakeholders, its work has not addressed charter and choice policies as yet. As charter schools continue to occupy a central position in school district politics, this chapter raises questions about how notions of equity get constructed, studied empirically, and promoted in research evidence, blogs, and media. Moreover, our findings point to the continued importance for scholars of the politics of charter school reform to think more broadly about how public and private policy actors are shaping what we know about the reform.

References

Ansell, C., Reckhow, S., & Kelly, A. (2009). How to reform a reform coalition: Outreach, agenda expansion, and brokerage in urban school reform. *Policy Studies Journal*, *37*(4), 717–43.

Au, W. & Ferrare, J. (2014). Sponsors of policy: A network analysis of wealthy elites, their affiliated philanthropies, and charter school reform in Washington State. *Teachers College Record*, *116*(8), 1–24.

Au, W. & Ferrare, J. (2015). *Mapping corporate education reform: Power and policy networks in the neoliberal state*. New York: Routledge.

Ball, S. J. (2012). *Global Education Inc.: New policy networks and the neo-liberal imaginary*. London: Routledge.

Ball, S. & Junemann, C. (2012). *Networks, new governance, and education*. Chicago, IL: The Policy Press.

Berkshire, J. (2017, March 4). Schools of LAst resort. [Web log post]. Retrieved from http://haveyouheardblog.com/schools-of-last-resort/.

Bermudez, C. (2016, April 5). Steve Barr on weighing a mayoral run and what education reform is getting wrong. *LA School Report*. Retrieved from http://laschoolreport.com/steve-barr-on-weighing-a-mayoral-run-and-what-education-reform-is-getting-wrong/.

Blume, H. (2015a, September 21). $490-million plan would put half of LAUSD students in charter schools. *Los Angeles Times*. Retrieved from http://www.latimes.com/local/education/la-me-lausd-charter-20150922-story.html.

Blume, H. (2015b, November 18). Nonprofit is formed to advance charter-school plan in Los Angeles. *Los Angeles Times*. Retrieved from http://www.latimes.com/local/education/la-me-charter-nonprofit-20151118-story.html.

Blume, H. (2016, November 22). Two L.A. schools get grants to clone their success. The amount is small, but the symbolism is huge. *Los Angeles Times*. Retrieved from http://www.latimes.com/local/education/la-me-edu-gpsn-planning-grants-lausd-20161122-story.html.

Blume, H. (2017, February 17). Grants go to charters and a traditional school to help teachers stay on the job. *Los Angeles Times*. Retrieved from http://www.latimes.com/local/lanow/la-me-ed-teacher-retention-grants-20170217-story.html.

Blume, H. & Resmovits, J. (2018, January 5). LAUSD chief Michelle King won't return from medical leave for cancer, plans to retire. *Los Angeles Times*. Retrieved from http://www.latimes.com/local/lanow/la-me-michelle-king-departs-20180105-story.html.

Castillo, E., Lalonde, P., Owens, S., DeBray, E., Scott, J., & Lubienski, C. (2015, April). *E-advocacy among intermediary organizations: Brokering knowledge through blogs*. Paper presented at the annual meeting of the American Educational Research Association, Chicago, IL.

Center for Research on Education Outcomes (2009). *Charter school performance in Louisiana*. Palo Alto, CA: Stanford University.

Center for Research on Education Outcomes (2013). *Charter school performance in Louisiana*. Palo Alto, CA: Stanford University.

Center for Research on Education Outcomes (2014). *Charter school performance in Los Angeles*. Palo Alto, CA: Stanford University.

Chubb, J. E. & Moe, T. M. (1990). *Politics, markets, and America's schools*. Washington, DC: Brookings Institution.

Coleman, J. S. (1997). The design of schools as output-driven organizations. In *Autonomy and choice in context: An international perspective* (pp. 249–70), edited by R. Shapira & P.W. Cookson: Pergamon.

Cucchiara, M. (2013). *Marketing schools, marketing cities*. Chicago: University of Chicago Press.

DeBray, E., Scott, J., Lubienski, C., & Jabbar, H. (2014). Intermediary organizations in charter school policy coalitions: Evidence from New Orleans. *Educational Policy, 28*(2): 175–206.

Davies, H.T. O. & Nutley, S. M. (2008). *Learning more about how research-based knowledge gets used: Guidance in the development of new empirical research*. New York: William T. Grant Foundation.

Favot, S. (2016a, June 16). Great Public Schools Now grants go to Teach for America, charter school and after-school program. *LA School Report*. Retrieved from http://laschoolreport.com/great-public-schools-now-grants-go-to-teach-for-america-charter-school-and-after-school-program/.

Favot, S. (2016b, June 21). Internal document shows LA Unified disputes some findings of UTLA-funded study on charter schools. *LA School Report*. Retrieved from http://laschoolreport.com/internal-document-shows-la-unified-disputes-some-findings-of-utla-funded-study-on-charter-schools/.

Favot, S. (2016c, November 15). Can these two women save thousands of LA students from failing schools? Behind the scenes with Michelle King and Myrna Castrejon. *LA School Report.* Retrieved from http://laschoolreport.com/can-these-two-women-save-thousands-of-la-students-from-failing-schools/.

Favot, S. (2017a, February 17). Fighting teacher burnout: Great Public Schools Now grants aim to retain effective educators. *LA School Report.* Retrieved from http://laschoolreport.com/fighting-teacher-burnout-great-public-schools-now-grants-aim-to-retain-effective-educators/.

Favot, S. (2017b). UTLA campaign supporting Zimmer now under full investigation; outside spending jumps $1 million in a week to $5.4 million. *LA School Report.* Retrieved from http://laschoolreport.com/utla-campaign-supporting-zimmer-now-under-full-investigation-outside-spending-jumps-1-million-in-a-week-to-5-4-million/.

Favot, S. (2017c). Final election results show voter turnout in LA races was 21 percent. *LA School Report.* Retrieved from http://laschoolreport.com/final-election-results-show-voter-turnout-in-la-races-was-21-percent/.

Gold, E., Simon, E., Cucchiara, M., Mitchell, C., & Riffer, M. (2007). *A Philadelphia story: Building civic capacity for school reform in a privatizing system.* Philadelphia, PA: Research for Action.

Great Public Schools Now (2016). *High-quality public schools for Los Angeles students.* Retrieved from Great Public Schools Now website: http://www.greatpublicschoolsnow.org/.

Gunter, H.M. & Mills, C. (2016). Knowledge production and the rise of consultocracy in education policymaking in England. In *The global education industry*, edited by A. Verger, C. Lubienski, & G. Steiner-Khamsi. London: Routledge.

Hacker, J. S. & Pierson, P. (2010). *Winner-take-all politics: How Washington made the rich richer—and turned its back on the middle class.* New York, NY: Simon and Schuster Paperbacks.

Hassel, B. C., Brinson, D., Boast, L., & Kingsland, N. (2012). *New Orleans-style education reform: A guide for cities. lessons learned 2004–2010.* Public Impact and New Schools for New Orleans.

Henig, J. (2013). *The end of exceptionalism: The changing politics of school reform.* Cambridge: Harvard Education Press.

Henig, J. R., Hula, R. C., Orr, M., & Pedescleax, D. (1999). Civic capacity, race, and education in Black-led cities. In *The color of school reform: Race, politics, and the challenge of urban education* (pp. 3–29). Princeton, NJ: Princeton University Press.

Hess, F. M., Palmieri, S., & Scull, J. (2010). *America's best (and worst) cities for school reform: Attracting entrepreneurs and change agents.* Washington, DC: Thomas B. Fordham Institute.

Hodge, E. & Benko, S. (2014). A "common" vision of instruction? An analysis of English/Language Arts professional development materials related to the Common Core State Standards. *English Teaching: Practice and Critique,* 13(1), 169– 96.

Hollyday, K. (2017, February 17). Amid teacher shortage, group aims to keep best educators in the classroom with increased training and independent projects (press release). Retrieved from GPSN website: http://www.greatpublicschoolsnow.org/gpsn_announces_funding_to_help_schools_retain_high_quality_teachers.

Janofsky, M. (2015, September 22). Zimmer accuses Broad charter plan of strategy to 'bring down' LAUSD. *LA School Report.* Retrieved from http://laschoolreport.com/zimmer-accuses-broad-charter-plan-of-strategy-to-bring-down-lausd/.

Kerchner, C. T., Menefee-Libey, D., Mulfinger, L., & Clayton, S. (2008). Learning from L.A.: Institutional change in American public education. Cambridge, MA: Harvard Education Publishing Group.

Kingdon, J. (1995). *Agendas, alternatives, and public policies.* New York: Harper Collins.

Leung, V. & Alejandre, R. H. (2016). *Unequal access: How some California charter schools illegally restrict enrollment.* Retrieved from American Civil Liberties Union of Southern California website: https://www.aclusocal.org/unequal-access/.

McCann, E. & Ward, K. (2013). A multi-disciplinary approach to policy transfer research: Geographies, assemblages, mobilities and mutations. *Policy Studies, 34*(1), 2–18.

McDonnell, L. & Weatherford, S. (2013). Evidence use and the Common Core State Standards movement: From problem definition to policy adoption. *American Journal of Education, 120.*

McGuinn, P. (2012). Fight club: Are advocacy organizations changing the politics of education? *Education Next, 12,* 25–31.

Marsh, J. (2016). The political dynamics of district reform: the form and fate of the Los Angeles Public School Initiative. *Teachers College Record, 118*(9), 1–54

Martinez, R. A. & Quartz, K. H. (2012). Zoned for change: A historical case study of the Belmont Zone of Choice. *Teachers College Record, 114,* 1–40.

MGT of America Consulting, LLC. (2016, May). United Teachers Los Angeles: Fiscal impact of charter schools on LAUSD. Retrieved from http://www.utla.net/sites/default/files/EIR_0.pdf.

Miles, M. & Huberman, A. (1994). *Qualitative data analysis: An expanded sourcebook* (2nd ed.). Thousand Oaks: Sage Publications.

Peck, J. & Theodore, N. (2010). Mobilizing policy: Models, methods, and mutations. *Geoforum, 41,* 169–74.

Orfield, G., Kuscera, J., & Siegel-Hawley, G. (2012). E Pluribus. Separation: Deepening double segregation for more students. Los Angeles: UCLA, The Civil Rights Project/Proyecto Derechos Civiles.

Qi, J. & Levin, B. (2013). Assessing organizational efforts to mobilize research knowledge in education. *Education Policy Analysis Archives, 21*(2), 1–24.

Quinn, R., Tompkins-Stange, M., and Meyerson, D. (2014). Beyond grantmaking: Philanthropic foundations as agents of change and institutional entrepreneurs. *Nonprofit and Voluntary Sector Quarterly, 43*(6): 950–68.

Reardon, S., Grewal, E., Kalogrides, D., & Greenberg, E. (2012). Brown Fades: The end of court-ordered school desegregation and the resegregation of American public schools. *Journal of Policy Analysis and Management, 31,* 876–904.

Reckhow, S. (2013). *Follow the money: How foundation dollars change public school politics.* New York: Oxford University Press.

Reckhow, S. & Tompkins-Stange, M. (2015). "Singing from the same hymnbook" at Gates and Broad. In *The New Education Philanthropy: Politics, Policy, and Reform* (pp. 55–78), edited by Hess, F. & Henig, J. Cambridge, MA: Harvard Education Press.

Reckhow, S., Henig, J. R., Jacobsen, R., & Litt, J. A. (2016). "Outsiders with deep pockets": The nationalization of local school board elections. *Urban Affairs Review,* 1–29. doi:10.1177/1078087416663004

Rogers, J., Lubienski, C., Scott, J., & Welner, K. (2015). Missing the target? The Parent Trigger as a strategy for parental engagement and school reform. *Teachers College Record, 117*(6).

Schneider, A. & Ingram, H. (1997). *Policy design for democracy.* Lawrence: University Press of Kansas.

Scott, J. (2009). The politics of venture philanthropy in charter school policy and advocacy. *Educational Policy, 23*(1), 106–36. doi:10.1177/0895904808328531

Scott, J. & Jabbar, H. (2013). Money and measures: Foundations as knowledge brokers. In *The infrastructure of accountability: Mapping data use and its consequences across the American education system* (pp. 75–92), edited by D. Anagnostopoulos, S. Rutledge, & R. Jacobsen. Cambridge, UK: Harvard Education Press.

Scott, J. & Jabbar, H. (2014). The hub and the spokes: Foundations, intermediary organizations, incentivist reforms, and the politics of research evidence. *Educational Policy*, 1–25.

Scott, J., DeBray, E., Lubienski, C., Lalonde, P., Castillo, E. & Owens, S. (2016). Urban regimes, intermediary organization networks, and research use: Patterns across three school districts. *Peabody Journal of Education*. Retrieved from http://www.tandfonline.com/doi/full/10.1080/0161956X.2016.1264800.

Shaker, P. & Heilman, E. E. (2004). The new common sense of education: Advocacy research versus academic authority. *Teachers College Record, 106*(7), 1444–70.

Shin, H. J., Fuller, B., & Dauter, L. (2015). Differing effects from diverse charter schools: Uneven student selection and achievement growth in Los Angeles. Retrieved from https://gse.berkeley.edu/sites/default/files/docs/FINAL%20Berkeley%20L.A.%20Charter%20Report%20-%20December%202015.pdf.

Shipps, D. (2003). Pulling together: Civic capacity and urban school reform. *American Educational Research Journal, 40*(4), 841–78.

Siders, D. (2017). Democrats link party rivals to DeVos as 2018 fights emerge. *Politico*, April 16, 2017. Retrieved from http://www.politico.com/story/2017/04/pro-charter-democrats-branded-as-trump-devos-allies-237257.

Skocpol, T., Evans, P., & Rueschemeyer, D. (1985). *Bringing the state back in*. New York, NY and Cambridge, UK: Cambridge University Press.

Stone, C. N., Henig, J., Jones, B., & Pierannunzi, C. (2001). *Building civic capacity*. Lawrence, KS: University Press of Kansas.

Szymanski, M. (2017a, March 29). Arne Duncan endorses Melvoin and Gonez in LAUSD races. *LA School Report*. Retrieved from http://laschoolreport.com/just-in-arne-duncan-endorses-melvoin-and-gonez-in-lausd-races/.

Syymanski, M. (2017b, April 12). Monica Ratliff endorses Kelly Gonez as an 'independent voice' to take over her seat. *LA School Report*. Retrieved from http://laschoolreport.com/monica-ratliff-endorses-kelly-gonez-as-an-independent-voice-to-take-over-her-seat/.

Tully, S. (2016, June 16). New plan in L.A. would support all types of public schools, not just charters. *Education Week*. Retrieved from http://blogs.edweek.org/edweek/parentsandthepublic/2016/06/plan_to_expand_la_charter_schools_altered_to_support_all_types_of_public_schools.html.

Walberg, H. J. & Bast, J. L. (2003). *Education and capitalism: How overcoming our fear of markets and economics can improve America's schools*. Stanford, California: Hoover Institution Press.

Weaver-Hightower, M. (2008). An ecology metaphor for educational policy analysis: A call for complexity. *Educational Researcher, 37*(3), 153–67.

Weiss, C. (1980). Knowledge creep and decision accretion. *Knowledge: Creation, Diffusion, Utilization 1*(3), 381–404.

Whitmire, R. (2016). Ed reform battle in Los Angeles: Conflict escalates as charter schools thrive. *Education Next, 16*(4).

Wohlstetter, P. & Houston, D. (2015). Rage against the regime: The reform of education policy in New York City. *Teachers College Record*.

Wong, M. D., Coller, K. M., Dudovitz, R. N., Kennedy, D. P., Buddin, R., Shapiro, M. F., Kataoka, S. H., Brown, A. F., Tseng, C., Bergman, P., & Chung, P. J. (2014). Successful schools and risky behaviors among low-income adolescents. *Pediatrics, 134*(2), 389–96.

Yin, R. K. (2009). Case study research: Design and methods. Thousand Oaks, CA: Sage Publications.

13

SELF-GOVERNING SCHOOLS, PARENTAL CHOICE, AND THE PUBLIC INTEREST

Helen F. Ladd

In the early twentieth century, the primary goal of U.S. education policy was to provide mass education to prepare workers, including large numbers of immigrants, for an industrial economy. Following the managerial tenets of Frederick Winslow Taylor, policymakers built the system around the concept that one size school fits all children. In addition, to promote efficiencies in the planning and use of school facilities, they typically assigned students to the school in the neighborhood in which they lived. One size fits all simply meant that the local school district would establish similar policies and funding across schools, with little operational flexibility for variation at the school level and limited attention to the mix of students in the school. Of course, even if they had access to the same funding, schools in wealthy neighborhoods were often able to offer higher quality schooling than those in low income neighborhoods because they were able to attract higher quality teachers and because children from higher income families are typically easier to teach than their less advantaged peers.

In recent decades, with the growth of a more complex economic system, policymakers have increasingly recognized the potential benefits of giving schools flexibility to manage their own operations. That flexibility initially took the form of site-based management within traditional public schools and more recently has taken the form in many U.S. states of self-governing charter schools operated by non-governmental organizations with their own boards of directors. In addition, parents have increasingly been given more choice over the school their child attends. Affluent families have always enjoyed the freedom to choose a school through their choice of residential neighborhood, but less affluent families have been more restricted in their residential and schooling decisions. The expansion of parental choice—whether in the form of magnet schools, multiple options among traditional public schools either within or across districts, charter schools, or publicly funded vouchers for use in private schools—serves to break the link between a family's neighborhood of residence and the child's school.

Because of the significant private benefits of education to the individuals who receive it, the combination of self-governing schools and expanded parental choice of schools greatly exacerbates the challenges that education policymakers face in promoting the public, or shared, interest in education. It is this shared interest that justifies public funding for schooling and laws requiring all children to attend school.

Symbiotic Relationship of Self-Governing Schools and Parental Choice

A major argument for self-governing schools is that school personnel are in a better position to understand and respond to the needs of their students than are more distant policymakers at the district or the state level. By analogy to separate plants or outlets within a private sector company, it makes sense to locate operating responsibility as close to the ground as possible in order to promote the most productive use of the available resources. Local managers can respond flexibly and quickly to particular challenges that arise at the local level.

In the education context, the case for self-governance often extends beyond productive efficiency to responsiveness to local interests in education, interests that may differ across local communities. One community, for example, may be most interested in the development of the academic skills necessary for pursuit of a college degree and another in the balance between academics and other activities such as sports or vocational programs. Similarly, a community of African American or Hispanic families might want somewhat different things from their local school than a community of White families. As long as the average preferences of members of local school communities differ one from another, self-governing schools have the potential to generate educational benefits—a fact that holds independently of whether parents are allowed to choose a school other than their assigned school. At the same time, once schools are empowered to differentiate their offerings, it is hard to defend a policy of assigning children to specific neighborhood schools if other schools would provide a better educational fit for the particular child. Consequently, policymakers typically combine self-governance of schools with expanded parental choice of school. U.S. charter schools are illustrative. States that enable charter schools give them substantial operating autonomy, but at the same time make them schools of choice in the sense that no children are assigned to them. Instead, families have to choose to enroll their child in a charter school.

The goal of providing greater choice of school for parents also logically leads to a symbiotic relationship between choice and self-governing schools. Among the various justifications for supporting expanded parental choice of school is the expectation that parents will use that flexibility to choose schools whose offerings are better matched to the educational needs or preferences of their children than otherwise would be the case. If the only difference among schools is the socio-economic status of the students they serve, parental choice will inevitably foster inequality. If schools are empowered to differentiate themselves one from another through the programs they offer, however, parental choice has more potential to improve the educational fit. Moreover, when combined with school autonomy, parental choice may induce schools to operate more efficiently than they otherwise would as they try to attract students by responding to parental demands. In sum, for parental choice to work well, and not simply to promote inequality, schools must have significant autonomy over their operations so that they can differentiate their programs and offer them in an efficient manner. In sum, parental choice and school autonomy go together.

The Private and Public, or Collective, Interests in Education

Schooling clearly generates benefits for the children who receive the education and their families. These benefits, which are often referred to as private benefits, are in the form of both consumption and returns on investment. The children themselves benefit from being in a safe, engaging, and potentially enjoyable school environment and their parents benefit from avoiding child care expenses and obtaining satisfaction from their children's development. Long-run returns on investment in education come in the form of access to better jobs with high wages, more opportunities for advancement, and lower rates of unemployment. In addition to these labor market returns, educated individuals tend to have better health, to be more civically engaged, and to have more fulfilling lives (Haveman & Wolfe, 1984; Oreopoulos & Salvanes, 2009. These private benefits—both the consumption and the investment benefits—can also be categorized as intrinsic or extrinsic. Intrinsic benefits arise when education is valued for its own sake such as the pleasure of being able to solve a complex problem or appreciate artistic expression, and extrinsic benefits arise when education serves as an instrument for the attainment of other valued outcomes such as the potential for the recipients of education to seek higher paying jobs and fulfilling careers than would otherwise be possible. Regardless of the classification, it is clear that education provides a variety of different types of private benefits, many of which accrue long after the students have been in school.

The benefits to schooling, however, accrue to more than just the child and the child's parents. Hence, the public interest in education is not simply the sum of the private benefits (Levin, 1987). Among the public benefits of schooling are short-run benefits for others that arise from keeping idle children off the streets and away from crime or other antisocial behaviors, and the longer-run benefits of having an educated citizenry capable of participating effectively in the democratic system and a workforce that is productive and innovative. These longer-run benefits accrue not only to the residents of the local community in which the children live, but also to the broader society. Low educational investments in students in one jurisdiction have spillovers to other jurisdictions because people move across jurisdictions, citizens participate in the political life of the nation as well as that of their local community, and the productivity of one geographic area of the country can affect overall productivity.

Another public or collective interest takes a different form. Although it is individuals who have interests, such interests become collective when they are shared. Most people, I suspect, would agree that as a society, we have a shared interest in providing all children, regardless of the income or inclinations of their parents, an opportunity to flourish. After all, the fact that a child is growing up in a low income or dysfunctional family is not the child's fault, nor can the child do anything about it. Given the importance of education to a child's life chances, there is a collective interest in assuring that all children have access to a quality education. In addition, we all have a shared interest in raising children to treat other children as equals.[1] Regarding others as equals does not require that we care about strangers as much as we do about our family members or ourselves. Nor does it rule out judgments that people are unequal with respect to attributes like strength, intelligence, or virtue. It means simply that we treat all people with dignity and as moral equals. In the U.S. context, treating others as equals is particularly salient with respect to race. The experience of slights grounded in assumptions of racial superiority—as also with gender, sexuality, or physical or mental abilities—undermines the self-respect and self-confidence of the slighted, making it harder for them to flourish. The impact is worse if the slighted themselves share the attitude that they are inferior, or, while not sharing it, are nonetheless disposed to accept the slights as their due. What this capacity implies for education policy may differ across cultures. For example, given the U.S. history of slavery and Jim Crow laws, the Brown v. Board pronouncement that racially separate schools are not equal provides the basis for a collective U.S. interest in avoiding racially segregated schools.

Importantly, families and their children have a strong and legitimate interest in the quality of the education that the children receive. That is, they have strong private interests. Although the collective interests in high quality education for all students may be equally or perhaps more important overall—and are what justify public funding and making schools compulsory—they are typically far less salient to individual families than are the private interests. It is this imbalance that creates the challenge of promoting the public interest in the context of self-governing schools and parental choice.

Illustrative Example of the Challenges: Durham Public Schools and the Growth of Charter Schools

The tension between the private and public interests in education are not unique to the U.S. but arise in many countries in a variety of forms. In several prior books and articles, I have described the tensions and policy efforts to promote the public interest in New Zealand, the Netherlands, and England. Here I focus only on charter schools which represent one of the most common and fastest growing forms of self-governing schools in the United States. In this section, I use the growth of charter schools in my home county of Durham, North Carolina, to illustrate the challenges that arise in protecting the public interest with this form of self-governance and parental choice. In the following section, I turn to efforts around the country to address those challenges through the development of compacts.

With its total population of 263,000, Durham County, one of 100 counties in the southern state of North Carolina, has historically had to grapple with issues of race, and now is confronted with new challenges posed by the growth of charter schools. Until the early 1990s, the county's schools were split into two districts, a virtually all-Black city district and a far whiter county district. At that time, strong city leadership consolidated the two into the current countywide district known as the Durham Public Schools (DPS), with the goal of providing a sounder educational basis for countywide economic development. The current school population is 50 percent Black, 25 percent Hispanic, and about 20 percent White. In an effort to keep White students in the school system which has been experiencing moderate growth in recent years, DPS has provided various forms of choice for parents in the form of magnet and year-round schools and has, in practice, had a flexible transfer policy that often enabled parents to opt out of their assigned schools.

The situation is now changing because of state legislation in 1996 that enabled 100 charter schools to be established throughout the state, with the State Board of Education as the sole authorizer. The cap of 100 schools remained in place until 2011 at which time a conservative newly elected Republican Legislature eliminated the cap in part as a means of assuring the state would be eligible for $400 million in federal aid through the competitive Race to the Top Program. Since then the number of applications for charter schools has grown dramatically. As of the 2015–16 school year, 149 charter schools were operating throughout the state with additional charters approved for the following year. Durham County has proven to be a popular location for charter school operators partly because of perceived concerns about the low performance of its many disadvantaged students in the public school system and partly because the county relatively generously supplements state funding for schools with county-raised tax revenue. Such funding is appealing to charter operators who receive the average per-pupil funding available to the students based on the district in which they live. As of 2015/16, the county had 13 charter schools serving 15 percent of the student population, a proportion that could easily rise significantly in the next few years as the state approves more charter schools.

The emergence of charter schools poses multiple challenges to the public interest in Durham. The first is a fiscal challenge. As students opt out of the traditional public schools in favor of charters, the traditional school system has to transfer funds to the charter schools. That would not pose a fiscal problem for the DPS if it were able to reduce its own spending in line with the loss of students. In fact, though, that is not possible. Some of its costs, such as school facilities or the infrastructure needed to serve students with special needs, are fixed in the short run and are not easy to cut. Moreover, in any case, even if it were feasible to reduce them in proportion to the loss of students, the school system would not be in a position to do so because of its responsibility for assuring a school for every student in the district. The problem here is that students who opt of the public school system for a charter school may need to return to the traditional public system either because the charter school is not a good fit for them or because the charter school itself shuts down. As a result the traditional system has to maintain the flexibility to assure places for them, a responsibility that does not extend to the charter schools.

In addition, charters typically serve lower proportions of the most expensive-to-educate students, such as students with the more serious forms of special needs or from economically disadvantaged families. Although some charters specifically orient their programs to such students, others make it difficult for disadvantaged students to enroll by not providing transportation or not offering subsidized lunch programs. Hence, while the district transfers funds to the charters based on average per pupil funding, it is left with a group of students who require above-average spending. Further, whenever the charter schools attract students who otherwise would have attended private schools, they impose new costs on the district. A recent careful analysis of the current fiscal burden placed on the Durham public schools is about $500–$700 per traditional public school student, although the precise amount varies depending on the assumptions made (Ladd & Singleton, 2017).

Another challenge to the public interest arises because the growth of charter schools interferes with the ability of the district to plan for facilities and programs. Recall that the State Board of Education is the sole authorizer of charters. Although the districts never had a lot of input into the process, recent legislation eliminated completely any statements from them about the potential impact of new charter schools on their operations. In the past, DPS could make reasonable projections about the size of the public school population and could plan facilities and programs accordingly. Planning is essential with respect to facilities because of the lead time needed to assure their completion in a timely manner. Many investments, such as the development of sophisticated science programs within high schools, also require long-term planning. As more students opt out of the traditional public schools for charter schools, DPS is left in the situation of not knowing how many students it will need to serve and how best to meet their needs. The 2012 establishment of a science-tech charter school in nearby Research Triangle Park illustrates the problem. Though the new charter school may be great for the students who attend it, few of whom are likely be disadvantaged, it interfered with the District's development of a major new science-tech program within an historically African American high school located near the Research Triangle Park. Presumably the public interest would have been better served if the District had had a greater role in the establishment of and location of new charter schools.

A third threat to the public interest is the impact of charter schools on the racial segregation of the schools in Durham. Ever since the merger of the city and county school districts in the early 1990s, the School Board has worked hard to integrate the schools, albeit not fully successfully given the large proportion of African Americans and Hispanics in the county and the Board's relatively lenient transfer policy. As of the 2011–12 school year, 41 percent of the students in traditional public schools were in schools that were almost exclusively minority (defined as having 90–100 percent nonwhite students). Moreover, only 1.4 percent were in schools in which the proportion of nonwhite students was less than 30 percent. Contrast that, however, with the distribution of charter school students in that same year. Among them, an even higher percentage (51 percent) were in schools with almost no White students, and 32 percent were in schools that had less than 30 percent nonwhite students.

This racial bifurcation of the charter schools reflects a combination of parental preferences and the offerings of the charter schools. In recent work based on the choices of all North Carolina families who switched their child from a traditional public school to a charter school in the 2014–15 school year, my coauthors and I have documented that minority families prefer charter schools that are majority minority, while White parents prefer predominantly White charters (Ladd et al., 2018). In addition, we found that in making their choices minority parents—and especially those with low family income, but not White families—placed positive values on whether the charter school provided transportation services and subsidized lunches.[2] This asymmetry of parental preferences means that charter schools that aim for an even mix of Black and White students are likely to tip toward being exclusively Black, while those that are primarily White will remain so. Moreover, within Durham, the charter schools increasingly appear to be serving as a means for White families to avoid the heavily non-White traditional public schools.

One logical way to address these challenges would be to try to get the two sectors—the charter sector and the traditional public school sector—to collaborate in the interests of serving all children in the county rather than competing with each other for students and the funding that follows them. That would mean, among other things, that the charter schools would have to take more responsibility for educating their fair share of expensive-to-educate students and the District would have to make a number of services, such as professional development or transportation, available to the charter schools, presumably for a fee. A few years ago, the chair of the DPS School Board supported a proposal to set up a task force of representatives from the board and the charter schools to develop a common enrollment system, a common school accountability framework, and a shared transportation and meal program. In addition, the task force was to be charged with establishing a common lobbying effort at the state level directed toward giving the local district more control over the charter schools within the district. (Thigpen, 2014) Collaboration of this type, however, turned out to be very difficult and it was not successful in Durham.

It is difficult in part because of the hostility and antagonism between the two types of schools and also because, in contrast to the traditional public schools which are organized under a single school board, the charter schools are separate entities not organized into a coherent unit. Even if representatives of the two types of schools could be brought together, some of the charters would have limited incentive to participate. As self-governing schools, they would have little incentive to put the general public interest above the more narrow private interests of many of the families they serve. That is particularly true for charter schools serving relatively advantaged students whose parents may have chosen the charter school specifically because it was not serving large numbers of disadvantaged students. For other charters, it could mean subjecting themselves to more regulations or bureaucratic decision-making that would interfere with their governing philosophy or with the financial or other interests of their sponsors.

One of the few potential benefits to the existing charters comes from the possibility that the resulting agreement might somehow help to slow the entry of new charter schools into the county that would otherwise dilute the demand for their schools. At the same time the potential for new charter schools to enter the Durham market, as is quite likely during the next few years, greatly reduces the incentive for the established schools to participate in agreements that might reduce their ability to compete successfully with new charters not bound by the same agreements.

Are Cross-Sector Compacts the Solution?

In contrast to Durham, more than 20 other cities have managed to put together some form of cross-sector compact designed to encourage schools of different types within a district to work together toward common ends.

Sixteen of them were supported by a 2010 initiative funded by the Gates Foundation. Bolstered by $100,000 grants, each city signed a formal compact with its charter schools to undertake a variety of cooperative activities. Despite some noteworthy progress in a few places in a few activities, a 2013 interim report showed limited progress in most of the compact cities (Yatsko et al., 2013). Among the 15 districts that had agreed to set up shared service agreements, for example, only three had made progress. Similarly, among the 14 districts that had agreed to improve access to and the quality of special education services, only five had made significant progress, and among the eight districts that had agreed to implement a common and coordinated enrollment system only four had made progress.

Despite this limited success, the Gates Foundation supported seven cities with large multimillion dollar grants in 2012. The funded compacts are in Boston,

Denver, Hartford, New Orleans New York, Philadelphia and Spring Branch (TX).[3] The goal of these Gates-funded compacts is to increase the supply of high quality schools and to raise student achievement throughout the district by supporting cross-sector activities of two types. One type is collaborative cross-sector partnerships for schools or individuals with the goal of sharing best practices and improving the quality of education. The other is district-wide collaborative activities or policies designed to ensure greater equity for schools and students. Such activities might include common enrollment systems, uniform accountability metrics, and efforts to promote a more even distribution of special needs students across sectors (Tuttle et al., 2016, Figure 2.1, p. 3). Both types of activities are intended, among other things, to reduce the distrust between district and charter schools that can interfere with the education of children.

Determining the overall effectiveness of these or other compacts is difficult because compacts take different forms in different cities. All I can do here is to draw on the existing descriptive and analytical work of others to make a few observations related to their progress in promoting the public interest in education.

The most careful empirical work is a 2016 Mathematica research report on the seven Gates-funded compacts, although that study focuses only on the partnership activities to the exclusion of the community-wide activities (Tuttle et al., 2016). In addition, studies by the Center for Reinventing Public Education (CRPE) and other researchers or reports from individual compacts are also available. The Denver compact is more developed than others and has received the most attention. That city is of particular interest to policy analysts who support the concept of a "portfolio district," that is, one that delivers education through a portfolio of district and charter schools. In Denver, the public school system is the sole authorizer of charters (which serve about 17 percent of the district students) and for many years, the leadership of the school board has embraced charters and promoted the compact approach. A distinctive element of the Denver model is the use of an enhanced cross-sector accountability system to shut down low performing schools in favor of schools deemed to be more effective, many of which are charter schools. As of 2016, CRPE labeled the Denver compact "mature" (CRPE, 2016).

Cross-Sector Partnership Activities

The 2016 evaluation of the Gates-funded compacts concludes that compacts have successfully promoted cross-sector school and individual partnerships and provides evidence that such activities have successfully transferred some effective practices from one sector to another, and in some cases improved participant attitudes toward the other sector. At the same time, though, the evaluators conclude that the scope and impact of such activities has been small and limited to the small number of direct participants. In Boston, for example, only six schools participated in school partnership activities, and in Spring Branch only four. Denver had the most school partnership activity, with 25 schools participating. (Tuttle et al., 2016, p. 9). Other cross-sector collaborations at the individual or school level such as teacher coaching and leadership development activities, though successful in some, were similarly limited in most compact cities. Based on surveys and interviews of participants, the evaluators identified time and resource constraints among the barriers to greater collaboration. Significantly though, they concluded that one of the most notable barriers to collaboration was the competitive environment. In partieular, many interviewees found it difficult to collaborate in an environment in which they viewed schools as competing for a finite level of resources, students, and facilities (Tuttle et al., 2016, p. 25). Given that competition is a driving force behind the growth of the charter sector and the success of individual charter schools, this finding does not bode well for the expansion of collaborative partnerships in the context of districts with large and growing numbers of charter schools.

District-Wide Activities to Promote Equity and Other Community Goals

Some of the compacts have worked to develop district-wide policies in pursuit of equity. Despite some successes, doing so has been difficult largely because of some of the structural differences described above for Durham. The compact brings together on the one side a group of traditional public schools that are all part of a single organization and single leadership and on the other a set of more autonomous charter schools or charter school chains that have individually agreed to participate in the compact. In compact meetings, charter school representatives cannot always speak on behalf of the other charter school compact members, much less those who chose not to join the compact, who have their own interests and concerns. In some cases, policies that may work well for some of the larger and more effective charter chains may work to the disadvantage of other charter schools. In Denver, for example, top charters were initially given access to Denver Public School facilities in return for serving more special education students. That approach worked well for the favored charters but not for those who were left out.

One of the most logical district-wide policies for promoting equity across schools would seem to be common enrollment systems and aligned transportation systems. A fully developed common enrollment system would include: a common calendar for applications, acceptances and registration; common application materials; a centralized matching mechanism with each child allocated to a specific school; and comprehensive information for families (Gross & Campbell, 2017). Only a few cities, such as Denver and New Orleans, have achieved such a system while some, such as Boston, have adopted some of the elements such as a common calendar for district and charter schools.

By providing a simpler and more transparent system for families to apply and enroll in specific schools. a common enrollment system has the potential to generate social benefits in the form of more equal access to all schools. An early study of Denver's common enrollment system, for example, showed that it increased the share of disadvantaged students in charter schools (Winters, 2015). At the same time, because the quality of schools often differs across areas of a city, a common enrollment system may disappoint some parents for whom the enrollment system raised hopes but who are not able to access the higher quality schools.

Despite their potential social benefits, such systems are often difficult to enact because they impose significant costs on both of the sectors (Gross and Campbell, 2017) By participating in a common enrollment system, for example, individual charter schools give up control over some of the strategies that they would otherwise use to give them a competitive advantage. These strategies include control over the timing of their application processes, and over recruiting methods and messaging to families that help them attract more motivated students and to minimize their share of expensive-to-educate students. District schools also give up something of value, namely some protection from parents easily opting out of their zoned (assigned) neighborhood school. The danger of such opting out for district schools is that they may lose students from the more engaged families, with the result that they may be shut down, as many district schools have been, for example, in Denver, to the consternation of many families.

Given these potential costs, evidence suggests that establishing such a system requires significant stakeholder engagement over a period of time and strong leadership (Gross & Campbell, 2017). Denver's ability to introduce a common enrollment system most likely reflects the proactive role of its school superintendent and New Orleans' ability the fact that almost all of the city's schools were charter schools under the control of the state, with few district schools. In both cities, the decision of a few charters to opt out of participating, which they can do because they are self-governing, weakens somewhat the effectiveness of the common system.

Although the Boston compact takes credit for introducing a common set of application deadlines for district and charter schools, which permitted a more aligned transportation system that serves children in both district and charter schools, the city has not gone the next step of implementing a common cross-sector enrollment system. Among other things, that complicates planning for its transportation system to the extent that many children continue to register in multiple schools before they decide on a final school and forces the transportation department to make costly and inconvenient changes to bus routes in the early fall.

The verdict on cross-sector compacts as a solution to the tension between public and private interests in an environment of self-governing schools and parental choice is still out. Although some cities have demonstrated successes in some specific policy areas (Whitmire, 2014; Tuttle et al., 2016), many have found it difficult to make substantial progress in bringing the two sectors together

(Education Counsel, 2017). Even in Denver, it is not clear what the future will bring, particularly with the end of Gates funding, and the eventual departure of the current superintendent. The compacts do not by themselves solve the fundamental challenge of promoting community-wide public interests in the context of competition among schools.

Concluding Discussion

This chapter does not provide a thorough overview or evaluation of self-governing schools and parental choice. Instead, the more limited—but highly policy relevant—purpose is to draw attention to some of the conflicts between pursuit of those policies and the public interest. Such conflicts arise because of the large and salient individual benefits of education that accrue to individuals relative to the potentially large—but far less salient to individual families or to the operators of individual schools—public benefits that justify the public funding of schools and making it compulsory. The existence of such conflicts need not imply that policymakers should completely avoid policies such as expanded parental choice and school autonomy. Instead, it means that they need to use caution in moving forward with policy initiatives of this type, and to incorporate mechanisms and provisions specifically designed to promote the public interest.

Useful provisions might include, for example, a system-wide accountability program that focuses attention on the internal school process and practices, including admission practices, of each school; extra funding and support for schools serving large proportions of disadvantaged students; and district-wide provision of services such as transportation, special education services, and professional development to take advantage of economies of scale. In addition, the provisions might include controls or limits on the exercise of choice by parents to keep schools from becoming more segregated than is consistent with the public interest. In district-based systems in which a higher level unit authorizes the charters, mechanisms for each district to provide input into the types and locations of new self-governing schools would be desirable. Such mechanisms would help the district foster a single coherent, but flexible, school system that addresses the needs of all the district's children.

Although I have not directly discussed voucher programs—that is, programs that provide public funding for privately operated schools—the reader would be correct in inferring that vouchers would generate even greater threats to the public interest than the charter schools described here. That follows first because of the extreme difficulty of holding individual schools, which are privately owned and operated, accountable for public purposes. Many, for example, may not even be willing to report how they spend the public dollars. In addition, depending on the size of the vouchers and the scale of the program, voucher programs may well generate even greater pressures for large concentrations of disadvantaged students.

If the program is large, the concentrations may emerge in the traditional public schools. Otherwise, or in addition, they may occur in low-quality private schools established primarily to take advantage of the public funding. Further, given that private schools are likely to refuse to give up their control over whom they accept, what starts out as parental choice among private schools is even more likely to morph into a system in which the schools are choosing which publicly funded students they want to enroll. Finally, any difficulties of the type discussed above associated with getting charter schools to work collaboratively with traditional public schools would undoubtedly be magnified in the context of private schools.

In sum, the challenge for education policymakers inclined to move policy in the direction of self-governing schools and expanded parental choice of school is to keep their eyes on the public or collective interest in education. In the natural pursuit of their own self-interest, families and self-governing schools will look out for their own private interests. If the education policymakers do not watch out for the public interest, who will?

Notes

1 Brighouse, Ladd, Loeb, and Swift (2018) explicitly draw attention to this benefit of education in their elaboration of "educational goods", which they define as the knowledge, skills, attitudes, and dispositions than enable an individual to flourish and to contribute to the flourishing of others.
2 Charter schools in North Carolina are not required to provide either of these services. While some do provide them, many others, especially those serving economically advantaged students do not.
3 In most cases the compacts are between traditional public schools and charter schools, but in Boston they also include Catholic schools.

References

Brighouse, M. H., Ladd, H. F., Loeb, S., & Swift, A. (2018). *Educational goods: Values, evidence and decision-making*. University of Chicago Press.

Center for Reinventing Public Education (CRPE) (2016). *Denver district-collaboration compact, 2016 city summary*.

Education Counsel (2017). Cross-sector collaboration case studies: Preliminary research findings for the DC cross-sector collaboration task force meeting. (working draft 3.17.16).

Gross, B. & Campbell, C. (2017). *A guide to unifying enrollment: The what, why, and how for those considering it*. Center for Reinventing Public Education. May.

Haveman, R. H. & Wolfe, B. (1984). Schooling and economic well-being: The role of non-market effects. *Journal of Human Resources, 19*(3), 377–407.

Ladd, H. F. & Singleton, J. (2017). The fiscal externalities of charter schools: Evidence from North Carolina. SSRI working paper. November.

Ladd, H. F., Clotfelter, C., Hemelt, S., & Turaeva, M. (2018). Choosing charter schools in North Carolina: What do parents value? Working paper in progress.

Levin, H. M. (1987). Education as a public and private good. *Journal of Policy Analysis and Management, 6*(4), 628–41.

Oreopoulos, P. & Salvanes, K. G. (2009). How large are returns to schooling? Hint: Money isn't everything. NBER working paper 15339. September.

Thigpen, M. (2014). Promising strategies for partnership: Can Durham district and charter schools collaborate to improve opportunities for all children. Master's thesis, Sanford School of Public Policy, Duke University.

Tuttle, C., McCullough, M., Richaman, S., Booker, K., Burnett, A., Keating, B., & Cavanaugh, M. (2016). Mathematical policy research report. August.

Whitmire, R. (2014). Inside successful district-charter compacts. *Education Next, 14,* 42–8.

Winters, M. A. (2015). *Narrowing the charter–enrollment gap: Denver's common–enrollment system.* Civic Report. Manhattan Institute.

Yatsko, S., Nelson, E. C., & Lake, R. (2013). *District/charter collaboration compact; Interim report.* Center for Reinventing Public Education. June.

EDITOR BIOS

Mark Berends is a professor of sociology at the University of Notre Dame, where he directs the Center for Research on Educational Opportunity. Dr. Berends' research focuses on the effects of school organization and classroom instruction on student achievement, and he has written extensively on school choice, educational reform, and achievement gaps. Dr. Berends earned his Ph.D. in sociology from the University of Wisconsin-Madison.

R. Joseph Waddington is an assistant professor in the Department of Educational Policy Studies and Evaluation at the University of Kentucky's College of Education. In his research, Dr. Waddington quantitatively studies school choice programs and policies, with a focus on the effectiveness of charter schools and school voucher programs. Dr. Waddington earned his Ph.D. in educational studies and his M.A. in statistics from the University of Michigan.

John Schoenig is the senior director of Teacher Formation and Educational Policy for the Alliance for Catholic Education (ACE) at the University of Notre Dame. A former ACE teacher himself, Mr. Schoenig now leads ACE's Teaching Fellows Program and Program for Educational Access. Mr. Schoenig earned his M.Ed. at the University of Notre Dame and his J.D. at Notre Dame Law School.

CONTRIBUTOR BIOS

EDITOR BIOS

Megan Austin is a researcher at the American Institutes for Research (AIR). Dr. Austin's research focuses on how educational policies and schools' organizational responses to policy shape student outcomes. Dr. Austin earned her Ph.D. in sociology at the University of Notre Dame.

Julian R. Betts is a professor in the Department of Economics at the University of California, San Diego and a research associate at the National Bureau of Economic Research. Dr. Betts studies the economics of education and has written extensively on the link between measures of public school spending and student outcomes. Dr. Betts earned his Ph.D. in economics from Queen's University at Kingston in Ontario, Canada.

Marisa Cannata is a research associate professor in the Department of Leadership, Policy, and Organizations at Vanderbilt University's Peabody College and the director of the National Center on Scaling Up Effective Schools. Dr. Cannata studies the organizational and social conditions that shape the work experiences of teachers, including teacher hiring and career decisions, professional climate, and teacher evaluation. She earned her Ph.D. in educational policy from Michigan State University.

Elise Castillo is a policy, organizations, measurement, and evaluation doctoral candidate in the Graduate School of Education at the University of California, Berkley. A former middle school and high school English teacher, Ms. Castillo now studies the political and social dimensions of public education policymaking, with a focus on market-oriented education reforms. Ms. Castillo holds an M.S. in teaching from Pace University and an M.A. in educational policy from the University of California, Berkley.

Elizabeth DeBray is a professor in the Department of Lifelong Education, Administration, and Policy at the University of Georgia College of Education and a fellow at the University of Colorado's National Education Policy Center. Her research interests include school desegregation, compensatory education, and the use of research evidence in policymaking. Dr. DeBray earned her Ed.D. in Administration, Planning, and Social Policy from Harvard University.

Anna J. Egalite is an assistant professor in the Department of Educational Leadership, Policy, and Human Development in the College of Education at North Carolina State University. Dr. Egalite's research focuses on the evaluation of education policies and programs intended to close racial and economic achievement gaps. She earned her Ph.D. in education policy from the University of Arkansas.

Philip M. Gleason is a senior fellow at Mathematica Policy Research, where he also serves as associate director of human services research. Dr. Gleason's research interests include charter schools and school choice, evaluation design and methodological issues, and federal nutrition programs. He earned his Ph.D. in economics from the University of Wisconsin, Madison.

Ellen B. Goldring is a professor of educational policy and leadership and the Patricia and Rodes Hart Chair of the Department of Leadership, Policy, and Organizations at Vanderbilt University's Peabody College. Dr. Goldring studies the intersection of education policy and school improvement, with an emphasis on educational leadership. She earned her Ph.D. in education from the University of Chicago.

Johanna Hanley is an educational administration and policy doctoral candidate at the University of Georgia College of Education. Her research interests include K–12 educational policy and politics, locally elected school boards, school choice, and educational equity and opportunity. She earned her M.Ed. in curriculum and instruction from the University of Virginia's Curry School of Education.

Samantha L. Hedges is a doctoral candidate in the Department of Educational Leadership and Policy Studies at the Indiana University School of Education. Her research interests include the politics of education, K–12 educational philanthropy, and the role of constituent voices in educational policymaking. She holds a master's degree in social work from the University of Illinois at Chicago.

Collin Hitt is an assistant professor of medical education and research director of continuing professional development at Southern Illinois University School of Medicine. Among his many research interests are character skills, survey methods, medical education, program evaluation, school choice, education finance, and arts enrichment. Dr. Hitt earned his Ph.D. in education policy from the University of Arkansas.

Helen F. Ladd is the Susan B. King Professor Emerita of Public Policy and professor of economics at Duke University. Dr. Ladd's research focuses on school finance and accountability, teacher labor markets, school choice, and early childhood programs. Dr. Ladd earned her Ph.D. in economics from Harvard University.

Christopher Lubienski is a professor in Department of Educational Leadership and Policy Studies at the Indiana University School of Education. Dr. Lubienski studies education reform and equity, the political economy of school choice, and the use of research evidence in policymaking. He earned his Ph.D. in educational policy from Michigan State University.

Madeline Mavrogordato is an assistant professor of K–12 educational administration in the College of Education at Michigan State University. Dr. Mavrogordato uses both qualitative and quantitative methods to study how the social context of education, the implementation of educational policies, and school leadership shape educational outcomes for underserved students. She earned her Ph.D. in leadership and policy studies from Vanderbilt University.

Michael Q. McShane is the director of national research at EdChoice. A former high school English and religion teacher, Dr. McShane has authored, edited, and co-edited a number of books on education reform. He earned his Ph.D. in education policy from the University of Arkansas.

Roberto V. Peñaloza is a research scientist at the Center for Research on Educational Opportunity (CREO) at the University of Notre Dame. His research focuses on statistical methodology and data analysis techniques for examining student achievement in U.S. schools, teacher quality, and the relationships among school, principal, and teacher practices and policies. Dr. Peñaloza earned his Ph.D. in economics from Vanderbilt University.

Janelle Scott is a chancellor's associate professor in the Graduate School of Education and the Department of African American Studies at the University of California, Berkeley. Dr. Scott studies the racial politics of public education; the politics of school choice, marketization, and privatization; and the role of elite and community-based advocacy in shaping public education. Dr. Scott earned her Ph.D. in education policy from the University of California, Los Angeles.

Claire Smrekar is an associate professor of public policy and education at Vanderbilt University. Dr. Smrekar uses qualitative methods to study the social context of education and public policy, with a specific focus on the impact of desegregation plans and choice policies on families, schools, and neighborhoods. Dr. Smrekar earned her Ph.D. in administration and policy analysis from Stanford University.

Y. Emily Tang is a lecturer in the Department of Economics at the University of California, San Diego. Dr. Tang's interests include the economics of education and the effects of charter schools on student achievement. She earned her Ph.D. in economics from the University of California, San Diego.

John F. Witte is a professor emeritus of political science and public affairs at the University of Wisconsin-Madison. Dr. Witte's research interests include tax policy, politics, and education, with a focus on school choice, vouchers, and charter schools. Dr. Witte earned his Ph.D. in political science at Yale University.

Patrick J. Wolf is a distinguished professor of education policy and the 21st Century Endowed Chair in School Choice of the Department of Education Reform at the University of Arkansas College of Education and Health Professions. Dr. Wolf has led or co-led a number of major studies on school choice initiatives and he has written extensively on school choice, civic values, special education, public management, and campaign finance. Dr. Wolf earned his Ph.D. in government from Harvard University.

INDEX

Page numbers in **bold** denote tables, in *italic* denote figures